Modelling the World
with Objects

Modelling the World with Objects

Phil Sully

PRENTICE HALL
New York London Toronto Sydney Tokyo Singapore

First published 1993 by
Prentice Hall International (UK) Ltd
Campus 400, Maylands Avenue
Hemel Hempstead
Hertfordshire, HP2 7EZ
A division of
Simon & Schuster International Group

Typeset in 10 pt Times
by Columns Design and Production Services Limited

Printed and bound in Great Britain
at the University Press, Cambridge

Library of Congress Cataloging-in-Publication Data

Sully, Phil.
  Modelling the world with objects / Phil Sully.
    p.   cm.
  Includes bibliographical references and index.
  ISBN 0–13–587791–1
    1. Object-oriented programming (Computer science)   I. Title.
QA76.64.S84   1993
005.1'1—dc20   92–22607
                                                                           CIP

British Library Cataloguing in Publication Data

A catalogue record for this book is available from the British Library

ISBN 0–13–587791–1

---

2   3   4   5   97   96   95   94   93

With love to Janet and our sons, Greg and Gene

Contents

Preface   ix

Acknowledgements   x

1   The object-oriented paradigm and its origins   1

2   Object-oriented development as an economically useful style of development   9

3   An object-oriented notation   17

4   Systems analysis and the object-oriented paradigm   31

5   Modelling systems   40

6   Approaches to object-oriented systems development   49

7   The synthesist approach   56

8   The direct approach   77

9   Modelling human activity systems with objects   98

10   The documentation of objects and their operations   113

11   Object-oriented databases   125

12   Modelling knowledge-based systems with object orientation   142

13   Object-oriented programming languages   154

14   Prototyping an object-oriented development   171

15   Human factors and an object-oriented approach   185

16   Object-oriented implementational units   197

17   CASE tools for effective development   211

18   Object-oriented development and the project manager   225

19   Conclusions   236

     Appendix 1   Glossary of terms   241

     Appendix 2   Case study: Continental Containers Inc.   246

     Appendix 3   Heuristics   274

     Index   280

Preface

In *Modelling the World with Objects* I have described what objects are and why they are useful. I have described the origins of object-oriented development and how an object-oriented development works.

This book is focused upon the systems developer who wishes to appraise him/herself as to various ways of developing in an object-oriented style. The early chapters outline the origins of object-oriented development and the rudiments of a notation. There is only one chapter that requires previous knowledge as to the Yourdon structured methods (Chapter 7).

Chapters 1 to 12 are concerned with the construction. Chapter 13 addresses object-oriented programming languages (OOPL) and what constitutes an ideal OOPL; it also compares various OOPLs and makes the distinction between object-based, object-oriented and class-based. Chapters 14 to 18 cover aspects of object-oriented development, such as HCI (human–computer interaction) and prototyping.

The Appendices have much rich material in them. Appendix 1 contains a comprehensive glossary of terms used in object-oriented development. Appendix 2 has a case study based upon a series of interviews in which the reader develops parts of the object-oriented model as a result of each of the interviews. An outline prototype of facets of the system is developed using Smalltalk. The source for key aspects is listed. Appendix 3 lists all the heuristics (rules of thumb) that are related with an object-oriented approach.

Phil Sully   *May 1992*

Acknowledgements

Appreciation and thanks are extended to Julian Morgan (Yourdon Inc.) for providing the stimulus for working on object-oriented development. In fact, I have much thanks to offer those I have worked with in Yourdon International and Yourdon Inc., with whom I have had many interesting discussions and arguments. I wish also to thank my boss of long standing, John Bowen, for his assistance and regular support. In many ways Yourdon Inc./International has served as a kind of finishing school, for which I am eternally grateful.

Credit also must be given to folks at Kodak Inc. (at Rochester, New York) for their contribution to many early ideas and extensions to the notation.

Hearty thanks are extended to the plethora of seminar attendees who have contributed consciously and, in some cases, subconsciously, to some of the ideas introduced in this book. Appreciation and thanks are extended to the production and editorial staff at Prentice Hall International.

CHAPTER 1

The object-oriented paradigm and its origins

The world cannot be understood from a single view.
(Eleanor Roosevelt)

If we are to build systems that accomplish their true intended purpose, it is desirable that we attend to the real essence of the requirement with the minimum of unnecessary clutter.

During the late 1970s and 1980s, structured methods gave developers useful tools to aid effective requirement building. This, in essence, looked at the problem space in terms of three major dimensions – the processing (i.e. the work), the information (i.e. the memory structure) and the time (i.e. time sequence) to service each of these domains. A set of very effective tools focused upon each of these regimes, namely, the data flow diagram (DFD), which addressed the processing; the entity relationship diagram (ERD), which addressed the information structure (as a map of memory) and the sequence behaviour, which was addressed by the state transition diagram (STD). These are depicted below in Fig. 1.1.

These separate viewpoints allow the modeller to concentrate on the processing, information structure and sequence whilst retaining the capability to integrate the three views into a whole.

Requirements expressed in this form were easily constructed by the analyst and were potentially comprehensible to the client. In fact they encouraged participation by the client. However, solutions derived from this style of expression of requirement, even though effective in their own right, were not so resilient to change and also became not so easy to extend.

Why were they more difficult to extend? My answer is that they did not focus upon the concept, they focused upon the processing view. People believe that most systems are there to perform work, so therefore the processing (i.e. the work view) must be important, possibly because it closely identifies with that aspect of the system. True it has importance but it is not an overriding importance. The nature of the processing of the system, i.e. the work, is potentially the most volatile aspect of the system, unlike the

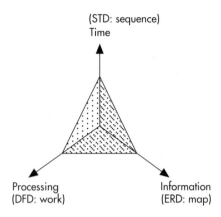

Figure 1.1   The three axes of emphasis.

concepts of the system, which change least over time. If we were to draw a concept diagram of, say, a business system constructed in the 1960s, and compare it to a concept diagram of that same system 20 years on, we would find that there was a strong resemblance between the two. In all probability the later model will have developed more specialised concepts, within general classes. A processing diagram for the same situation will probably look very different because of the nature of work, i.e. the processing changes more rapidly than the concept. It is also likely that some processes, which may be thought to be happening, will have long since ceased to do effective service.

How can we build systems that are more resilient to change? The short answer is that we should organise all the processing units around the concept, as opposed to any specific process domain. An object-oriented approach assists this aim because it is based on the natural concept whilst postponing attention as to the object's real detailed technical implementation.

An object-oriented approach is one in which we take a viewpoint that encourages the recognition of objects. Why is this useful? First, let us look in a dictionary: an object is defined in the *American Heritage Dictionary* as:

1. Anything perceptible by the senses; a material thing.
2. *Phil* Anything intelligible, or perceptible by the mind.

In the process of our recognition and development of objects we must try and keep this in mind. The emphasis is upon a perceived unit, in other words a concept.

Theoreticians in eighteenth century medicine often considered that some physiological processes were carried out by mythical little folk (called 'homunculi') whose behaviour could only be explained in aggregate terms. For example, the visual system was perceived as being 'handled' by homunculi operating just behind the eyes. These homunculi transcribed what they saw into messages that the 'brain' homunculus could interpret and operate upon. The collection of homunculi would then model an understanding of physiological behaviour (De Marco, 1986).

This was a useful working hypothesis for analysis and explanation. Each unit's behaviour was acting as a system 'black box', exhibiting only limited visibility to an external observer.

How could we effectively recognise objects and use them as a stepping stone? To show how it could be useful, we shall go back to the basics in our systems philosophy and I shall use a model 'world' to illustrate. Models in general are very useful abstractions in which we can manipulate a representation and explore the model to find out more information about its innate nature. All the man-made systems we require should be organised to generate responses to external events. An event is something significant that occurs in the environment to which our system should respond.

Events act as a sort of raw message, which 'tells' the system something significant has occurred. In our object paradigm I shall give our system the title of an object, because it is the system at its highest level of abstraction. Referring back to our definition of the object, it is a 'perceived' unit. Additionally, it encapsulates all of its processing behaviour as one unit, that is to say it has all the memory, services and time sequence behaviour incorporated in one! In Fig. 1.2, I have depicted the object as a cloud, to indicate metaphorically that it is tentative at this stage. Now, our object will attend to the raw messages from the environment and respond in an organised way by means of the message being received by a service receptor (a processor), which then, according to its prescribed algorithm, makes the appropriate response. This is the model of the system at its highest level.

In a system of significant size, we would be able to identify whole families of types of messages that require responses. The nature of the messages may suggest certain types of objects that are required to organise a response.

To achieve this end we must extend our model where we may identify a raw message entering the system boundary and then connect it to other objects inside, just like little cellules. Each object at this level will be addressing a particular subject area of the system, and each object may need the services of another object to assist it in accomplishing its response by acting as a server.

In our model situation, the objects within our system boundary may intercommunicate through a perfect communication medium, and show that things are organised in our 'model world' and that there is a message protocol in use, which acts like an address code:

> Object (name of the object class for example Patient class)
> + instance (the particular occurrence for example 'Jones')
> + service required (for example surgery)
> + arguments (for example parameters like sex, date of birth, last operation, operation type, physician, duration, date).

When each object receives a message, the object itself will be sensitive enough to

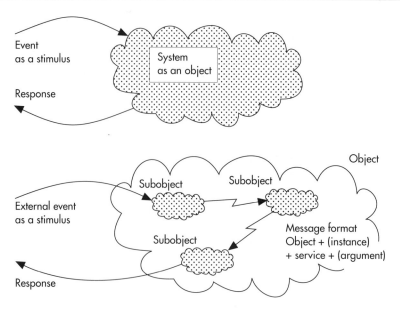

Figure 1.2   Objects and the layering of objects.

'know' whether the message is for the same class or some superclass. A superclass is a grouping that embodies common characteristics over some more specialised groups. If the message is for a superclass, the object itself will automatically have available the inherited facilities. If the message is for a specialisation (i.e. a subclass) then an inheritance mechanism automatically gathers the general supertype characteristics and presents it ready for use.

For example, if one of our objects is a specialist Physician, e.g. a Paediatrician, then this object will inherit all the basic General Physician information and skills will all be presented ready for use. In many ways this is just like the homunculus metaphor with little folk living in these 'cloud' units, each inheriting general characteristics from a superclass, when necessary, and telegraphing other cloud units when they require services.

This scheme is like each object being able to telegraph the others by means of the protocol, mentioned above, and it presents a limited but effective interface for exchange.

The model also shows limited visibility, which is desirable. Each object is assumed to be an encapsulation of memory (knowledge), processes (work) and time/sequence behaviour (control). External observers will only see what concerns them; there are no internal details visible to distract them. The model also shows ideal behaviour and there is no encumbrance with specific types of technology possibly being involved.

Another principle involved with the object-oriented approach is the fact that the models that are constructed with objects are actually mimicking the real world. Object-oriented solutions are simulations of the real world. This principle was 'discovered' when using the computer source language 'Simula', which was primarily designed for simulation systems. It was then perceived that Simula could be applied to a much wider range of solutions because all computer solutions could be perceived as simulations of an aspect of the real world.

If we take as an example an air traffic control system, controlling aircraft, their courses, takeoffs and landings, we will see that if we are to make a computerised solution, the real-world units such as aircraft, runways, courses, surveillance and controllers will all be represented (Fig. 1.3). These objects represent classes (e.g. an aircraft as a representative of all aircraft rather than one in particular) and will interact by means of exchange of messages. The objects will generally be of a type that provides services or objects, the role of which is to coordinate the behaviour of various objects. All of this is accomplished by communication between the objects according to an established protocol. The closer the object model corresponds to the real world, the more closely the behaviour has been mapped.

An object-oriented view of the world has also been adopted by other disciplines for

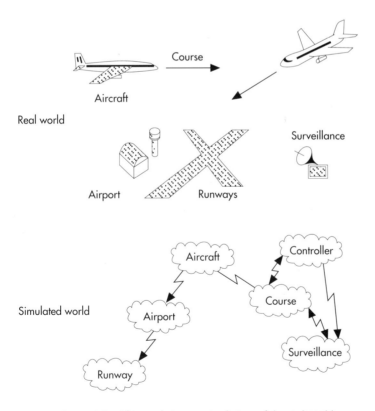

Figure 1.3 Object solutions as simulations of the real world.

some significant period of time. If we look at the field of knowledge cognitive psychology, and the subspecialisation concerned with knowledge representation, the concept of objects is richly used. Collins and Quillian (1969) showed that the majority of cultures on the earth represent knowledge in terms of a hierarchy; animals are embodied with certain general characteristics (Fig. 1.4). The normal and more general situation is that the specialisations inherit most characteristics from the more general classes. The lower parts of the hierarchy are specialisations of the animal class and may have characteristics that override those of the general animal class. For example, specialisations of the class bird, such as canary and ostrich, have certain characteristics that override the general bird characteristics.

This raises the whole idea of how we represent information as economically as possible. This was explored by the psychologist Labov, who experimented with categorisation and found that people categorise by a typicality template (i.e. a general schema for mapping the general characteristics) (Labov, 1973). The more the item resembles a cup, the more it is categorised in that group. The closer it is perceived to resemble a soup bowl the more it is categorised into that category (Fig. 1.5).

Eleanor Rosch, a psychologist working in the area of concept representation, experimented with knowledge representation and subject recall. In her view (Rosch, 1975) memory of objects is represented in terms of a prototypical example, which incorporates all the key representative characteristics in the form of a generalised

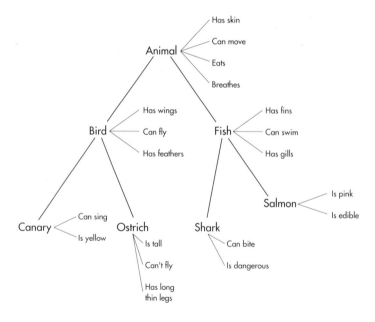

Figure 1.4   Object class hierarchy (reproduced by kind permission of Open University Press).

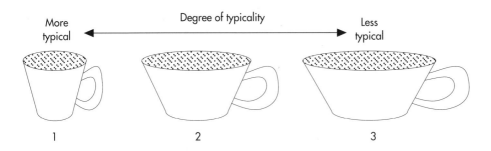

Figure 1.5 Typicality and classification.

abstract schema. This prototypical example (abstract schema) becomes the root of a hierarchy that possesses specialisations, subclasses.

Figure 1.6 shows an example drawn from families of fruit. At the top of the hierarchy there would be an exemplar of a typical fruit – the abstract schema. This fruit abstraction is an exemplar of the typical fruit characteristics of a banana cum apple cum orange. It is, in fact, an abstraction. Now an orange, *per se*, will be one of those specialisations of the fruit abstraction, i.e. typical orange. Then, in turn, there will be yet further specialisations of oranges such as Jaffa and Navel.

Additionally each of the specialisations inherits some characteristics and overrides others. For example, the orange itself overrides some fruit characteristics, such as the skin, but inherits some characteristics, such as the leaves attached to the fruit. This process of memory and knowledge representation is an economical way of arranging information and gives rise to the concept of cognitive economy, i.e. storing of information with the least possible effort.

If we turn to man-made systems, in the electrical engineering industry products are arranged in a class structure that allows effective product development and the automatic 'inheritance' of general types of behaviour. In the telecommunications industry an object view of the world has been taken where the telecommunication activity between users may be expressed in terms of the seven OSI layers. Each layer exhibits limited visibility to the previous layer and, as one delves deeper into the layer structure, there is an inheritance of the previous layer's characteristics. By describing the problem in terms of these layers one has parcelled up the problem into nice digestible chunks of information (e.g. cognitive economy).

Conclusions

In conclusion, an object view of the world is a natural one, as exhibited by its use in other disciplines such as cognitive psychology and electrical engineering. Our objects are abstractions of classes, which exhibit limited visibility, and encapsulations of memory, services and state behaviour. They additionally have a communication

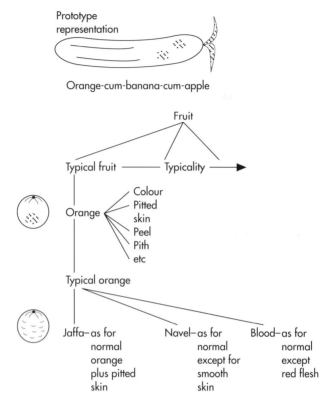

Figure 1.6   Rosch's abstraction as a prototype.

protocol to allow messaging between one another. Where specialisations of an object class were in use, they would automatically inherit the general characteristics. The cloud model is a generalised schema exhibiting most of these principles, plus the idea that our models for developing solutions are simulations of the real world.

References and further reading

Collins, A. and Quillian, M.R. (1969) 'Retrieval time from semantic memory.' *Journal of Verbal Learning and Verbal Behaviour*, **8**, 240–7.

De Marco, T. (1986) 'Object-oriented design and structured analysis.' *Atlantic Guild Notes*, **26**, 1–8.

Labov, W. (1973) 'The boundaries of words and meanings.' In C.J. Bailey and R. Shuy (Eds), *New Ways of Analysing Variations in English*. Washington, DC: Georgetown University Press.

Rosch, E. (1975) 'Cognitive representations of semantic categories.' *Journal of Experimental Psychology: General*, **104**(3), 192–233.

CHAPTER 2

Object-oriented development as an economically useful style of development

Software design is a system – not a secret
(L. Peters)

First, I intend to expand upon the concepts associated with object-oriented systems development. The whole idea of an object is that it is an abstraction that more closely mimics the real world. The original ideas on objects emanated from Simula 67 which, as a simulation system, worked effectively. Simulation could be applied to more general problems. If the system were perceived as if it were mimicking the real world it would be beneficial. For the developers these were the earliest examples of an object-oriented paradigm at work; these ideas actually predate the early ideas of the structured revolution. As software is the end solution of the majority of the software projects we ought also address what the software product should have.

The next questions relate to what are the desirable characteristics that our systems should exhibit. The following is a possible checklist of those desired characteristics:

Robustness: the ability to function in abnormal circumstances or in an unintended manner.

Extendibility: the ease of adaptation of a product, so it may be easily extended to capture new behaviour.

Reusability: the capability to be reused in part or whole and when used in another context it has all the appropriate behaviour as a unit.

Compatibility: the ease with which products may be combined.

In achieving the above desired behaviour, from our objects, it is recognised that there

9

will be tradeoffs between these factors, depending on how each of the individual factors are weighed.

In the working definition cited, it has been mentioned that the very character of *objectness* requires an encapsulation of process and data. Which is the anchor around which one encapsulates: process or data? The encapsulation ought take place around a more general abstraction, which is data, and that relates to the concept. It is upon a selected concept that all the functions should be grouped. They are then grouped under a minimal number of concepts.

Processes (functions) tend to be more prone to change in functionality with time but the concept (data) tends to have less volatility with time. Processes organised as a group suffer from the lack of an overall binding concept. Additionally there is much debate on whether the objects recognised at an early analysis phase are class- or instance-based.

There are some writers on the subject who posit organising *objects* on a completely different basis, namely by organising around the roles that they perform (DeMarco, 1986). This is only useful as a second order of organisation, the conclusion being that the data is the prime means of recognising objects.

It appears from the literature that a definition of what object-oriented software development might be (Meyer, 1988) is as follows:

> **Object-oriented design is the construction of software systems as structured collections of abstract data type implementations.**

It is possibly, at this stage, worth justifying the definition, with some background as to the nature of object-oriented systems development. It is considered a desirable trait that systems are developed as economically as possible, with the minimum of duplication of effort and with as much resilience to change as possible. To be able to manufacture units of software whilst obeying the previously stated objectives requires a useful, easily applicable approach, where one can recognise the key constituents at as early a stage as possible. Object-oriented programming has as a style of development the concept of the package whereby the process and the data is bound together as a unit. This becomes a useful entity in terms of development, because of reusability. Furthermore, it is resilient to change because it localises change to as few places as possible. Object-oriented programming and software development has these principles as part of its working practices, but so far the links to the previous stages of development (requirements, systems analysis) are not present. So, in lieu of a definition for object-oriented systems development, the following definition is being suggested:

> **Object-oriented systems development is a style of development of applications where the potential and actual encapsulation of process and data is recognised at an early stage of development and at a high level of abstraction with a view to build systems economically that will mimic the real world more faithfully.**

The economic justification for object-oriented development derives from the following driving forces:

The 'software crisis'

This is the apparent problem related to a shortfall between the growing 'mountain' of working code in existence and the shortfall in the development personnel to maintain that 'mountain'. This is further compounded by an accelerating demand for yet more software. This view derives from writers on the subject such as Barry Boehm (1987) and Grady Booch (1983) in his writings on Ada and software engineering. Responses to this crisis have come in the form of higher productivity environments (Boehm) or, in the case of Booch, by making software more reusable, implying that subsequent development should require less effort.

Reuse of system components

Much of the effort of serious system building requires that a system should be built from a library of ready-to-use components. This raises the question as to what is the ideal size of system component for reuse. At its most granular there is the function, and at its most lumped form there is the whole system. The intervening stages ranging from library units to packages (Fig. 2.1). What is the most effective reusable unit?

In the nineteenth century, manufacturers noted that to be responsive to a customer's needs it was more practicable to have a range of products that could be manufactured from a repertoire of core components; new products would be generated from different combinations of these components. In other words, interchangeable parts. This is in contrast to highly specific components that could be manufactured in volume, and very cheaply, and which were specific to one product. Many modern automobile manufacturers use this principle of interchangeable components at a level significantly above that of plain nuts and bolts. These components are, in many cases, complete self-contained units, which are well proven. This allows a manufacturer to respond flexibly to revised customer demand by 'assembling' a new product from proven components.

Returning to software building, what we need to do is to recognise that the effective unit of software building is between the function-based library unit and the application, and that is the class/object.

The 'maintenance mountain'

To maintain the mountain, maintenance must be more efficient. Where changes occur their effect must be as limited as possible. Meyer would, one believes, recommend that maintenance effects be taken into account at the design stage.

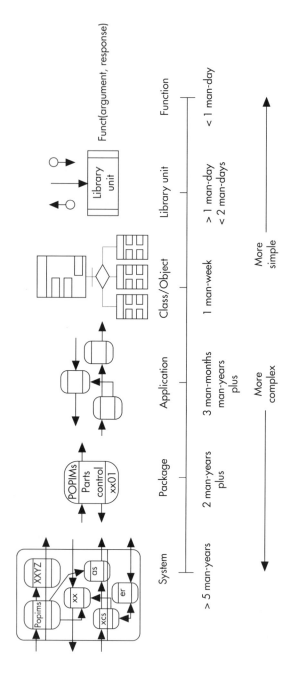

Figure 2.1   A scale of granularity for systems components.

The re-engineering of existing systems into object-oriented (OO) systems could become a desired reality in the near future if the economies from an object-oriented approach warrant it. There is still the opinion that throwing away an existing elderly system and starting anew is a valid option. However, this genre of system, which has been added to layer by layer as each new innovation vogue occurred, will be bound to have processing artefacts that no longer have a useful role to play.

Human dependence upon man-made systems

Increasingly systems are being developed upon which human lives depend (e.g. fly-by-wire systems for future generations of airliners with many hundreds of people). The quality of development must be higher and the consequences or maintenance changes to systems must be limited, hence the argument for tighter encapsulation of process and data, to limit the span of unforeseen effects.

Reliability of object-oriented systems

Formal proofs are logically rigorous analyses of a system's logical behaviour, are certainly needed for safety-critical systems. The derivation of formal proofs of the system's components is a notoriously labour-intensive activity. Ideally it requires that the system's processing functions have their behaviour prescribed in a language such as Z or VDM (Vienna Development Method), with a procedure to prove its behaviour formally in formal logic. In object-oriented development, components that are built would have their behaviour prescribed and proven once. This would, in effect, be a guarantee of performance. This is to encourage people to use components from a library (class browser). This is again similar to the automobile manufacturers using well proven fuel injection systems and well proven instrumentation systems.

Organisational issues

These also contribute to the software crisis through a lack of recognition, by many organisations, that there is a software development cycle. Additionally, there is the lack of an agreement as to what those particular stages are. For organised development to take place it is essential that a software developer focuses upon what actually constitutes this life-cycle, what should be delivered at each stage and what resource mix is required at each phase.

It is recommended that organisations follow a consistent life-cycle view for each of their development projects. The one life-cycle that appears to work for most projects is that suggested by Boehm (1981) which defines the main stages. These stages are RD (requirements definition), SD (structural design), DD (detail design), CUT (code and unit test), IT (integrate and test), M (maintenance) and R (replacement) (Fig. 2.2). This

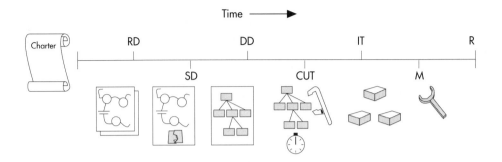

Figure 2.2   A linear view of the development activity.

view of development is essentially linear and is not necessarily the case in reality, but at least we have a view as to what the various phases are and what they should do for us all.

This is a simplified and linear view of the development cycle. Boehm (1986, 1988) has developed his model of the life-cycle to reflect the more general vogue in development, where it is represented in a spiral form (Fig. 2.3).

The spiral form is a more realistic representation of what occurs in systems development. It is in essence the linear model of the previous page extended into a spiral to accept iterative development.

What is actually occurring is that both parties (developer and client/user) are not 100 per cent sure of the validity and degree of realism of their requirement. To reduce the uncertainty (risk) the iterative steps by means of models are welcomed. Prototyping has a role to play in this realm. Many prototyping tools are object-oriented and offer a lower cost for the client/user and developer to refine the requirements.

Additionally, the spiral view of an application development is a vast simplification. The group that is developing an application requires more comprehensive support from the infrastructure of an organisation. This infrastructure would have to supply and maintain a repertoire of objects with the suitable documention about the objects

Figure 2.3   A spiral view of the development activity.

available and their behaviour. This needs comprehensive indexing to allow more complex searches for suitable object categories.

There are additional aspects of object-oriented development, which ought to be recognised at this stage. These issues all relate to how one will go about the system-building activity:

Item 1. Is there an exclusive choice between whether object-oriented development supplements or replacing existing structured analysis and design practices?

Item 2. Objects ought to be recognised by a set of easy-to-use heuristics (rules of thumb), which must also be easy to quality check. Furthermore, there must be traceability through a development cycle (step *i* linking to step *j*).

Item 3. Where would code generators fit in? Are they relevant?

Item 4. Where do computer-aided software engineering tools (CASE tools) fit in? What should one be expecting from a CASE tool? Would it be reasonable for the CASE tool to have automated object recognition facilities?

Item 5. Are subspecialisms such as object-oriented databases, object-oriented man–machine interfaces and object-oriented knowledge-based systems relevant? If they are relevant, where do they fit in?

Item 6. Roles of the parties. What would each party expect to see and check? The user (client) must comprehend what is being presented; what should he/she see? What would the technicians develop? What would the quality assurers check?

If one accepts the working definition of object-oriented development (posited earlier) one will perceive many specialisms of systems development, which beg the question of what these flavours are and how they are likely to be affected.

For example, how are object-oriented knowledge bases (OOKBs) to be addressed within object-oriented systems development? The concepts are preserved in the OOKB, which is a collection of objects, and there is still the knowledge concept, which is the OBJECT. This in turn encapsulates the RULES and DATA together, so they may be held as one concept. Additionally in this area, concepts of inheritance are recognised (i.e. where a descendant object inherits the rules and data from its ancestor). Here limited visibility is being depicted.

In the case of object-oriented databases (OODBs), similar concepts are being expounded where the data entities (defined by the data description language (DDL)) are encapsulated with the process part (data manipulation language (DML)) to give greater resilience to change along with more effective development. Such developments as ObjectSQL have removed the distinction between DDLs and DMLs into one coherent language. A database such as the Ontos VBASE exhibits this characteristic, and later versions of Ingres exhibit the object-oriented concepts.

Object-oriented office automation systems are another version of the concepts already met. For example, by identifying useful office objects one may find a truly flexible system. The publication object is actually a way of representing communications objects, along with business graphics, which may in turn be derived from spreadsheets (a pie chart being a rendition of a spreadsheet). Again the concept of DATA and PROCESS have been expressed in a flexible architecture.

Conclusions

Essentially these specialisms do not radically alter any of the main concepts and how they relate to object-oriented development. These are the packaging together of DATA and PROCESS and, wherever a class system has been defined, the descendant object inherits DATA and PROCESS from its ancestor. If we are to have some means of attending to objects they should be available across all the major areas where an object-oriented conceptualisation is used.

References and further reading

Boehm, B. (1981) *Software Engineering Economics*. Englewood Cliffs, NJ: Prentice Hall.
Boehm, B. (1987) 'Improving software productivity', *IEEE Computer*, September, 43–57.
Boehm, B. (1988) 'A spiral model of software development and enhancement.' *IEEE Computer*, May, 61–72.
Booch, G. (1983) *Software Engineering and Ada*. Menlo Park, CA: Benjamin Cummings Publishing Inc.
DeMarco, T. (1986) 'Object-oriented design and structured analysis.' *Atlantic Guild Notes*, **26**, 4/9186.
Meyer, B. (1988) *Object-oriented Software Construction*. Hemel Hempstead, UK: Prentice Hall.

CHAPTER 3

An object-oriented notation

Newton's fourth law: If I have seen further it is by standing on the shoulders of giants
(the *New York Times*, February 16th 1976)

For the candidate objects to be identified, developed and used as a means for discourse with possible developers, there must be some standardised way of expressing objects and their behaviour. The cloud model with the lightning strike served as an introductory metaphor expressing the main ideas behind objects, but it lacks rigour. This chapter outlines a more rigorous notation.

A notation

A good notation ought be a good metaphor, based around graphics, and should ideally have textual support to augment these graphics. The notation should depict a series of layers to allow decomposition into simpler units for discourse. Much of the structured diagram notation contains these characteristics, although they are focused upon separate aspects of a system such as the process, data and state views.

This fragmentation – into a variety of differently focused diagrams – causes a lack of continuity. If we return to the metaphor, it is helpful to employ a notation that people are able to apply, a notation that involves the least number of 'mental somersaults'. This is true particularly when considering objects and the symbol representing an object and its relationship to other objects.

If we recall our model object discussion from Chapter 1 we are still considering our objects as encapsulations of processing, memory and state behaviour. These object units are a sort of packaged unit from which we require services. Our object is a type of module that encapsulates all the desired behaviour within one unit, as opposed to focusing on just one aspect. In the everyday world, we meet a similar situation with services packaged together in the form of a vending machine (automat). This is, in a way, an object engine. We have a protocol to communicate with it, namely inserting money (a message) and making a selection of a service by depressing a button (a second message) whereupon a service is performed and a beverage is delivered (a response). This is a good metaphor for an object because we are not concerned with its internal workings (i.e. we have limited visibility) and our buttons are labelled with the services that are being offered. This external view of the object may be a collection of human activities in an organisational unit, a software unit or even a hardware unit.

The symbol – the external view

The notation for an object is deliberately chosen to look like an object 'vending machine'. It is a rectangle with the name of the object at the top then a series of metaphorical 'buttons' along each edge, appropriately labelled with the services it is offering (Fig. 3.1). These are publicly available services. This is also the view that most users of the object would get, the users here being the end-user and the analyst as a user of the notation. The visibility of the object does not show the detailed workings nor the individual data items that are being used; this reduces visibility to the publicly offered object with services (Fig. 3.2). This information is retained by means of textual definition, which we will see later defining all the aspects of the object and its services.

The symbol – the internal view

However, the detailed workings of the object may be required for the developer of the object and, of course, in its documentation. The metaphor of the vending machine is taken still further if the front of the vending machine is unscrewed and a more detailed yet consistent internal view is displayed (Fig. 3.3). Wherever an external service was offered, there is an operational process to perform that service. Flows depict connections from the outside world (to the button) and depict the messages and responses from the operation process. Inside the flow itself are arguments upon which the operation would work. The operation process is where some useful transformation

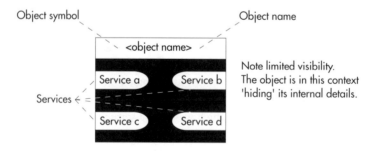

Figure 3.1   An external view of an object.

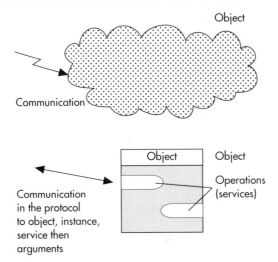

Figure 3.2   Communication with the object.

is performed. The memory is represented by a data store symbol (i.e. a file). This is the collection of data that has to be retained to provide services to users. One of the operations in its own right may need the services of other objects (servers). This is depicted in the lower part of the object internal view and shows a message from an operation to the 'button' of the server object and a response from it. The server object is only depicting its publicly available services, which would probably be documented somewhere in the enterprise's library.

Messages to objects

Within an object, and kept from public view, there may be extra processing operations that are required for the object to preserve its public services. These are quite rightly not depicted as visible 'buttons'. Communication to and from an object is straightforward and in general it is by means of a flow depicting a message to and from the object's operation button in the form of a dialogue. This message would be labelled and its structure (i.e. the arguments) defined in the appropriate repository providing definition for subsequent persual.

In many ways this style of describing various systems is similar to opening the bonnet of a car to see the various systems and their interconnection, which in turn can then be decomposed. This whole activity of layering permits cognitive economy in dealing with complex systems.

This form of notation for the external view of the object and its internal view is useful. However, it is necessary to augment the internal view. For example, there may be occasions when the behaviour of the object requires the modelling of state behaviour. This is where the object will behave in a manner dependent upon what

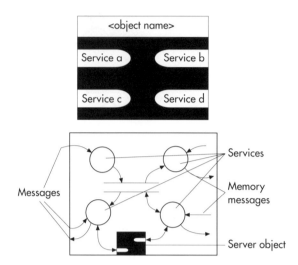

Figure 3.3   The external and corresponding internal view of an object.

'state' the object is in. This is particularly the case where the object is coordinating activities performed by various object classes. Ideally a state transition diagram can augment the type of behaviour (this type of diagram will be described in more depth in Chapter 5). The state transition diagram is a well established modelling tool for this type of behaviour. This diagram becomes an annexe to the main object internal view diagram. As far as the object internal view is concerned, it is associated with a control operation (depicted by a circle prescribed by a dashed line). Operations (services) may be triggered by control flows (again dashed lines) or may yield control information in the form of yet another dashed line. The state transition diagram may be seen as an annexe to the object's internal view.

Organisation of objects

At another level, it is useful to be able to describe how the objects are organised within an application and how they may be organised within the enterprise's resources.

Each of the diagrams depict objects and their interrelationships with others. The icon representing an external view of the object will appear on each of the diagrams.

There are four types of diagrams: the object internal view, the object dependency diagram, the object inheritance diagram and the object interconnection net. Each diagram is focused to servicing a particular development cycle need. The diagrams themselves are models inasmuch as they are representations that can be analysed, and they should be examined actively to ensure the models are properly tested. It is envisaged that all development project members are able to participate in the building and testing of these models.

Object internal view (OIV)

This is the view that a designer develops. It corresponds to the external view of an individual object (Fig. 3.1), and all the externally visible operations will be represented as operations, with all the appropriate connections to memory and possibly to other server objects. This diagram is particularly useful when designing an object. It will show all the operations and server objects required. This view would be available from any object that presented an external view.

Object dependency diagram (ODD)

This diagram shows how objects are organised within an application. It is in essence a hierarchical view of the objects (Fig. 3.4). The diagram depicts client–supplier relationships. Client object is the caller of object services from an object that supplies (supplier) the services. There are no information messages being shown explicitly. The directed arc indicates the direction of the client–supplier relationship. If one needed to know the detail of the message he/she would look at the associated object internal view. Remember that each object icon can be decomposed into an internal view depicting all the specific messages and connections. This type of diagram closely corresponds to the object-oriented program units that may be employed in the software implementation.

Object inheritance diagram (OID)

This diagram depicts the native organisation of an object (Fig. 3.5). It depicts the inheritance structure of a set of objects and maps how the enterprise's resource library may be organised. This diagram may look superficially like the object dependency diagram but it performs an essentially different role, showing the general classes and the specialisations (subtypes). It is often the case that a subtype (specialisation) may be

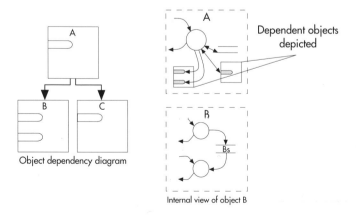

Figure 3.4 Object dependency diagrams and their corresponding internal views.

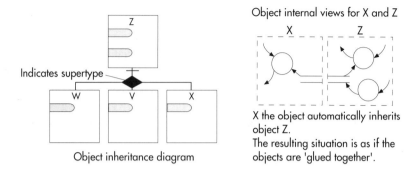

Figure 3.5   Object inheritance diagrams and their corresponding internal views.

used in an application and we would like it to have automatically inherited data and operations available. This actually occurs. It is as if the subtype object has the general class memory and behaviour 'glued' alongside it.

Distinctions between ODDs and OIDs

At first view both diagrams look similar, but they have different purposes and they are modelling different aspects. The ODD is, in effect, an execution model showing the various objects and their calling structure. The OID shows each object and its inheritance structure. For unit, as a subtype, it implies the supertype behaviour and memory. The supertype 'diamond' symbol and the cross tick show the reader that these are different diagrams.

Networks of objects

So far the diagrams depicted have been, in essence, organised hierarchically, and this has suggested that these diagrams are predominantly implementational in character. It is useful to show diagrams that are as free of implementation as possible. These diagrams are used in the analysis phases and models of objects collaborating via messages (object interconnection diagrams (OIN)) (Fig. 3.6) and the other, the object relationship diagram (ORD) (Fig. 3.7), shows objects and their interrelationships.

Object interconnection net (OIN)

This diagram shows how objects may be interconnected based on ideal (perfect) technology (Fig. 3.6). This view of objects is useful for the initial recognition and development of the candidate objects. The objects are first identified and then arranged so that specific operations accept external flows and produce appropriate responses. To perform such actions messages may have to be sent to other objects' operations to supply the appropriate response. In fact, the objects are collaborating via messages.

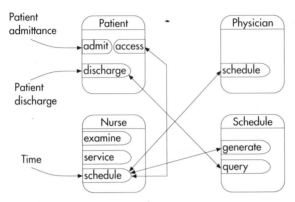

Figure 3.6   An object interconnection net.

This form of diagram is ideal for depicting the objects and interconnections without being constrained by implementational considerations.

The OIN is a natural way to describe how the various objects may collaborate to provide a response. The flows from the edge of the Fig. 3.6 represent messages directed to an object. Each message is met by an operation as a receptor, which, in making its response, may construct a 'dialogue' with other objects' operations; this is depicted by a bidirectional dialogue flow.

Relationships amongst objects

Object relationship diagram (ORD)

This diagram shows how objects may be arranged as a preliminary step prior to the definition of an object-oriented database (Fig. 3.7). This diagram is used in conjunction with an object interconnection net. The ORD depicts the external view of an object with visible services, as defined before. The objects are interconnected by a relationship diamond, which expresses a real-world connection between the objects. On the connecting links between the diamond and the objects there is a definition of the threshold and limit of the objects' participation in a relationship. No message flows are shown on this diagram.

This diagram is useful for modelling the structure of objects in a style free from implementation.

Textual definition material

The object diagrams can express only so much of the message and textual specification is an efficient way to supplement the graphics. The specific textual definitions required are for the object itself and its operations (services).

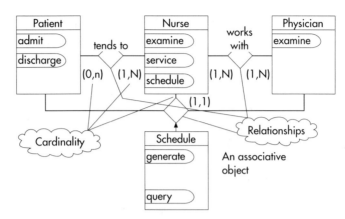

Figure 3.7   An object relationship diagram.

In the case of an object the minimum following items are required:

> Object name, an identifier for the object concerned; note it is a class.
> Object description, some friendly description of the object.
> Inheritance, the objects that supply supertype data and operations.
> Data items, these are the attributes that are used by the object.
> Operations, a list of the available services from this object.
> Invariant, this is a list of the true assertions concerning the object's behaviour.

The ideal arrangement for this information is as a text frame with appropriate slots to cater for all of the categories of information (as stated above). It would be likely that the diagrams associated with this text frame would be implemented on a CASE tool.

Alternative arrangements for object definitions can use the data dictionary language, as introduced by Tom DeMarco, but I believe a text frame is more contemporary (Fig. 3.8).

More detail of the text frame contents and rules defined is in Chapter 10.

The definition of the services offered

The operations themselves are like the program modules that are available for use within the object. The prescription of their behaviour is achieved by means of structured language, pre- and post-condition specification or even formal specification. Structured language is a subset of natural language that uses some standard constructions for conditions, repetitive procedures and procedural blocks. Pre- and post-condition specification takes an external view of the operation using logical declarations. The logical declarations describe the pre-condition that exists prior to the operation 'firing' and the post-condition declarations describe the logical assertions that are held true after the operation has 'fired'.

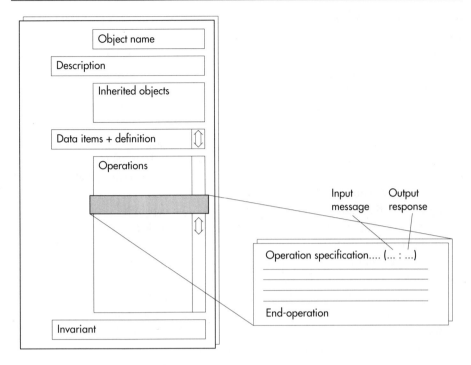

Figure 3.8   An object text frame.

Consistency between all the components

If a notation is being used, it is imperative that there are some balancing rules to ensure consistency between the various models. The external view of the object is the most frequently used view of an object. Its external 'buttons' must map directly to at least a subset of the operation visible within the internal view of the object.

Each internally visible operation process must have some message connection input to it and output from it. Each of the messages must be labelled with a subject area name. Operations are always communicated with by messages. Each object will, as a rule, have memory depicted by a store. This memory is based upon a class of object, for example a Patient object is catering for the class of Patients, of which one instance may be 'Bowen'.

If an operation uses another object to provide services, it is depicted by a dialogue flow line connecting the operation to the 'button' of the server object's operation. This usage of a server object sets up a form of dependence – a client requiring a supplier's service. This will balance with a fragment of the object dependency diagram, where one object (the client) will have a directed arc pointing to the top of another object (the supplier).

If the operation used is of the control variety (i.e. coordinating time sequence behaviour) then there should be a state transition diagram annexed to the object internal view.

The object's internal view should balance against the text frame defining the object. Each internally visible operation should balance with an entry in the object frame's operations list; each introduced operation should have an operation specification and each object should have each data item within the object defined in the object frame, e.g. name, range of values and units of measure.

If a given object inherits from other objects, the objects from which it inherits directly must be introduced. Note that an object can inherit from more than one object. Each of the introduced objects must be defined in its own right. That is, general classes must be defined before specialisations.

Any models that have been created should have the capability of being examined comprehensively to test that the model matches the intended view of a reality. The object models may be tested by performing a 'message thread'.

The message thread is a trace through all the activities from an event through the various links between objects, i.e. messages between objects, until it produces the response to the outside world. The thread is usually described in the form of a table listing external events through the series of object operations to the production of the external responses. For a complete analysis of the behaviour, each object operation's behaviour should be threaded in the form of using pre- and post-condition logical assertions. This assists with the perceptions of the before and after situation of the operation, which, of course, is the equivalent of a program. What is actually happening is that the object-oriented notation is acting as a means to help someone simulate an intended solution (Fig. 3.9).

OINs and ORDs

These two diagrams are networks and they represent complementary views of objects. They differ in scope, an ORD typically being more extensive than an OIN. The OIN shows all the messages and interactions for an application view. The ORD depicts a static view (Fig. 3.10). The flows are depicted as directed arcs. Any object shown on the diagram will have a text frame with associated operation frames. Any object shown in the ORD or OIN form may be decomposed into an internal view.

ODDs and OIDs

These two diagrams depict a complementary view of a situation through implementational means. Both are essentially hierarchical diagrams (Fig. 3.11). The OIDs are, in effect, showing objects as resources to be reused in application to application.

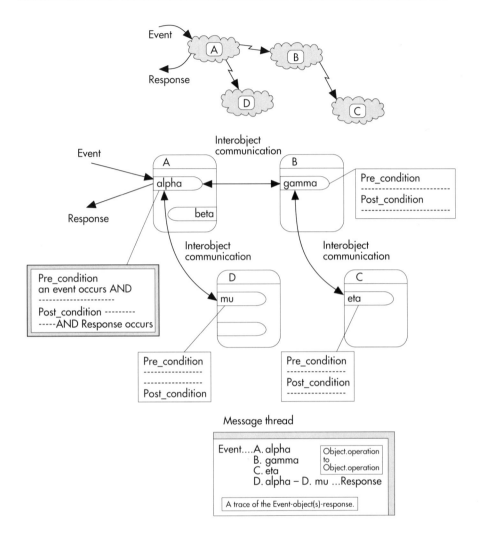

Figure 3.9   Objects, messages and collaboration.

OINs and OIDs

Any object depicted on an OIN may be a supertype or subtype in an OID (inheritance diagram). To indicate this situation the objects in an OID may show that they are subtypes of a specialisation by use of a roundel symbol (Fig. 3.10, right-hand diagram). An object may also show that it is a supertype with many subtypes by means of a roundel with an 'X' inside. Figure 3.12 shows the complementary views of each diagram.

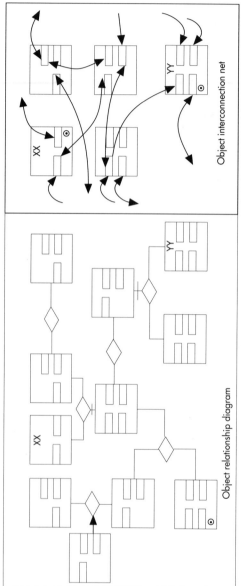

Object interconnection net

Object relationship diagram

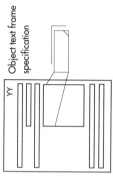

YY

Object text frame
specification

Figure 3.10 Object relationship and network diagrams.

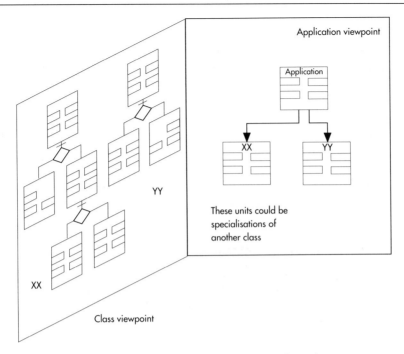

Figure 3.11 Object inheritance and object dependency diagrams.

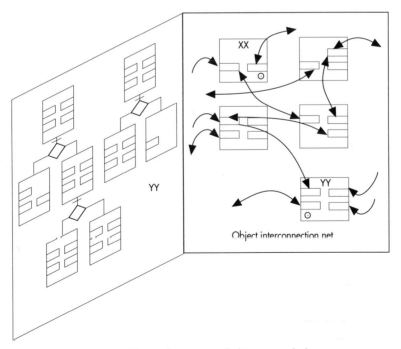

Figure 3.12 Object inheritance and object network diagrams.

Conclusion

The notation introduced has been based upon the metaphor of an object engine with buttons to represent the services that the object can supply. This view deliberately hides the internal complexities; it is this view that the users will see. At another level the developers will need to see the internal components. The object is defined textually by an object frame. Objects may be arranged into various organisations, such as the object dependency diagram, object inheritance diagram and the object interconnection net. All the object diagrams are models in their own right and should be subjected to a message threading test to ensure continuity. There are some diagrams which augment the description of the object's behaviour, such as the state transition diagram and entity state transition diagram; these will be covered in Chapters 7 and 8.

References and further reading

Coad, P. and Yourdon, E. (1990) *Object Oriented Analysis*. Englewood Cliffs, NJ: Prentice Hall.
Shlaer, S. and Mellor, S. (1988) *Object-Oriented Systems Analysis*. Englewood Cliffs, NJ: Prentice Hall.

CHAPTER 4

Systems analysis and the object-oriented paradigm

There are only two ways open to man for attaining a certain knowledge of truth: clear intuition and necessary deduction

(Rene Descartes)

This chapter addresses such questions such as: What does an object-oriented approach offer the systems analyst? What happens to the role of the user? What should he or she see in the form of the documentation and how should he/she respond to it?

The systems analysis activity

What the systems analysis activity actually does for the enterprise that is employing it has been debated over and over again. My view is that the systems analyst should be the person who ascertains what the client's real effective requirement is. The representation of that requirement has often been in the form of a textual report. However, text-based reports have the drawback that the client is susceptible to the analyst's expression style. The users are inclined not to realise the full consequences of their choices. Of course, all this presumes that people have read the report in the first place. There are many jokes about requirements being so weighty that they have been dubbed 'Victorian novels'; such reports are not always inviting to read!

Additionally, there is the tendency for some requirements specifications to be written in a guise that preserves the 'mystic arts' of systems analysis.

We should also look at the sort of problems that users have with software systems. The prevalence of the maintenance activity for software indicates a form of problem that originates in the requirements capture time. Chapin (1979) reported that 80 per cent of software errors originate in the requirements phase. The types of failure are caused by:

1. Failure to communicate the requirements effectively.
2. Lack of methods inviting enough for the user to actively participate with.
3. Failure to define the performance attributes of the product at requirements time.
4. Failure to handle the evolution of the user's requirement.
5. Failure to provide a set of tools to allow the users to visualise the projected product at early stages.

The client/user will not necessarily have formulated in his/her mind what the real requirement is at the requirements phase. Additionally there is often much uncertainty associated with the requirement. It is true to say that a requirement actually evolves through the process of getting started then working through the requirement, visualising options, identifying inconsistencies, correcting them and then refining the requirement. It is not a one stop activity.

Structured analysis

Tom DeMarco's book on structured analysis (DeMarco, 1978) focused attention upon using a structured form of diagramming to illustrate the specification. The diagramming notation (data flow diagrams) and structured text demystified the activity of systems analysis, allowing participation by the client/user alongside the analyst. The overall aim with requirements specification is to reduce the uncertainty in specification whilst not constraining technical choice. The user/client was now able to participate effectively. The mix of graphics plus text is one that, I believe, is effective. Human beings have limited channel capacity to think, and using the mix of graphics plus text uses both left and right sides of the brain effectively (Edwards, 1979).

The analyst's role

The analyst's role is to define a requirement that accepts the user/client's needs and structures them in such a way that the solution is not constrained technologically. The client/user has one set of knowledge specialised in a specific subject area and the analyst has another set of knowledge specialised in systems technology. The systems analyst is practised at distilling subject area knowledge fed to him/her into a form that becomes a viable solution. There is an underlap in the knowledge set, which is to do with a domain of discourse. The analyst must be sure that he/she has understood the problem area well and this requires an echoing of the solution to the client/user. He/she must, in turn, must be able to comprehend what is put in front of them. The vehicle cited as definitely useful is the structured model which includes data flow diagrams (DFD), entity relationship diagrams (ERD) and state transition diagrams (STD). These

diagrams, along with the appropriate textual specifications assist in providing a vehicle for discourse.

The client/user's role

Where does the user/client fit in? The client/users must take responsibility for their own set of systems that they will use. They will probably use these systems as tools to assist them in their day-to-day business activities. They are 'stakeholders', whether they like it or not. Most client/users whom I know of, welcome the chance to participate actively in the analysis stages. The role of the analyst is as a facilitator and integrator of all of the various pieces of the subject area puzzle. Participative vehicles like 'JAD' (joint application design), 'Blitzing' (a process of rapidly capturing requirements) and 'walk-throughs' aim at animating the discourse between analysts and client/users and improving the quality of discourse.

The structured models work by providing diagrams that are easy to construct and that represent the appropriate viewpoint quickly for validation and verification. The notation for each of the cited diagrams (DFDs, ERDs and STDs) is straightforward, namely only four symbol types in each! The graphic diagrams are now assembled, along with the textual specification, into models. It is the model that is the subject of the detailed systems analysis and its definition ideally becomes part of the requirements definition.

If the structured models work why consider changing them? The structured models work well but suffer from varying degrees of participation and contribution from the diagrams. Let's look at some of the criticisms.

Viewpoints

There are three different viewpoints, processing (work), structure (a concept map) and time/sequence behaviour. This requires of client/users to have to integrate these three viewpoints in their own minds before having a complete 'picture'. Engineering diagrams have the same problem: plan, side elevation and front elevation. One needs to integrate the three views to get the picture (Fig. 4.1). To some people this is not a problem!

The diagrams have differing degrees of friendliness to the users. The DFD is friendly in its own right. People can usually visualise work to be done, be it logical or physical, or even a unit that has the capacity to perform work. The STD is friendly because it is easy to represent discrete control behaviour or even the human–machine interface with such a diagramming notation. With both the DFD and STD there is a direct cognitive mapping between the perceived world and its representation in the diagram notation. The ERD, however, is a representation of the concepts and their interconnections. It is static, i.e. not showing work; it is also abstract. Users/clients often have difficulty in

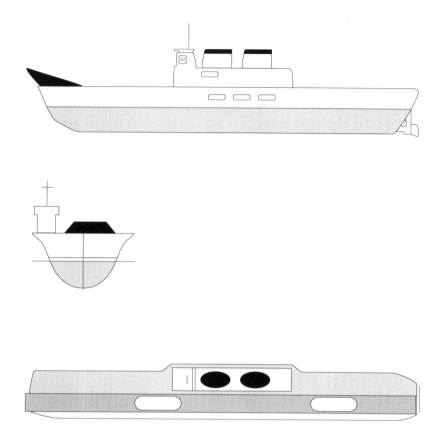

Figure 4.1 Orthogonal views.

creating a conceptual representation of a situation. I suspect it is because of an apparent lack of visual cues. With the DFD and the STD there is a direct mapping to something tangible that is associated with work. The ERD does not exhibit this phenomenon. However, once an ERD is created it becomes useful in showing how the various conceptual sets of information are arranged and how one can easily navigate from set to set. The only difficulty is in the creation of the ERD. This is actually only a matter of practice for client/users to become effective at constructing ERDs.

What could an object-oriented viewpoint give the analysis activity?

The object-oriented activity gives a notation in which one symbol predominates rather than three interlocking views. A client/user can get a good complete view of the system by means of a collection of objects rather than a collection of diagrams each exhibiting one viewpoint. There are less cognitive units for our client/user to deal with. This

principle is similar to the engineering diagrams with the three orthogonal views and is useful for technicians, but an isometric view encapsulates the picture in one fell swoop (Fig. 4.2).

Economic justification of an object-oriented approach is based upon more economic construction of systems, through the reuse of components. In the analysis activity reuse comes about by means of conceptual specification units that may be redeployed. The objects identified are assumed to have a close correspondence with implementation objects in the form of language units in an object-oriented programming language (OOPL). Extension of the system then becomes a much easier activity. It is, in fact, a form of modularising based on a conceptual unit rather than just on one aspect like a function.

What does the object-oriented approach give the client/user and analyst?

The unit of discourse would be the object with appropriate configurations of objects to display the appropriate behaviour. This is, I believe, a more natural representation for the client/user and the analyst to deal with. With appropriate training I would expect that client/users would be more comfortable with objects as representations. This degree of participation would extend to being able to use objects as the main items of discourse in JAD, blitzing or even walk-through sessions.

Paradigm shift

A paradigm shift is a radical change in the axioms that were held valid previously. Robert Pirsig (1979), in his book *Zen and the Art of Motorcycle Maintenance* describes a paradigm shift. His example concerns a monkey that traps its hand in a coconut whilst getting peanuts. Now, for as long as the monkey is determined to grab the peanuts it cannot withdraw its hand because the space constrains its withdrawal together with the peanuts. If the monkey changes its objectives and is concerned only with withdrawing its hand then it will release the peanuts and will be able to physically withdraw its hand. The paradigm shift is the basic change in the fundamentals.

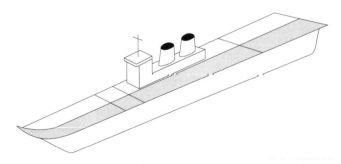

Figure 4.2   An isometric view.

There is shift in the emphasis as to what are the units of interest between the structured and object based requirements. The scale of solution posited is capable of being much grander than originally envisaged. Models based upon enterprise needs rather than highly localised application project needs.

The best analogy comes from Bertrand Meyer, who focused upon the difference in analysis perception, and the example is drawn from the construction industry.

The movement from a *project culture* with such accoutrements as:

Outcome	Result
Economies	Profit
Unit	Department
Time	Short term
Bricks	Programs
Method	Top/down, functional
Language	C, Pascal, etc.

The distinctions emanate from Bertrand Meyer, and he contrasts this with a *product culture*.

Outcome	Components/libraries
Economies	Investment
Unit	Company/industry
Time	Long term (viz 3 years plus)
Goal	Systems
Bricks	Software components
Method	Strategy bottom-up
Language	OOPLs such as Smalltalk, C++, Oberon

These are the main distinctions between a project and a product culture. In systems development there is the tendency to take a view that closely corresponds to the application as a project unit. All organisational effort tends to be focused to realising the project unit without due recognition to enterprise fabric and the possible infrastructure that may contribute positively (Fig. 4.3). In addition, what is also ignored is what the individual project may contribute positively to the enterprise's infrastructure.

The majority of the expressed requirements would be in terms of objects, which would be depicted in the following forms:

1. A layered family of objects. The topmost diagram, the object context, along with events (raw messages) listed.
2. Object interconnection diagrams showing the objects with visible (therefore available) operations (services) along with a depiction of the flows (messages) from the external world and appropriate responses to the external world.
3. All of the diagrams would be depicted with comprehensive text organised for the product. All of this would be shown with messages that are required between objects.

Figure 4.3 Perceived units as objects.

Other items required, such as a project dictionary defining all the objects and their contents and a specification for each visible operation, would augment the diagrams. This would allow a user/client to predict the behaviour of the collection of objects and act as a definition for subsequent stages of development.

It should be considered desirable that a client/user, along with the analyst, uses the object model as a means to build an active, or animated model of their requirements expressed in the form of a prototype.

By expending effort with expression of requirements in terms of objects it is a much more flexible unit for analyst and client/user to work with. The perceived goal is not a simple extrapolation from a point in time but one that is gradually evolving on the basis of new evidence and the dynamics of the environment (Fig. 4.4).

Systems would be seen as much more adaptable and the building specifications would become related to drawing-out of browser libraries appropriate documentary

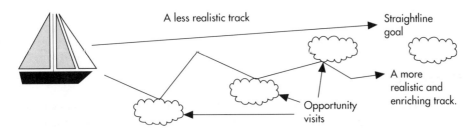

Figure 4.4 Real and perceived goals through time.

items and then the 'assembly' requirement specifications, which become the basis of further development. The so-called 'end-product' does not become an issue of prime focus, the revised focus is towards evolutionary systems, ones that will be adaptive to future requirements.

The systems may be seen as comprising firm and flexible components. The concrete section could be said to be concerned with the aspects of the systems that are based on the concept. The more object-oriented specified systems are likely to have a greater proportion of their behaviour in flexible form and correspondingly be more focused to human and environmental needs (Fig. 4.5).

Hitherto, the factors related to reuse have addressed the detailed functional components. This is rather like reuse in the manufacturing industry being based at the elemental item level such as screws, grommets, washers, etc. Greater economy can be derived from reuse at the level of whole assemblies and structures. The electronics industry has already seen this sort of revolution from reuse at the transistor level through to reuse of whole systems as components in which a whole plethora of more effective systems may be designed.

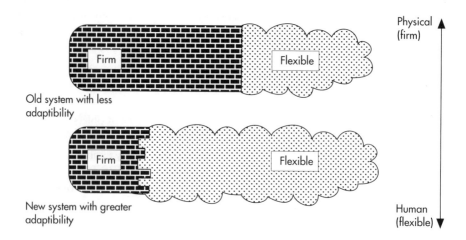

Figure 4.5   Relative proportions of firmness and flexibility.

Conclusions

The whole analysis activity is capable of reaping benefits from perceiving organisation needs at a higher level, which is the object level. The greater economy comes from reuse at the higher level with the items of reuse at component level or even higher. All this requires a reperception of the modelled views of the world (Fig. 4.6).

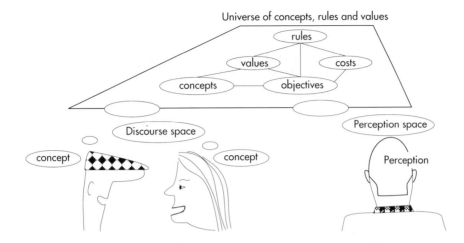

Figure 4.6   Discourse and perception spaces.

References and further reading

Chapin, N. (1979) 'Software lifecycle,' *InfoTec Conference in Structured Development. Proc. NCC*, New York.

DeMarco, T. (1978) *Structured Analysis and Systems Specification*. New York, NY: Yourdon Press.

Edwards, B. (1979) *Drawing on the Right Side of the Brain*. Los Angeles, CA: J.P. Tarcher, Inc.

Hodgson, R. (1990), 'Object-oriented approaches to reuse', Unscom seminar *Exploiting object-Oriented Technologies*, Uxbridge, UK.

Norman, D. (1988) *The Psychology of Everyday Things*. New York, NY: Basic Books, Inc.

Persig, R. (1979) *Zen and the Art of Motorcycle Maintenance: An Inquiry into Values*. New York, NY: Morrow Publishing Co.

CHAPTER 5

Modelling systems

Knowledge is that area of ignorance that we arrange and classify

(Ambrose Bierce)

This chapter outlines what a model is and what it should contain, and it introduces the basic ideas behind modelling. It introduces some of the structured diagramming notation and its family of associated models and outlines the benefits and disadvantages of each.

Models

In most technologies developed since Victorian times, models have been seen as a developmental step prior to actual implementation of the ideas. The idea has been to emphasise some aspect of the projected item and de-emphasise other aspects. The British Admiralty used models of the warships, provided by contractors, as a means of ensuring that the appropriate specifications were being upheld by the contractors. In fact the model served as part of the contractual agreement. Usually the model became part of the documentation.

Since Boehm (1981) recognised the importance of modelling and its benefit in systems development, modelling has been recognised as an appropriate activity to undertake in software building. Correction of specification errors at downstream stages are often orders of magnitude more expensive to correct at later stages of development.

In other industries, such as aerospace, shipbuilding and industrial plant, models of the projected solution have been seen as cost-effective activities. The majority of industries have insisted that there be a graphic representation, whether in two or three dimensions. Alternatively an appropriate graphic notation is used. Some industries have insisted on an 'active model' being produced. This active model is a very close representation to the projected end item, and the client can use it to comprehend fully the benefits and limitations. This is, in fact, a form of prototyping that I fully endorse (see Chapter 14).

What form should a model take?

The models that we are likely to be interested in are of systems that we are about to build. These systems will in essence be performing useful work. The models that we may make of this projected system may be static or dynamic. Static models use a notation to express the configuration of the intended situation. This may be expressed by means of graphics and text. Now, I personally believe that one needs both graphics *and* text to express a static model. This uses both image and logic processing of the reviewer's central nervous system. Pictures are all very well, but there is a variance in artistry and interpretation from pictures. So a graphic message requires formalisation and this is catered for by means of a notation that restricts meaning to a set of standard interpretations and makes it easier for the author to express his/her intentions. These graphic messages may be expressing the sequence of activities, the interdependence of activities or even the geographic relationships of pieces of knowledge. Text, which can be formatted, according to rules, supplements the graphic message. The graphics and the text then become a model.

Models can be made to be dynamic by being animated. This requires possibly some simulation on a mechanised system, such as a CASE tool. It is still a representation for communicational purposes.

Last, our models should convey a view of a projected system that is consistent and that allows prediction of behaviour which can also be documentation for subsequent developmental steps.

Stages of modelling

The essentials of a modelling approach require that the models are partitionable, i.e. allow an overall view to be broken down into more detailed viewpoints. An appropriate graphic notation is used along with suitable textual support. Care is taken here not to overload the viewer. The models should allow prediction of the system's behaviour. Additionally, the models should have sufficient logical rigour to demonstrate consistency.

A suitable modelling notation should be used when modelling systems. Commensurate with separating a user's view of a man-made system there are the three orthogonal views: structure, processing and behaviour, introduced earlier. To fully address each dimension a separate graphic notation was used with each. One for the structure the entity relationship diagram (ERD), one for the processing the data flow diagram (DFD) and one to express behaviour the state transition diagram (STD). Each of these diagrams has some object contribution to make.

Information structure

This is a geographical map of the concepts for which we are going to hold information in a projected or existing system. It is expressed by means of the entity relationship diagram (Fig. 5.1).

The entity relationship diagram (ERD) is a means of expressing how all of the subject area concepts (along with their attributes) are interconnected. Again, only four symbols are used. The rectangle represents a concept (a candidate object) that is of a tangible nature. The diamond represents a connection between *n* entities. The remaining symbols are more specific cases of the previous. The associative entity is a link entity whose existence is derived from the relationship which links a specific set of entities. This type of entity has the additional charm of automatically resolving directly *n:m* relationships. This type of entity is usually of a transactional nature. The supertype/subtype is an indication of a hierarchy amongst a set of objects. The relationships are also defined as to their cardinality. The ERD is used as a development step prior to formulating a schema for its subsequent implementation on a database. The entity itself is relevant to an object-oriented approach because it is a valid candidate object to be recognised. The relationship itself can be traced back to some real world connection between entities. This relationship is preserved in the form of a part of an operation that an entity will provide when it becomes an object. An entity

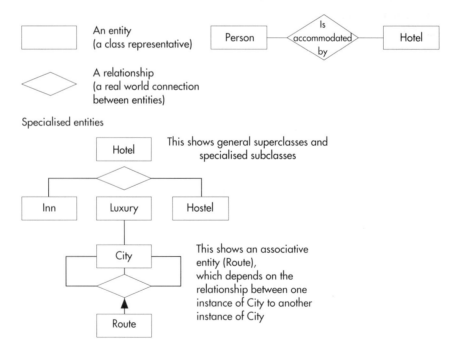

Figure 5.1   The entity relationship diagram notation (ERD).

may become an object once all the behaviour is collected and encapsulated with the entity.

Transformation of data (i.e. processing)

Transformation means the work that the system is actually undertaking. The data flow diagram expresses the transformations for a system. It is of interest because it is a representation of useful work that is or will be performed by a system. The PROCESS symbol expresses the logical unit of work or a 'thing' that is capable of performing work or in the last case a task. The FLOW is represented by the directed arc (Fig. 5.2).

There are three types of flow that may be represented: information, control and material (or energy). The latter group can only usually be used in survey work. There

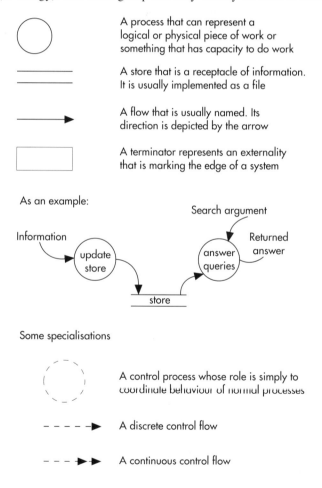

Figure 5.2   The data flow diagram notation (DFD).

are also two modes of flow: discrete (single-headed arrow) and continuous (double-headed arrow) (Fig. 5.3). The STORE symbol is represented by a flow that has been 'parked' for subsequent use. The last symbol in this group is the TERMINATOR. This symbol marks the edge of the system (or area of interest). DFDs may be levelled so as to abbreviate diagrams for checking. The DFD (as the method stands) has many heuristics in place to encourage well constructed diagrams. Most CASE representations have the majority of these heuristics embedded within the tool.

The DFD provides a model of the work that is to be performed by the systems. In the object-oriented development it has a relationship to the operations that an object may provide. However, it is not always a one-for-one relationship between processes and operations. DFDs are optimised to the depiction of flows and functions. The object is based on data, which is represented by the store, and in many cases each process introduced on a DFD will be associated with two or more processes. This will require that the individual processes are 'factored-out' to the appropriate object.

Additionally, this process of redistribution from the DFD to the object representation is accomplished by a series of steps so as to collect fundamental processing and custodial processing which in turn become the operations. The segmentation of the processing behaviour is made easier by use of pre- and post-condition specification of behaviour. The actual steps for this redistribution of behaviour are described in Chapter 7.

Time/sequence behaviour

The state transition diagram is a means of expressing finite state behaviour (STD). This diagram is for determining the conditions when specific transformations are 'triggered' and in what specified sequence. Finite state behaviour may be used to represent discrete

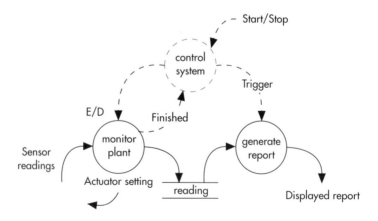

Figure 5.3   An example of a DFD.

control, human interaction or even the life-cycle for a candidate entity. The notation comprises four symbols. The state (a mode of behaviour) is represented by a long thin rectangle with an appropriately named state (Fig. 5.4). The transition is represented by a directed arc connecting the state symbol. Associated with the transition is the condition/action pair. The condition is the logical condition that gives rise to a transition. Associated with the condition is the action set, which is a set of processing actions. Different sequencing of the states is undertaken by a transitory state which acts in the role of a decision point.

From the object-oriented development side, the STD provides control behaviour for a role-based object called the coordinator object. The actions with the STD suffer little change, apart from referring to enabling, disabling or triggering processes. The STD, in an object-oriented sense, has an action set which corresponds to operations instead of processes.

Additionally, a derivation of the STD called the entity state transition diagram (eSTD) allows exploration of the life history behaviour of an object and is a first-rate tool for deriving the custodial behavioural operations that an object must provide. It represents a life history of a representation instance. It retains the same notational aspects with an alteration in viewpoint, namely each state is an 'entity state' and our focus is upon the life-cycle of an entity. The conditions are still related to 'events'. Figure 5.5 shows a 'life history' of a patient in a hospital administration system. The

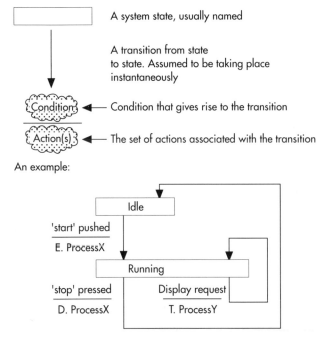

Figure 5.4 The state transition diagram notation (STD).

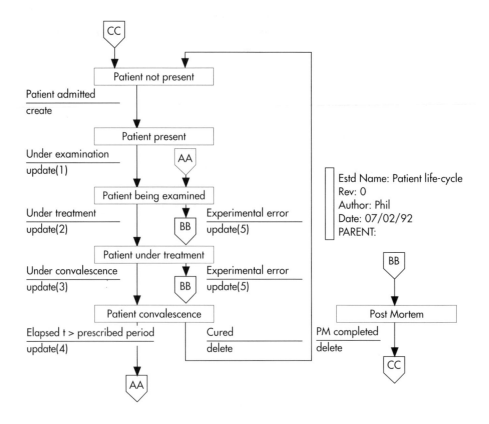

Figure 5.5   An example of an eSTD for a patient.

fully developed eSTD provides all the custodial behaviour that our patient 'object' representation will require. The only processes/operations not depicted are any matches or reads made against a specific patient.

The textual definition

The symbols for all of the diagram types are easy to draw freehand. Moreover, an external viewer to the method is not easily confused between the diagram types. Textual specification is seen as supporting the graphics and takes the form of:

1. Data dictionary: a catalogue/repository of all the data items.
2. Process specifications: a prescription as to the behaviour of each lowest level data flow diagram process (structured language or pre- and post-condition specification or even by means of a formal language).

Both the textual tools have direct contributions to the object frames and the operation specifications. The graphics and the textual components are a complementary set ready for review by developers and users.

Models as collected sets of views

At the next level above the diagrams we must think of the product development cycle showing all the appropriate phases – the development cycle. The Yourdon view of the development cycle is one of splitting the development phases into two major models: the logical and the physical. The logical model is rephrased as the ESSENTIAL because of the need to view the intrinsic quality of the system without technology 'clouding' the issue. It assumes that there is perfect technology. It is the essential model that is used as a vehicle for checking with the user/client that the represention has the essence of the requirement (the WHAT). The physical model is also rephrased as the IMPLEMENTATIONAL model because it is going to recognise the tangible physical implementation units be they processors, tasks or modules. It is focused upon resolving the HOW of the system. Checks are included in the construction rules to preserve the essential content in its implementation.

The essential and implementational models link to become the Yourdon view of the development cycle. The stages beyond the implementation (i.e. code and unit test, integration and test along with maintenance) are considered to be attended to by the local organisational culture.

Each model is derived from a previous one, with the exception of the first (which is tied to the charter). Each model should be a complete set of diagrams. There is traceability through the model. From the project manager's point of view, he/she may easily partition the units of the models into useful work breakdown structures. The earlier views of systems development used functional decomposition, which resulted in a wide variance of types of solutions whilst much effort is expended in the successive decompositions. The solution specification from this approach was consistently larger than the advocated route, which is the event partitioning approach. The Yourdon development cycle assumes a minimalist posture (it only recognises what a user identifies as being needed) and it does not immediately recognise any character directly related with object-oriented development. The minimalist approach is also only the development of a single product.

Limitations

In the majority of development cultures there is an embracing facility called infrastructure, which serves an enterprise as a whole by providing service functions. It is a collection of all the concepts and how they are interconnected within an enterprise. This function is not directly recognised by the structured approach, however it is important to recognise that it should exist for object-oriented development. It is from this infrastructure that much reuse may be derived, hence saving much development effort. The reuse of components from some centrally shared repository of resources available to all development shops. However, this in turn requires facilities to be put in place to assist in the navigation around these valuable resources. Additionally, much encouragement must be given to people to reuse rather than build anew.

Conclusions

Modelling is useful, we must have a notation that uses graphics and text and with appropriate rules to ensure consistency. The models can be static representations, which are suitable for pencil and paper outlines with representation in a CASE tool, they may also be animated as prototypes. The idea is the same – a representation for review. The representations can be optimised to depict *what* should be undertaken and separate models to depict *how*. Each model should link to the next as a series of developmental steps.

References and further reading

Boehm, B. (1981) *Software Engineering Economics*. Englewood Cliffs, NJ: Prentice Hall.

McMenamin, S. and Palmer, J. (1984) *Essential Systems Analysis*. New York, NY: Yourdon Press.

Ward, P. (1984) *Systems Development Without Pain: A User's Guide to Modelling Organisational Patterns*. New York, NY: Yourdon Press.

Ward, P. and Mellor, S. (1984) *Structured Development for Real Time Systems*. New York, NY: Yourdon Press.

CHAPTER 6

Approaches to object-oriented systems development

Every revolutionary idea – science, politics, art or whatever – evokes the same stages of reaction:
– it is impossible – don't waste my time
– it is possible but it is not worth doing
– I said it was a good idea all along

(Anon)

This chapter describes the various approaches that are possible in adopting an object-oriented approach. It includes the radical revolutionary approach and, as a contrast, the synthetic approach. Then, as a result of the development of the two previous approaches, we have the mutually shaped approach. The benefits and disadvantages of each are discussed.

What are the various approaches that are available?

An object-oriented approach offers much flexibility in the types of systems it may address. This may be from information systems through to real-time control. To say that we have a systematic way of applying our object-oriented development there must be a methodology. A methodology is a systematic set of principles and procedures applied to a technology. A methodology must be the following:

1. It must be a rational set of practices and must produce consistent results.
2. It must be able to deal with a wide band of problem sizes.
3. It must allow easy partitioning of the problem area.
4. It must allow easy checking for correctness.
5. It should allow a stepwise refinement.
6. It will have some theoretical foundations and reproducible results.

For example, it means that we can apply the methodology to a given situation and have a high degree of reproducibility between the following combinations:

	Day	
Person	**Monday**	**Friday**
Sydney	result*i*	result*j*
Gladwys	result*k*	result*l*

Where the results *i* to *l* have a high degree of congruance.

This means that we can say that we have a methodology in place when we can state the principles and can predict results. In software development the degree of rigour has not reached that of a robust science where the rules and practices have been rigorously applied and verified over a significant period of time. At the other end of the spectrum we have a weak craft, which means there are some techniques applied but little rigour involved. The remaining dimension is the degree of subjectivity involved ranging from one end of the scale being total flexibility and on the other end of the scale complete rigour. So far software engineering has moved from being totally flexible but has not reached the state of complete rigour (Fig. 6.1).

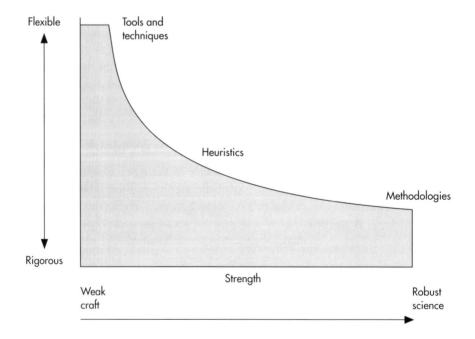

Figure 6.1   Methodologies and crafts (with thanks to David Tryon, Bell Pacific).

What should the ideal method do?

Returning to our object-oriented paradigm, an object-oriented methodology should allow our developer access to a set of procedures for recognising candidate objects along with an appropriate set of heuristics.

It should allow for development of those objects by means of a set of refinement steps. This refinement should enable all the desirable traits of behaviour required of the object to be captured, i.e. the appropriate fundamental services the object should provide along with the appropriate custodial services. 'Fundamental' here means those activities that are fundamental to the nature of the application; 'custodial' means those activities required to keep the object maintained (i.e. create, delete and change). There should be appropriate rules for ensuring consistency and correctness of the object's behaviour.

Has a similar sort of thing happened before?

At the advent of structured methods (the late 1960s and early 1970s) a similar 'disturbance' rippled through development shops. The mode of application was first into structuring programs into modules and arranging them into a hierarchy. This provided the basis for another layer of development – structured design. The advent of new modelling tools (such as DFDs) provided this basis in the mid-1970s. This in turn provided a basis for 'structured analysis' to look at all the prerequisite activities in structured terms. With this layering it was then time to integrate and order the structured techniques to accommodate DFDs, ERDs and STDs together with the textual material. Development of methods is a lengthy process and it occurs bottom up. Object development has, as I perceive, a similar ontology. OOPLs evolved first, then object-oriented design and then object-oriented analysis, and we are currently in an integrative phase. So far the object-oriented method of development has mimicked the structured methods in their mode of development.

The nature of change

With any innovation there are always difficulties introducing change. Some people will welcome change (for change's sake, possibly) and others are absolutely hostile to change and require the most burdensome proof before adopting change. In this particular context of change and object-oriented development there are the early adopters (the reds) and they usually will constitute about 10 per cent of the population, and then there are those that will go along with change once it has been demonstrated as effective. This group constitutes around 70 per cent of the population (the greens). The remaining 20 per cent (the laggards), as a general rule, are those who will be dragged 'kicking and screaming' to the new mode of development (the blues). Those early adopters (innovators) are ideal as apostles for the new development style and are the agents of change for the group that once convinced will convert over to the new development style.

Specific object-oriented development styles – direct

There are two major approaches to object-oriented development, with an emergent third approach. The first approach has been dubbed by Yourdon (1989) the 'revolutionary' approach. This approach operates on the belief that the structured methods are *passé* and should be jettisoned in favour of direct object-oriented methods. The object-oriented paradigm is the one and only paradigm. Additionally, it also sees structured methods as not contributing anything. Bertrand Meyer has intimated that 'objects are just there for the picking', giving apparent unbounded freedom to create one's useful objects.

A technique attributed to Abbott (1983), which involves textual analysis of material and collection and classification of nouns (which become object candidates or qualifiers) and verbs (which become related to the services that an object may offer), also offers a direct approach.

This viewpoint has much attraction to some prospective object-oriented developers. There are many followers and advocates of this direction, such as Grady Booch, Peter Coad, Sally Shlaer and Steve Mellor. The advantages of this approach are the directness to the development of objects. The disadvantages are related with the total freedom to create objects which leads to a lack of repeatability, which is important if we are to consider an object-oriented approach as being a methodology.

Specific object-oriented development styles – synthesist

An alternative direction, dubbed by Yourdon (1988) as the 'synthesist' direction, this presumes that the objects may be derived from the structured 'stuff' by means of a set of systematic actions based upon heuristics. Many serious developers now have much investment in structured methods with a good track record of success with this style of development. Their clients have also become convinced of the benefits. Can one realistically say to this group of practitioners 'Sayonara structured stuff' (Yourdon, 1988) and suggest that they should throw out all this old stuff and go with the new? Their first questions are likely to be 'Is this just a new fad?' or 'The structured stuff works for me. Why should I change?'.

By means of an anecdote, clients of mine in Scandinavia were excellent practitioners of the structured methods and produced effective systems. On one of their later contracts they were to use Ada as the solution language. Their development style appeared to be a normal structured series of models and then, just before the last model, there was a miraculous experience where apparent intuition took over and as a result there emanated Ada 'packages' (Fig. 6.2). Their request was 'Please would you document how these objects were recognised and developed into objects'. Their viewpoint was that there must be 'object material' sitting there quiescently in the structured material and there should be a set of rules to transform the artefacts of the structured diagrams into appropriate object components. A significant number of developers have come to this conclusion, e.g. Meillor Page-Jones, Steve Weiss and Tony Wassermann.

In essence the idea is that the data model (entity relationship diagram) yields the candidate objects to be worked with. The custodial activities – those related with maintenance – are all collected from the entity life-cycle diagram (eSTD). The processing for the objects is drawn from the data flow diagram. However, the processes often have to be decomposed and rearranged to be placed into the appropriate viable objects. Any discrete real-time behaviour is developed in the data flow diagram, along with the state transition diagram. For this type of coordination behaviour 'role'-based coordinator objects are created. There are additional rules related to inspection of the data flow diagrams looking for certain configurations, which can be directly mapped into object configurations. There is an additional activity that follows, which is the inspection of currently held objects, held in the form of an OID (object inheritance diagram), which may in turn be reused in this evolving application. The delivered object models are an OIV (object internal view) for each cited object and an ODD (object dependency diagram) for each application area inspected. There would be textual definition material to support the object and each of its operations.

There is a burden with this approach, which is that the developers will be expending more modelling effort to develop a structured set of models. Then there is an additional activity to derive the object-oriented version of the model and there is the burden of keeping the two models balanced (Fig. 6.3). However, there is also a significant benefit

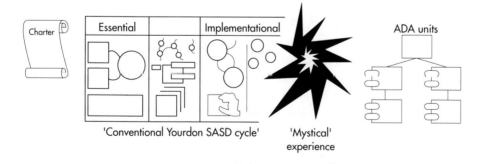

Figure 6.2 Object-oriented development as a 'mystical' experience.

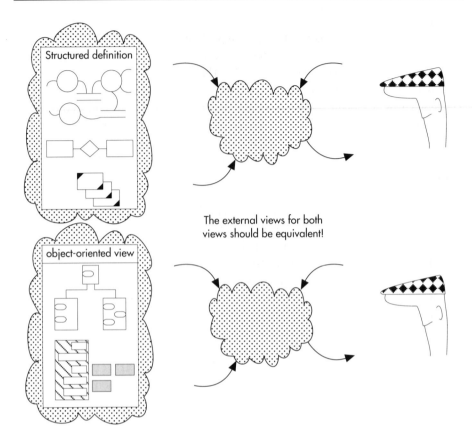

Figure 6.3   Consistency of external views.

from this approach, which is the repeatability and the preservation of an easy to follow trail. The detail of this approach with the specific heuristics is described in Chapter 7.

The mutually shaped option

As we have seen, we have two opposing groups with, in many ways, deeply held views. However, two distinct groups arguing very actively about the pros and cons of each approach will often influence one another indirectly. This is what has happened in the object-oriented approaches. I have dubbed it the *mutually shaped* approach because each of the major protagonists has 'shaped' one another to some extent. The directness of the revolutionaries has influenced the synthesists. The revolutionaries have seen benefits from some of the 'structured stuff'.

The synthesists have gained from this direction because they have cut down the amount of 'structured stuff' they work with whilst retaining the highly useful construction trail. The revolutionaries have gained the heuristics associated with constructing objects and the repeatability.

In essence, taking an application viewpoint, the context diagram becomes an object context at its topmost level. The events are perceived as 'raw' messages that the system must attend to. The events, once formatted, become source material for developing an object relationship diagram (ORD) and an object interconnection net (OIN). The custodial behaviour of the object is described by the entity state transition diagram, which is derived directly from the event list. Reuse is assisted by inspection of the object inheritance diagrams (OID). Should there be a need to expend an object for subsequent development, the object internal view (OIV) is still available. An implementation view is derived directly by use of the object dependency diagram (ODD), which is an application view, and maps directly to the object-oriented programming language (OOPL) units. Textual definition is retained by means of object frames to define the object and operations. This approach is described in more detail in Chapter 8.

Conclusions

There is no 'silver bullet' solution to systems development problems. The object-oriented development styles introduced are the similar posturings that occur with any innovation. The revolutionaries in full fervour will attempt to make sweeping changes. There are benefits from that approach but there are also disadvantages, in terms of making development a reproducible and systematic activity. The 'synthesis' approach builds on a foundation laid down by the structured methods. There are rules to assist in the development of objects from the products of the structured methods. These two views have influenced each other and the approach called 'mutually shaped' reaps the advantages of both plus the additional benefit that it is easier to introduce in to a development shop.

References and further reading

Abbot, R.J. (1983) 'Program design by informal English descriptions.' *Comm. of the ACM*, **26**(11), 882–94.

Bergland, G.D. (1987) 'Structured design methodologies: tutorial: software design strategies.' *IEEE Computer*, New York, NY: Society Press.

Brooks, F. (1986) 'No silver bullet: essence and accidents of software engineering.' In: H-J. Kluger (Ed.) *Information Processing '86*. Amsterdam: Elsevier.

Yourdon, E. (1988) 'Sayonara structured stuff.' *American Programmer*, **1**(6), 1, 4–11.

Yourdon, E. (1989) (Special issue devoted to object-oriented observations). *American Programmer* **2**(7–8), 3–108.

CHAPTER 7

The synthesist approach

> When the map and the terrain do not agree, trust the terrain
> (Swiss army maxim)

This chapter deals with how to develop a derived object model from the products of the structured models. It explains the principles and also depicts a roadmap to show suggested development stages. It also outlines the heuristics to assist in developing the object model. The only object models referred to are the ODD (dependency diagram), OID (inheritance diagram) and the object internal view (OIV). In addition, many of the rules refer to the Yourdon structured models. There is no reason why the rules cannot be applied to the SSADM approach, it is the general principles that is the important concern.

The essence

The essence of the synthesist approach is that the structured methods have within the various diagrams (DFDs, ERDs and STDs) material from which the appropriate object material may be derived, the object material being the object candidate itself along with the appropriate behaviour. The choice of the term 'derive' indicates that the object material is extracted by applying a set of rules to the various structured diagram in turn. These rules are introduced in this chapter.

The concept map

Candidate objects are selected on the basis of the concepts they are to represent rather than specific aspects of their processing. The concept itself is more resilient to change than its collection of functions. For example, concepts related to a business information system at one period of time tend to be the same as for that identical system viewed many years later. What tends to occur is that the concepts still exist but become more specialised. It is my view that an ERD (entity relationship diagram) is a good vehicle to represent the concepts and how they are interconnected.

As an example, a fragment of the business system would have the following two concepts represented: Bank Account and Customer at a period 1. Many years later the same conceptual structure will persist, except that the Bank account may 'sprout' specialisations, such as Current Account, Deposit Account and Special Reserve Account (Fig. 7.1).

The behaviour associated with each concept (entity) tends to be constructed from two types of activity – custodial and fundamental. The distinction is useful because the source of each is different. Custodial activities can be derived from an entity state transition diagram (eSTD) and fundamental activities can be derived from the DFD.

Custodial activities

Custodial behaviour is that behaviour associated with maintaining the integrity of the concept. These are functions to create instances, update instances and finally remove them (deletions). These activities may be explored by means of an entity state transition diagram (eSTD). These activities are independent of any one application. The operations associated with the entity may be taken directly from the action part of the eSTD and applied directly to the candidate object.

Fundamental activities

Fundamental activities are associated with the purpose of the system, such as those activities related to accessing and updating instances. The activities are related to the fundamental behaviour of an application and can be explored and developed by means of the data flow diagram. These activities are specific to any one application. These two regimes of behaviour do have some degree of overlap. The mapping of the DFD process behaviour to its equivalent object's operation is not a straightforward one to one mapping. Another form of fundamental behaviour may be the control of a system.

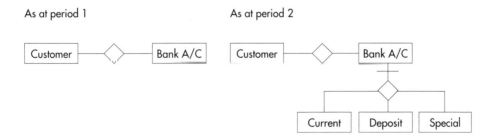

Figure 7.1   Constancy of data structures with time.

This is usually expressed in terms STDs and the DFDs. These two types of diagram contribute directly to the object-oriented model.

The textual definition material used to define the functionality of a system is also capable of redistribution in its object-related form. The data dictionary items are, for the main part, preserved along with some degree of rearrangement. The process specifications are used as source and rearranged into the appropriate operations specifications.

Entity relationship diagram

The entity relationship diagram (ERD) is the major modelling tool from which our candidate objects will be drawn. It is assumed that before gathering the possible object candidates the ERD model has been balanced against the complementary graphic tools such as the data flow diagram (DFD) and the STD. Additionally, it is expected that the full set of entity attributes have been defined.

Each ERD component has a role to play in the development of the object. The entity itself is a candidate object. It will already be accommodating the attributes that are required along with an identifier. An entity may become an object when all the appropriate behaviour has been gathered and encapsulated as one unit. This behaviour may come from two sources: custodial behaviour from an eSTD and fundamental behaviour from a DFD.

The relationship defines how an entity (concept) is linked with another entity. This relationship will map to some message that will connect one object to another. The relationship name will also have some suggestion as to a service that an object is expected to provide (Fig. 7.2).

Supertypes and subtypes depict a class of structures with specialisations; this is useful for recognising inheritance situations. Note that within the ERD notation a subtype may be connected to more than one supertype, which is equivalent to stating that we can recognise potential multi-inheritance situations. In object-oriented development environments it is useful to recognise potential inheritance within the project, as well as recognising within the enterprise that certain entities may be a specialisation of a concept already held within the enterprise's resources (Fig. 7.3).

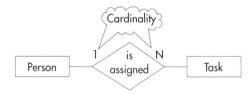

Figure 7.2   An entity relationship and cardinality.

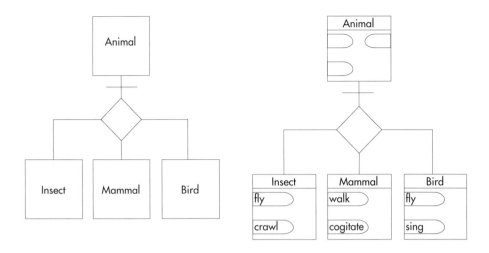

Figure 7.3   An ERD supertype/subtype and an inheritance diagram.

The ERD is a static model of the concepts – it does not depict any work at all. The relationship connections between entities gives only a suggestion as to the actual connection between the objects. In the case of a small ERD fragment (Fig. 7.4) Person is assigned Tasks. The 'is assigned' relationship will have some message equivalent. In this example 'Person' may be assigned to some activity in a 'schedule'. This is diagrammatically represented by a message from the 'assign' operation of 'Person' to the 'assign' operation of 'schedule'. This, then, completes the 'is assigned' relationship.

Each entity in turn will need to have defined all the operations with which it will deal. Each entity will have to cater for both custodial and fundamental processing. This activity is sometimes ascertained by means of an array depicting the various processes against the appropriate classified types of custodial activities:

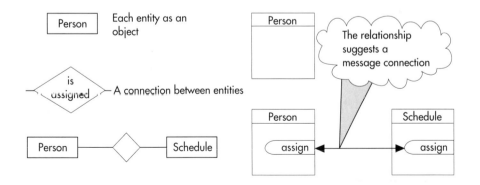

Figure 7.4   Entities as candidate objects.

For Entity: **Person**

Process:	Process 1.1	Process 1.2	Process 1.3	Process 1.4	Process 1.5
Create		X			
Read	X	X			
Update			X		X
Delete				X	

This assumes that we have already constructed a DFD to have identified the behaviour of each process. Whatever the behaviour, each process may not be restricted to just the store Person but may have involved other stores.

The DFD's contribution

The idea behind an object-oriented approach is that we have all the processing encapsulated within the object. The other major source of structure is the DFD and it is not necessarily organised just around one store but is typically focused on the transformation of flows from multiple stores.

The DFD is a friendly modelling tool, which can be used to depict the work that is to be accomplished by a system or the work of which a system is capable. There is a temptation by some to make an object out of a process. This does not, as a general rule, become a good object because it will often use many concepts to accomplish its role, which means it does not become a cohesive unit.

Let us take as an example a situation we can easily visualise in the real world and we express it with a DFD. We shall then show the equivalent object-oriented viewpoint by means of the object-oriented diagrams.

Our DFD (Fig. 7.5) is quite straightforward. There are two processes (1.1 and 1.2)

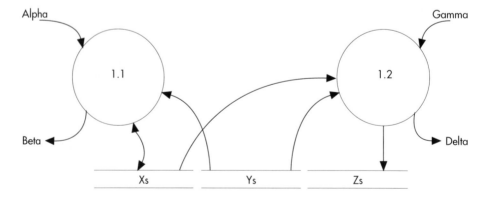

Figure 7.5   A generalised DFD.

which are driven by two separate flows (alpha and gamma). Three stores are accessed: X, Y and Z. An object-oriented representation of this situation will first identify the concepts being referred to which are Xs, Ys and Zs. These become our candidate objects X, Y and Z (note it usual to apply the singular name for an object as it is a class representative) (Fig. 7.6).

The DFD and equivalent object dependency diagram

The processing behaviour that we wish to put into the objects is derived from examining the processing that each process undertakes. We then extract the processing that is relevant to each store and insert it into each appropriate object (Fig. 7.7). Each process may be viewed as a set of processing in which there is a subset that should be extracted to be put into the appropriately named object. The different fill patterns show the mapping from the processes to the appropriate operations. This maps only the store-access-related behaviour from the DFD.

The remaining piece of behaviour is associated with accepting flow alpha and response flow beta and accepting flow gamma and producing response delta. To model this piece of behaviour we need a coordinator object, the role of which is to accept the inbound flows (alpha) and (gamma) and do the appropriate coordination to send suitable messages to the appropriate supplier objects (Fig. 7.8).

The directed arcs pointing from the coordinator object to the objects X, Y and Z indicates a client–supplier role. This type of diagram is an object dependency diagram (ODD). The behaviour of the objects X, Y and Z may not be complete because they do not have all the complete life-cycle behaviour within them. This behaviour may well be in other DFDs or can be derived as part of a life-cycle analysis of the particular object concerned.

If one is not quite sure of the behaviour and needs a more detailed viewpoint of the object, these objects may be opened to display their internals. Each object will become expanded into an object internal view (OIV). Note that each object can be expanded. The coordinator object has been expanded and is showing every externally visible operation as an internal operation in the brickwork fill and the polka-dot fill. The flows alpha and gamma are now in the role of messages to these operations. Emanating from the operations are dialogues to the appropriate operation of another object to provide operational services. These are, in turn, messages (Fig. 7.9).

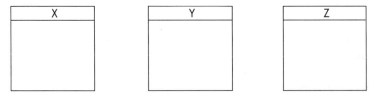

Figure 7.6 Candidate objects.

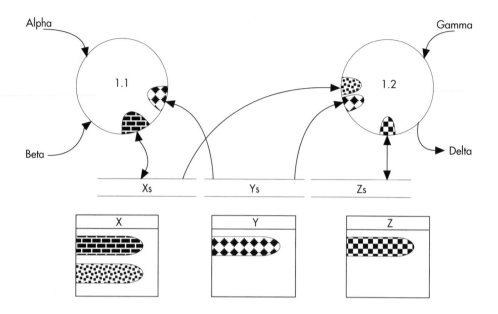

Figure 7.7   An equivalent ODD for a DFD.

Object X has also been expanded to show its internals, showing again the visible operations inside plus a store with the name of the object in plural form. The flows to the operation are expanded to depict whether they are truly a dialogue or simply a single flow. An internal view may depict extra operations to those shown externally. This may be for internal processing purposes or choosing not to show all the operations for clarity on the external view of the object. The action of opening the object may suggest extra pieces of processing that may be required which may duly be developed. The idea is that the object symbol is like a capsule of behaviour concentrated around a concept.

Objects based upon identified DFD roles

The DFD can yield additional candidate objects by means of configuration inspection. Two types of configuration can be easily recognised: a 'librarian' object and a transducer-type object.

The librarian-type object is an object that acts the role of custodian of the data and has clustered around it all the behaviour that uses or maintains that data. Its configuration is easy to spot on a DFD (Fig. 7.10). The name 'librarian' is borrowed from the types of objects recognised by DeMarco (1986).

Its configuration is, in fact, isomorphic with an internal view of the object. Of course,

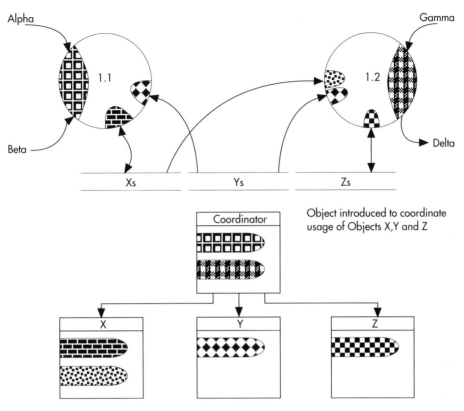

Figure 7.8   The correspondence between an ODD and DFD.

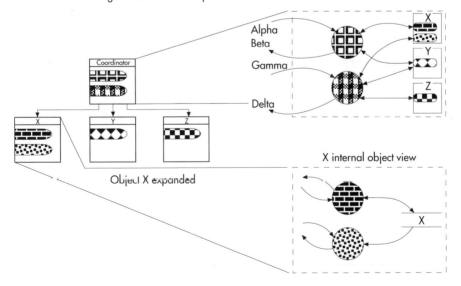

Figure 7.9   Decomposition of an ODD into internal views.

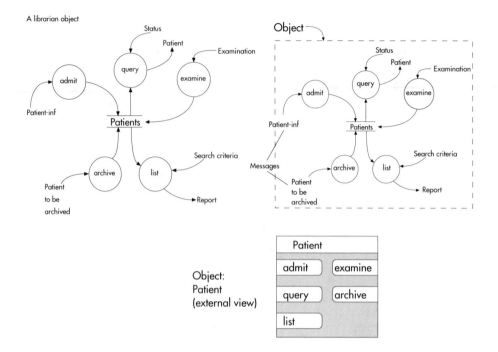

Figure 7.10   A librarian object and its DFD source.

each of the processes surrounding the store will likely become externally visible operations, all with the minimum of distortion.

Another configuration phenomenon that can be recognised is the transducer object. From inspection of a DFD we can recognise where we have processes that are strung in a line and all that is occurring is the transformation of the form of the information. These may be in the form of accepting inbound information from some sensor and transforming the raw physical information into some much cleaner system digestible form. This is depicted in Fig. 7.11, where we may see that some of the processing, such as the physical acceptance and filtering, has been buried in the object and so really the only essential activity is the presentation of the information on demand. Another situation may be sending information, which has in turn to be translated into a machine form for operation of an actuator.

Transduction

A similar situation exists for distributed systems where we wish to use a resource located on another machine. This could be represented by accessing a visibly available operation to connect to a specific resource on another machine. The object would

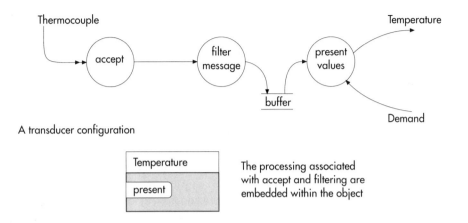

A transducer configuration

Temperature

present

The processing associated
with accept and filtering are
embedded within the object

Figure 7.11   A DFD configuration and a transducer.

encapsulate all the mysteries of connection and knowledge as to where resources were
and would just present the requested resource. This is again the concept of limited
visibility, where all extraneous mysteries are deliberately hidden. The object is a unit
with all the behaviour in one location.

Controllers

Another piece of the DFD that suggests an object is the control process, which is easily
distinguishable by the normal process symbol but with the dashed line. This type of
process describes coordination. The usage of objects requires an object to be a kind of
'conductor' demonstrating what object and services come into play in what situation.
There is a temptation to encapsulate as much as possible into as few objects as possible,
and this principle suggests that as much control as possible becomes encapsulated
within the object. This, in the long run, makes objects very specific and hence they tend
to become less reusable as opposed to highly granular objects which are potentially
reusable.

As an example I will borrow from Page-Jones and Weiss (1989), who recognised the
same problem. They cite an object-oriented farm where two candidate objects are: Cow
and Milk. Temptations may exist to make a composite object. Confusion then exists
when we wish to avail ourselves of services. Do we send a message 'milk yourself' or
is it 'uncow yourself'? Plainly it is confusing. So if we retain objects as objects Cow
and Milk they can have their own custodial activities and operations become easy to
recognise. We still, however, need another object to coordinate activities and that is by
way of the Farmer object. If we wish to expand more upon control it is best to look at
the state transition diagram and see the object-oriented consequences.

The STD's contribution

The STD itself suffers very little distortion as a result of a conversion from a structured (analysis or design) solution to an object-oriented solution. The states are in essence still the same control states we would wish to see in an object-oriented situation. The conditions are real world events that would have to be recognised. In many cases, in an object-oriented solution, it would be a form of message that was received. The actions are similar in the form of using the 'triggers', 'enables' and 'disables' when referring to pieces of processing. However, the individual pieces of processing, as operations, will have the same aggregate behaviour, the operations may not map one for one to original processes. The other forms of actions are raising and lowering flags. This is again the same as the object-oriented solution because it uses the coordinator object's own memory. The signal is a form of raw message to another device, which may be another coordinator object or an external device, which may in turn be perceived as another category of object to be used.

Textual specification

The textual specification material from the structured specification is capable of reuse in the object-oriented definition. All flows and their constituents become rearranged as messages and all storage definitions and relations are reused in the appropriate definition material for the objects.

Process and operation specifications

The process specifications of the processes, however, do not always have a neat one for one mapping to the operation specifications. As discussed before, this is because the 'processing' is relocated to the object that represents the concept. Typically a process is decomposed and the fragments are redistributed to the operations. With structured language, the specification, in all probability, will have to be rewritten because it does not fragment easily. However, with pre- and post-condition specification, because it is a declarative prescription with logical assertions connected by logical ANDs and ORs, the declarative behaviour may be more easily decomposed into logical fragments that will in turn populate the operation specifications.

The development cycle

There is a 'roadmap' of the likely development path that would be involved with the synthesist approach. In essence we would still recognise the principal modelling phases namely:

An essential modelling phase, which consists of modelling the environmental context to the system, followed by a detailing of the internal behaviour; this constitutes the logical model. This is followed by an implementational model, which comprises a model to allow exploration and detailing of processor choice (both hardware and liveware). This in turn is followed by a software architecture model, which details the task definitions. This becomes the basis to the construction of a code organisation model, which displays the arrangements of the code units (modules). This is a simplification and one recognises that there will of course be iteration between the various phases (Fig. 7.12).

With a synthesis approach the majority of the structured activities are preserved as a baseline. It is from this baseline that the object model is derived. The object model at this phase should have equivalent external behaviour. An external observer should perceive the same external behaviour (Fig. 7.13).

The generalised roadmap shown in Fig. 7.12 is to be read in a left to right direction. The vertical panels approximate to the modelling phase. The lower panels address the object-building activity and they 'draw' upon the structured items depicted in the upper panels using the derivation rules. This activity will in all probability mean deriving life-cycles for the candidate objects (i.e. ensuring complete custodial operations). When moving to an adjacent phase the structured models are used as a basis for development. The object-building phase will import material from the previous phase.

It will use the extra structured material from the current phase to elaborate the object model still further. The rightmost panel is the code organisation model and this will largely be an object dependency diagram depicting the client supplier configurations of the objects.

One of the economic justifications for an object-oriented approach is the concept of reuse. Along the bottom of the diagram you will see a panel called 'central supplier' running horizontally. This is a euphemism for the central repository of objects with a suitable 'browser' mechanism to assist a 'viewer/user' who can see what objects have the desired behaviour required for this application. Now the 'viewer/user' will be encouraged to gather as much as possible from this repository of objects.

Actually this repository of objects should be viewed as stretching across all the development projects, because it is a common resource. Figure 7.14 depicts this central supplier in the horizontal plane. Looking at the detail of the horizontal plane there is an extensive ERD, which extends over the domain of various single projects. There are eSTDs to depict the life-cycle of entities whose life-cycle may extend across many application boundaries. Systems development people should be encouraged to use this resource. Remember, this is the way of encouraging 'wheels' to be invented in one place and used everywhere.

Heuristics for the derivation of objects

To approach its derivation activity the heuristics must be stated. As mentioned, before a heuristic is a rule of thumb that is easy to apply:

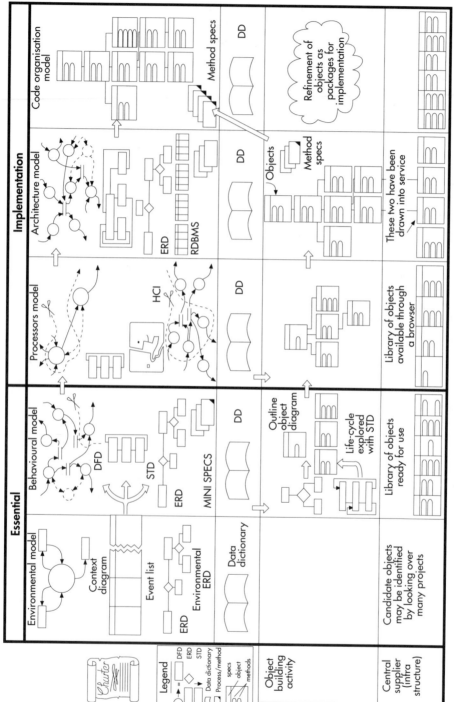

Figure 7.12 The synthesis development cycle (reproduced by kind permission of Yourdon Inc.).

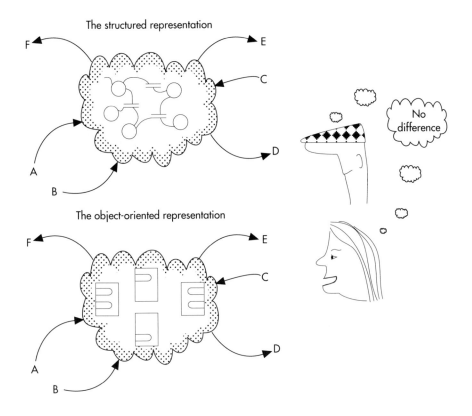

Figure 7.13 Constancy of external behaviour (reproduced by kind permission of Yourdon Inc.).

1. DFDs, if decomposed to their most primitive form (one flow input one flow output and a store access), may correspond directly to a method for that store reincarnated as an object.

2. DFDs are, as a rule, using more than one store. The process may become fragmented into *n* operations. Each operation will then be placed with the data. However, there are situations where a store is surrounded by processes, each of which is solely servicing the store. This is a 'librarian'-type object. (See Fig. 7.10 and note that the DFD configuration and the object internal view are isomorphic.)

3. DFDs in a processor model. For an asymmetric distribution of the essential model to *n* processors ($n \geqslant 2$) it is necessary to preserve the essence of the requirement. The cut to separate the processing must be a minimum weight cut across essential flows (minimum weight = importance, volume, frequency). Cuts across a process tend to be equivalent to cuts across flow, between processes at a lower level.

4. Processes in a serial relationship. A set of processes that are in a serial

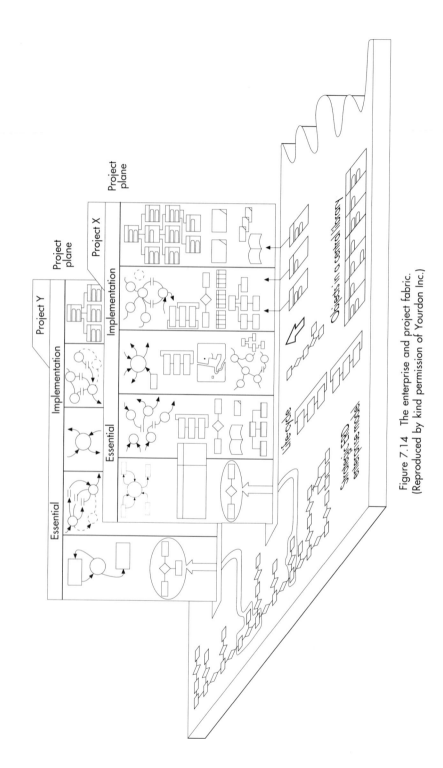

Figure 7.14 The enterprise and project fabric.
(Reproduced by kind permission of Yourdon Inc.)

relationship (see Fig. 7.11) may be considered as a transducer. All the behaviour may be encapsulated as one transducer named after the subject that is being transformed.

5. Control processes as controller objects. If a DFD uses a control process, this will be a candidate controller object. It will also gather the associated STD behaviour for that control process.

6. Process specifications written in pre- and post-condition specification form tend to be more easily rearranged during the object construction activity. The fragmentation is by assertion group so it can easily be 'copied' and 'pasted'.

7. ERDs. Each viable ERD entity is a candidate object. Supertype and subtype entities are candidate representations of inheritance. All the definition material for the entity is directly of use in the object definition.

8. ERDs. Each relationship between entities will trace out a message connection between the corresponding objects.

9. ERDs and processor models. As a provider of ERD services one will have to cut the ERD for each processor region. There will be a major portion of processing and a minor portion of processing:
   (a) cuts are made across relationships;
   (b) each cut will cause a 'ghost' entity to remain on the major portion ERD and a reduced entity on the minor portion ERD;
   (c) the service provider shall perceive a compressed entity that will migrate from the major processing portion to the minor portion periodically to retain system integrity.

10. The external event list is a source for candidate objects and operations. The event list is a list of external stimuli to which the system must respond. In object-oriented terms this is similar to the system being sensitive to certain messages originating from the environment. The event list takes the form of an external agent being the source of an event that has a relationship to some specific subject area of the system. This style of structured development is derived from McMenamin and Palmer (1984). This has the slot pattern of: Agent, Action and Subject area. This specific pattern maps directly to facilitating candidate objects and operations (Fig. 7.15). Each event becomes a candidate to be decomposed into appropriate ERD fragments.

11. The life-cycle of an entity is expressed by an eSTD. For a full life-cycle the actions associated with each transition condition become the operations for that entity. The source of the life-cycle is the external event list. The conditions correspond to external events and the actions are the minimal set of custodial operations (see Fig. 7.15 and heuristic number 10).

12. STDs. A state transition diagram is a representation of time and sequence (discrete control). For a translation of an essential STD to its corresponding object representation, states are preserved in a controlling object. Transitions

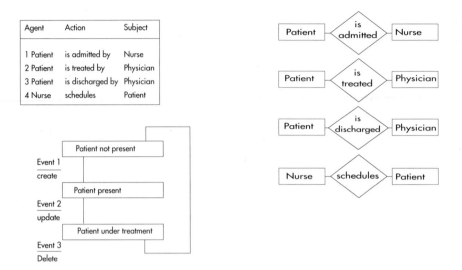

Agent	Action	Subject
1 Patient	is admitted by	Nurse
2 Patient	is treated by	Physician
3 Patient	is discharged by	Physician
4 Nurse	schedules	Patient

Figure 7.15   An external event list as source for ERDs and eSTDs.

remain as they were in the essential model. Conditions will be the same, actions, however, have different constituents (invoking *n* objects instead of *m* processes) to accomplish the same time sequence behaviour.

13. Processor model. In the case of asymmetric distributed processing (processors ≥ 2), one should think of a virtual observer, who is familiar with the essential required behaviour, and his/her view should remain the same. Therefore there will be a service object which will provide methods (services) that preserve the virtual observer's viewpoint (he/she should not see the join). Note heuristic number 3.

14. Refinement. This, in object-oriented terms, may be a measure of the set of operation cohesion. In a DFD, for an application, there may be a total of P_1 lines of process specification. This is an expression of the sum of all the transformations. This processing may be redistributed into objects' operations. There may be a degree of repeated behaviour in the processing when accessing stores, as expressed by a DFD. The sum of the operation processing lines may be expressed by O_1. The ratio P_1/O_1 represents index of compression of the process specification into operation specification. This ratio can be further increased by use of object operations that may be drawn from a central library (say O_c). This may be expressed by $P_1/(O_1 - O_c)$; this increases the ratio further. However, there is the burden that each time an object operation is called it introduces an extra prescription line in the form of an object operation message O_m. The revised ratio takes the form of $P_1/(O_1 - O_c) + O_m$.

15. Quality rules relating to traceability:

(a) an object model shall perform the same end–end 'transaction' threading as the original DFD. If positive it means there is equivalence, if negative it means there is incipient distortion.

(b) each essential process specification fragment shall be 'posted' to an operation specification. Unposted fragments from the essential model shall be considered an error. This is in effect a conservation of pre- and post-condition fragments.

(c) every ERD entity shall have as a minima a life-cycle, e.g. create, change, use and delete. The lack of any one of these operations should indicate possible omission of behaviour.

Worked example

By means of recapitulation of an extensive chapter, Fig. 7.16 depicts a small worked example to show derivation from an structured essential model into an ODD and associated OID. The example is for a Department of Motor Vehicles system controlling the registration of motor vehicles. The example is kept as simple as possible to optimise traceability.

On the left is the context diagram with the associated event list. The entity event table is a cross reference to external events and the associated entities. Each cell has an entry to depict its entity link 'c', 'r', 'm', 'u' and 'd' correspond to create, read, match, update and delete. The DFD and the ERD are as they would be displayed for an essential model. The lowest diagram is the eSTD, which depicts the life-cycle for the entity registration. This eSTD gives us the custodial actions associated with entity 'Registration'. All the entities in the diagram become candidate objects. The list in the diagram itemises the object operations and their sources from the DFD. To make the application effective a controlling (coordinating) object 'vehicle registration' is created, which uses the objects owner, vehicle and registration.

Conclusions

This synthetic approach is workable but it is labour intensive. So far the type of organisation that usually adopts this style of approach is one with a heavy investment in the structured methods, and one whose clients and users are also happy with this approach. Our discussion centred on the Yourdon structured methods as a source; most of the principles may be applied to SSADM. To gain the economic benefits of an object-oriented approach they favour this style of synthesis of object-oriented material from the structured material. There is also usually some variance as to the phase at which the object-oriented construction activity commences, some favouring object-oriented analysis and some favouring the object-oriented activity commencing as design in the physical construction phases.

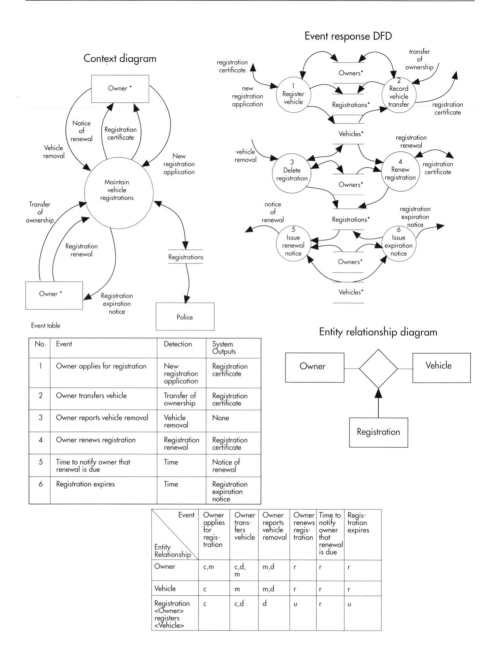

Figure 7.16 DMV – worked example (reproduced by kind permission of Yourdon Inc.).

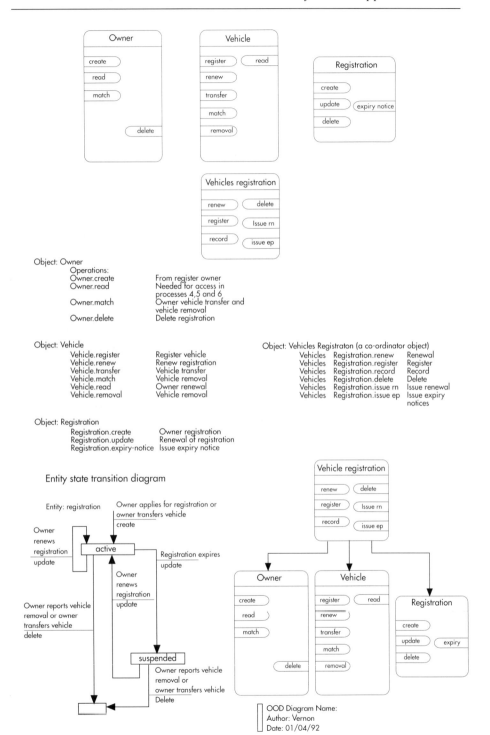

Owner

- create
- read
- match
- delete

Vehicle

- register   read
- renew
- transfer
- match
- removal

Registration

- create
- update   expiry notice
- delete

Vehicles registration

- renew   delete
- register   Issue rn
- record   issue ep

Object: Owner
Operations:

Owner.create	From register owner
Owner.read	Needed for access in processes 4,5 and 6
Owner.match	Owner vehicle transfer and vehicle removal
Owner.delete	Delete registration

Object: Vehicle

Vehicle.register	Register vehicle
Vehicle.renew	Renew registration
Vehicle.transfer	Vehicle transfer
Vehicle.match	Vehicle removal
Vehicle.read	Owner renewal
Vehicle.removal	Vehicle removal

Object: Vehicles Registraton (a co-ordinator object)

Vehicles	Registration.renew	Renewal
Vehicles	Registration.register	Register
Vehicles	Registration.record	Record
Vehicles	Registration.delete	Delete
Vehicles	Registration.issue rn	Issue renewal
Vehicles	Registration.issue ep	Issue expiry notices

Object: Registration

Registration.create	Owner registration
Registration.update	Renewal of registration
Registration.expiry-notice	Issue expiry notice

Entity state transition diagram

Entity: registration

Owner applies for registration or owner transfers vehicle
create

Owner renews registration
update

active

Registration expires
update

Owner renews registration
update

Owner reports vehicle removal or owner transfers vehicle
delete

suspended

Owner reports vehicle removal or owner transfers vehicle
Delete

Vehicle registration

- renew   delete
- register   Issue rn
- record   issue ep

Owner

- create
- read
- match
- delete

Vehicle

- register   read
- renew
- transfer
- match
- removal

Registration

- create
- update   expiry
- delete

OOD Diagram Name:
Author: Vernon
Date: 01/04/92

Table 7.1 lists all the various structured components against the object-oriented components they manifest themselves in.

Table 7.1 Synthesist sources

Structured source	Component	Corresponding object component
Entity relationship diagram	Entity Relationship Diagram	Candidate object Message connection between objects Class structure and inheritance
State transition diagram	State/transition Condition Action apply to processes	Same states and transition Same Similar: they now apply to specific object operations
Entity state transition diagram	Entity states/transitions Conditions Actions (custodial)	Same entity states/transitions Same These actions must be fully accommodated by the object create/update(s)/delete

Data flow diagram	Process (data)
	
	            (control)
	Store
	
	Flow (control)
	          (data)
		Operation for object though not always one for one
		This becomes a controller object
		Candidate object. Note it will have corresponding entity which will have been dealt with in the ERD
		Control message
		Data message

Data dictionary	All named items	All named items should be reincarnated in the object solution
Process specifications	Process specification Structured language Pre-/post-condition	Note each operation should represent a process or a subset of process behaviour

References and further reading

DeMarco, T. (1986) 'Object oriented design and structured analysis.' *Atlantic Guild Notes*, **26**, 1–8.

McMenamin, S. and Palmer, J. (1984) *Essential Systems Analysis.* New York, NY: Yourdon Press.

Page-Jones, M. and Weiss, S. (1989) 'OO synthesis.' *American Programmer*, **2**(7–8), 64–7.

CHAPTER 8

The direct approach

Ethnocentrism: thinking that life in our society is the only way of living, or worst still the only correct form

(Anon)

This chapter introduces the ideas related to working directly with objects as opposed to synthesising them from the products of structured analysis. The main diagram types we work with are the object interconnection net (OIN) and the object relationship diagram (ORD). Either of these diagrams may be augmented with the object internal view (OIV). The structured diagrams may be used as an annexe to help explain additional pieces of behaviour.

The concept

Instead of relying upon the structured diagrams and text having been worked upon first, we will look at an application at its top level, as if it is an object engine. This top level view of a system is often called the system's context diagram. In object terms this is the the topmost object and it has object behaviour at this level, i.e. all processing, state behaviour and memory as one unit (or capsule). The protocol for communication at this level is the event list, which may be perceived as a set of raw messages upon which the system must respond. Figure 8.1 shows that the context diagram and an object symbol at the top level are equivalent. The flows originate and terminate with rectangular symbols called terminators. The external event list is an inventory of appropriate stimuli (messages) to which the system must respond. The terminators are sources of events and likely recipients of responses from the system.

The flows are depicted as the conveyors of the message and we would name them appropriately from the application area. If we expand our view of the system context we may see associated with the terminator various types of flow (Fig. 8.2).

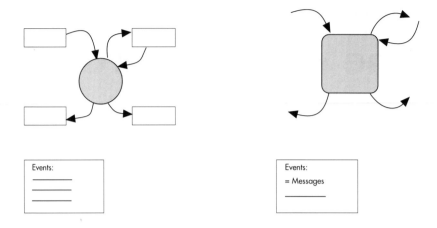

Figure 8.1   Systems context as a high level object engine.

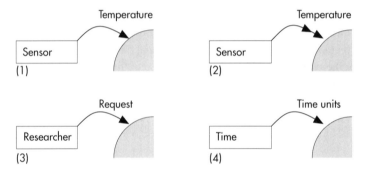

Figure 8.2   Source flows and the system's context.

Flows as messages

The flows can show their various characteristics. There are generally two types of flow: data and control. Additionally there are two dispositions of flows, such as discrete and continuous. Data flows are denoted by a solid flow line with an arrowhead. This is the information upon which an operation will transform into a response. Control flows are denoted by an abbreviated flow line and this denotes a stimulus to alter a control state.

The two dispositions are easy to describe. Discrete means a packet of information that arrives discretely. The message content is first the arrival of the packet itself. Continuous means that the information persists with time and the message itself is the value change or amplitude change (Fig. 8.3).

Once the boundary of the system is defined, we have to recognise the situation whereby those items (terminators) that are described as externalities will probably have to be described within the system. This is memory of the outside world. This is true

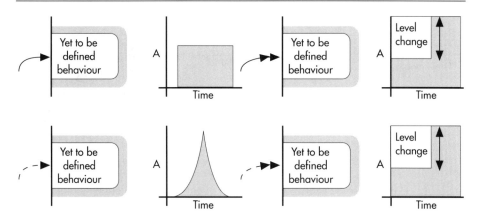

Figure 8.3   Types of flows and their reception by operations.

whilst we are recognising what we are going to keep records of. Where the externality is a human (or group of humans) the key question is: What are we going to have to keep data about (e.g. customer, supplier)? If, however, no information is required to be kept *per se*, then it is the interface we must represent. This is very similar to the situation with the human eye and perception, as described in Fig. 8.4, which is that information that is external in many cases will have to be re-represented within the system.

Events as messengers

The events themselves have a form of grammar or 'slot pattern', which should be adhered to; the events are indicators of messages. (Events were described in Chapter 7 and illustrated in Fig. 7.15.) It is useful to use a slot pattern to describe the main ingredients of an event as agent (the source) action and subject area.

The pattern is: agent (the originator) action, subject (specific area of the system) and instrument (grammatical instrument). Each of these items are easy to recognise in our system situation.

The agent is the originator and will map to a terminator that is representing that class. These may be people defined in a role, a device such as a sensor or actuator, or even another system.

The action is the verb phrase that will link the agent to something specific about the system. It is expected that this will be drawn from the subject area and makes sense to a subject area expert.

The subject area is the specific area to which the stimulus applies. This may be the system itself or a specific subject area, which in turn may be a superclass, subclass or even an attribute.

The instrument is a grammatical instrument where the agent operates on some subject area in conjunction with some other item (instrument). Not all events will have this situation.

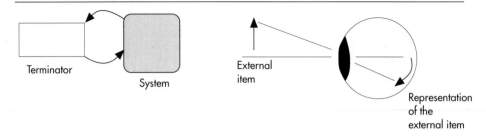

Terminator

System

External item

Representation of the external item

Figure 8.4   Representation of the external world inside a system.

For this event list to be useful, each external event should be defined along with its desired response.

The purpose of the OIN and ORD

The OIN and ORD diagrams are specifically for expressing the direct approach. The OIN is a diagram that depicts objects with externally visible operations connected to real world event flows and responses whilst also showing the intermediate responses required (i.e. the flows between object operations required to make a complete response). The OIN does not show, nor suggest, any form of hierarchy. All the objects and operations should be named and the flows to and from the 'outside' should be named. The dialogue flows between object operations does not need to be named as it is named in the operation specification. Any augmentation of the detailed behaviour of an object can be served by an OIV. It is intended that users be familiar with this notation to explain what the objects provide and how they may be coupled.

The event list is the inventory of stimuli to which the system should respond. The OIN may be threaded by tracking the event (message) through to the flow to the object operation and through to the other possible object operations participating in the response. Textual definition is provided for the object itself and each of the visible operations. The OIN itself can be developed into an ODD at a subsequent step of development.

The ORD depicts the interrelationship of the various objects. Each object will display its visible operations. Connecting the objects themselves is the relationship symbol, which should be named. It will also optionally depict the cardinality of the relationship (i.e. the correspondence of one object to another, in the form of $1 : n$ or more precisely $0, 1 : 1 : n$). The purpose of the ORD is to lay out the objects in a form where one can analyse whether there is a complete set of objects and operations and that this is likely to service all the foreseen needs and possibly suggest additional opportunities. The ORD is also seen as the precursory step to the formulation of an application on an object-oriented database (OODB). The subject of OODBs is dealt with in Chapter 11. The two diagram types OIN and ORD have a complementary nature, as we shall see later in this chapter (see p. 88).

ORDs and OINs – do we need both?

The ORD is a static view of the objects and is more extensive than the OIN. The OIN is optimised to show the flows to and from the environment and the collaboration between object operations. This may be checked with an event message thread.

Events and responses

The events are not only the source of messages but are also the source for some of the concepts about which we hold information. The format of agent (the originator) action, subject (specific area of the system) and instrument (grammatical instrument) become directly useful when introducing the concepts and showing how they are interrelated. If we take as an example the following set of events:

	Agent	Action	Subject area	Instrument
1	*Clerk*	*Creates*	*Ticket*	
2	*Clerk*	*Sells*	*Ticket*	*to Passenger*
3	*Passenger*	*Checks in with*	*Ticket*	
4	*Ticket*	*is Moved to*	*Archive*	

For each of the above events we can describe the appropriate response required:

1	*Clerk*	*Creates*	*Ticket*

Terminator (Clerk) initiating a creation.

2	*Clerk*	*Sells*	*Ticket*	*to Passenger*

Terminator (Clerk) modifying ticket.

3	*Passenger*	*Checks in with*	*Ticket*

Terminator (Passenger) having subject (Ticket) modified.

4	*Ticket*	*is Moved to*	*Archive*

Expiry of ticket requires removal to some archive.

We could have thought up many more actions related with the ticket and passengers but in the interests of keeping things simple we shall limit it to these four events.

To develop the problem area further we could build an entity relationship diagram (ERD) depicting how the concepts are interrelated. The appropriate ERD fragments area shown in Fig. 8.5.

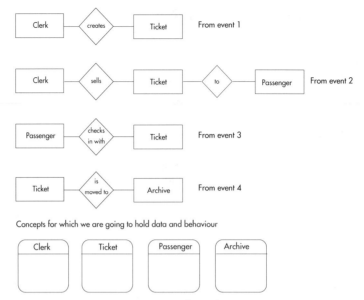

Figure 8.5   Events and ERD fragments.

Each of the entities can become object candidates in their own right. The key concepts taken from the ERD – Clerk, Ticket, Passenger and Archive will become candidate objects.

OIN construction

The OIN can now be started. Each event and its associated flow are drawn as connecting to the appropriate object and an appropriately named operation is chosen. The operation may require an associated operation to be used, which in turn requires a dialogue (message) with another object's operation.

1 Clerk Creates Ticket

This requires that a record of the ticket is created to keep track of the tickets, because a ticket is like a blank cheque and we want to curb the desire of clerks to write their own round the world trips.

A flow 'basic ticket detail' is the message to the object Ticket to have an operation create, and there is a message to object Clerk, which in turn has an operation create.

2 Clerk Sells Ticket to Passenger

This requires an update of the status of the ticket and an update to the object Passenger. The Flow 'Routing' (passenger's routing) is the event message to an operation sale, which in turn is connected to an object Passenger (a representation of the passenger because we are required to hold information concerning the passenger). The specific operation concerned is 'sale'.

3 Passenger Checks in with Ticket

This will require an update to the ticket and to the passenger reflecting the new status of the ticket. The stimulus message is 'Passenger check-in'; this is coupled to an operation 'check-in' within the object passenger.

4 Ticket is Moved to Archive

This requires the deletion of the ticket and its resurrection as an archive instance where it shall rest until time expiry. Time may be considered as a suitable message of an event to stimulate the removal of tickets that have been 'used' and their being placed in an archive. The Time message is connected to an operation 'Archive', which is connected to an operation 'create' with the object Archive.

Figure 8.6 depicts this updated situation.

OINs and control-type applications

There are other types of events, such as those that are related to a change in the state of the system or part of it. The 'slot pattern' is still the same for these types of events: agent, action, subject area and instrument. The agent may well be a sensor, actuator or an operator. The actions are verb links to a subject. Subject in this case will be some specific piece of state-sensitive equipment. The instrument can be something that is used in conjunction with the agent and the subject in this specific event.

By means of an example we can use a vending system (automat) and we shall describe the events that are relevant.

	Agent	Action	Subject area	Instrument
1	*Customer*	*Inserts*	*Coin*	
2	*Customer*	*Selects*	*Beverage*	
3	*Caterer*	*Replenishes*	*System*	
4	*Caterer*	*Collects*	*Revenue*	
5	*Caterer*	*Changes*	*Tariff*	

From the event list one can derive an ERD, even though it is primarily a control system (Fig. 8.7). We will describe the behaviour for each of these events (Fig. 8.8).

1 Customer Inserts Coin

The coin is validated against some rules held in the memory of a concept (object called

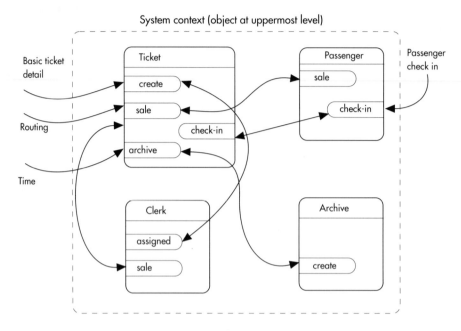

Figure 8.6   An OIN for the ticketing system.

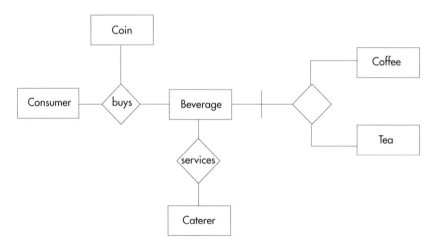

Figure 8.7   An ERD for the vending system.

COIN). The flow is the information related to a coin connecting to the operation 'accept'. This action also requires a control communication to the object Beverage and specifically to a constructed operation denoted 'coordinate'.

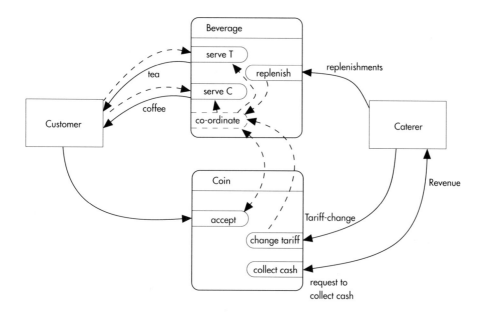

Figure 8.8   An OIN showing the terminators for the vending system.

2 Customer Selects Beverage

The customer's selection is a control flow to either serve tea or serve coffee. This in turn requires communication to the 'coordinate' operation to ascertain that it may proceed to serve the customer.

3 Caterer Replenishes System

This event signals that the machine is being replenished and that no drinks may be served whilst that is in progress. The Flow is connected to the operation called 'replenish' and it in turn has control communication to 'coordinate'. There is an event when the replenishment has finished whereupon the Beverage coordinate operation will become aware and allow continuing service.

4 Caterer Collects Revenue

This event requires that the caterer collect the cash without undue delay or hindrance of operation. The operation is appropriately called collect cash.

5 Caterer Changes Tariff

This event is associated with the caterer requiring a tariff change. This is coupled to an operation change tariff within the object coin. It in turn communicates with Beverage coordinate.

Further expansion of the behaviour of the objects concerned can be accomplished by means of an OIV. Further augmentation of the behaviour of the system can be exhibited by means of the STD. Figure 8.9 shows that the STD is seen as an annexe to the control operation of the OIV Beverage.

ORD construction

For applications where significant data storage is required, it is recommended that the ORD is used. The ORD's purpose is to depict how the information may be stored. Figure 8.10 shows the ticketing system as described earlier.

We may then populate Fig. 8.10 with the operations that we identified earlier, these being all the visible operations at this stage (Fig. 8.11).

As an example, we may have a situation where in a market trading system we have objects to depict Wholesaler and Commodity and we may show the visible operations for Wholesaler (buys and sells) and Commodity (increment and decrement). We may also show how these objects are related by means of relationships such as 'is restocked' and 'sells'. The OIN shows the equivalent situation *vis à vis* the message traffic (Fig. 8.12).

If we return to the Passenger ticketing system, we can draw the appropriate ORD

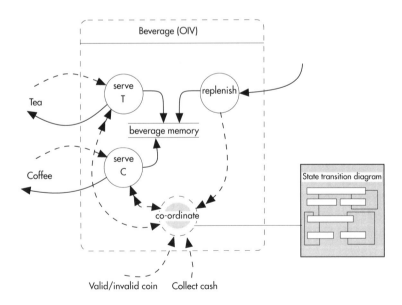

Figure 8.9   An OIV for the beverage object.

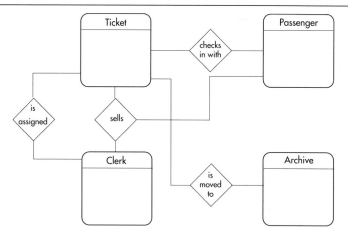

Figure 8.10   An ORD in initial skeletal form for the ticketing system.

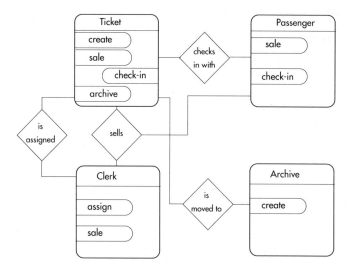

Figure 8.11   A more developed ORD for the ticketing system.

showing the various relationships that exist between the objects. If we take just two of the objects, Ticket and Clerk, we can see two of the relationships that are involved (Fig. 8.13). Relationship 'is assigned' connects Ticket and Clerk and corresponds to the message flow between Ticket create and Clerk assign. The relationship 'sells' is a three-way relationship because it connects Ticket, Passenger (not shown here) and Clerk and the associated Ticket Sale, Clerk Sale and Passenger Sale (Fig. 8.13).

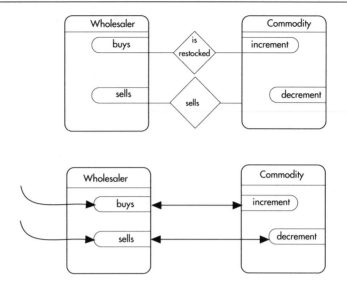

Figure 8.12   The relationship between an ORD and an OIN.

The relationship between OINs and ORDs

The OIN and the ORD are related but are optimised to show different things. The OIN is focused to show the message interconnections, to and from the external world and amongst the objects. The ORD shows how the objects may be arranged to service the various transactions as a possible precursory step to implementation on an OODB. Another way to link the two diagram types is to think of the ORD as providing generalised 'trunking' of the messages. The relationship symbol actually acts as a conduit for the messages between the objects. The Messages trace out the relationship paths between the objects (Fig. 8.14).

The direct route roadmap

At this point it is appropriate to describe the sequence through time for the development of objects with this style of development. The layout of the road map is described in Fig. 8.15. The chart is organised with time running left to right, and the panels depict stages in the development of objects. The lowest horizontal panel depicts the enterprise repository of objects.

The essential panels are comprised of an environmental view of the object, i.e. context diagram (object engine) plus event list (raw messages). The ERD is there to sketch out how the concepts may be arranged. The next panel is the behavioural model, depicting the OIN together with annexed material (OIVs) and STDs where behaviour is to be refined. ORDs may also be included where appropriate. The textual definition is supported by means of the object frames with associated operation specifications.

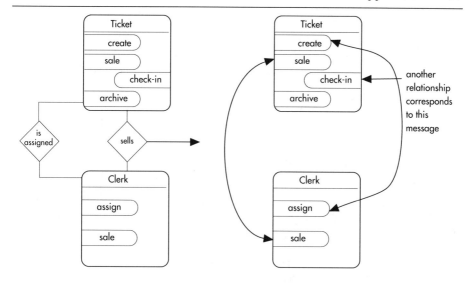

Figure 8.13   Flows and relationships.

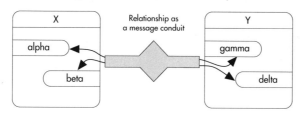

Figure 8.14   The relationship as a conduit for messages.

The next series of panels depicts the implementation in a series of progressively more detailed slices. The first is the processor model, where we may assign appropriate physical machinery to service our OIN. The general topology of the OIN may be presented, as from the analysis, by means of a transducer object. A transducer provides a transparent link between processes. A further, more detailed, behaviour of the human processors may be plotted with an object-oriented tool (see Chapter 14). The successive panels deal with the software architecture and tasking and the last panel deals with the OOPL code structure.

What is the relationship beween OINs and object dependency diagrams (ODDs)?

An OIN is a network of objects and shows how they relate amongst one another in an application or partitions of one; the object dependency diagram (ODD) is a physical realisation of one. The two diagrams have a correspondence. An OIN is developed into

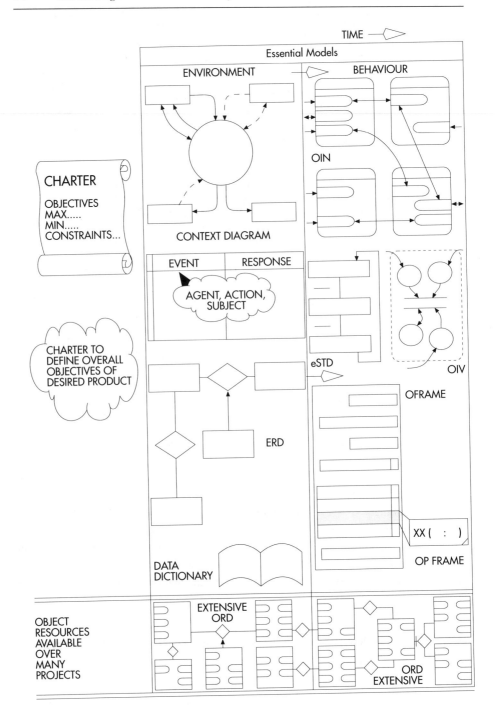

Figure 8.15   The direct development cycle.

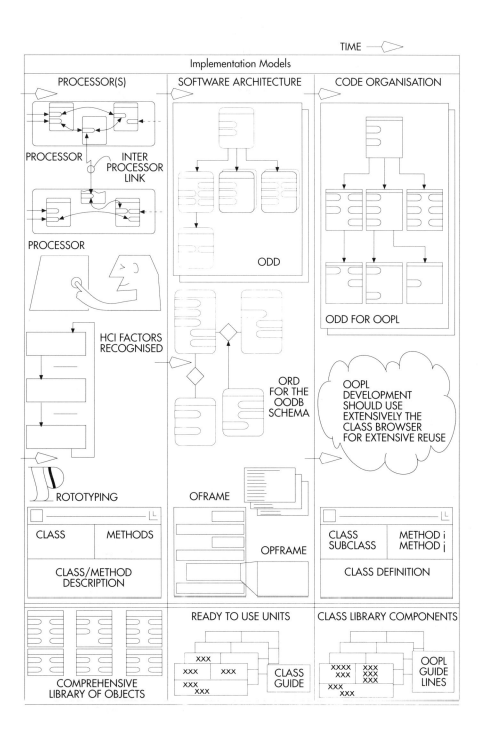

TIME ⟶

Implementation Models

PROCESSOR(S)   SOFTWARE ARCHITECTURE   CODE ORGANISATION

PROCESSOR   INTER PROCESSOR LINK

PROCESSOR

ODD

ODD FOR OOPL

HCI FACTORS RECOGNISED

ORD FOR THE OODB SCHEMA

OOPL DEVELOPMENT SHOULD USE EXTENSIVELY THE CLASS BROWSER FOR EXTENSIVE REUSE

PROTOTYPING

OFRAME

OPFRAME

CLASS	METHODS
CLASS/METHOD DESCRIPTION	

CLASS SUBCLASS	METHOD i METHOD j
CLASS DEFINITION	

COMPREHENSIVE LIBRARY OF OBJECTS

READY TO USE UNITS

xxx
xxx   xxx
xxx
CLASS GUIDE

CLASS LIBRARY COMPONENTS

xxxx
xxx   xxx
xxx   xxx
xxx
xxx
OOPL GUIDE LINES

an ODD by adding a coordinator (controller) object (Fig. 8.16). It is almost as if the controller (coordinator) object is in a plane above that of the OIN and, in effect, exerts control through linkages down into the plane of the OIN.

What is the relationship between ORDs and object inheritance diagrams (OIDs)?

An ORD is an extensive static representation of objects and their relationship. It is intended that it also acts as an augmented ERD (that is, depicting the operations associated with the entities). An object inheritance diagram (OID) depicts a class structure amongst objects; it is optimised to show this characteristic with a view to inheritance and intended reuse of components. The OID does overlap the class structure components of an ORD. The way to view two is to remember that the ORD is extensive and shows all relationships between objects whereas the OID is specialised to show just the class structures to assist with the documentation of class browsers.

Worked example

To illustrate the application of the direct approach, the DMV example from Chapter 7 is developed using the direct approach. Figure 8.17 depicts the working steps.

The context diagram and event list are shown on the left. The context may be perceived as an object engine at the topmost level, with a list of events as messages our system must attend to. The OIN is developed first by building an ERD that is relevant to this context; two ERDs are depicted at the bottom left. The leftmost ERD is extensive and the one to the right corresponds to the event list (i.e. narrower scope). The event/entity matrix is a useful source, along with the context diagram, to develop the OIN. Each entity becomes a candidate object. Each event is then responded to by connecting to a receptor operation and by linking associated object operations. The event threads are listed on the diagram. The eSTD, as before, can assist with the development of the custodial actions create, update and delete; the event list itself assists with the finding of the additional fundamental operations expiry notice and expiry.

Many systems have multiple contexts and it is useful to develop an ORD that, in general, is more extensive than the OIN. For the DMV system an ORD may be derived from the known entities that have been introduced at the bottom left of Fig. 8.16. The behaviour that has already been identified may be included in the objects. Anticipated objects may also be included, such as specialisations of vehicle, and it is also likely that we may have an object Driver (Fig. 8.18).

Conclusions

With the direct approach the objects are perceived without undue complication from physical details of an object-oriented solution. The OIN, along with the ORD and

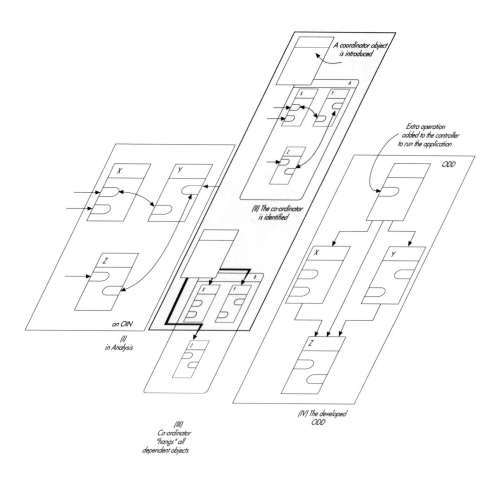

Figure 8.16   The correspondence between OINs (networks of objects) and ODDs (dependency)

appropriate expansion from the OIV, presents a view for users to appreciate the behaviour in essential terms. Table 8.1 shows the relationship between all the components described.

References and further reading

Graham, I. (1991) *Object-Oriented Methods*. Wokingham, UK: Addison-Wesley.

Context Diagram Answer

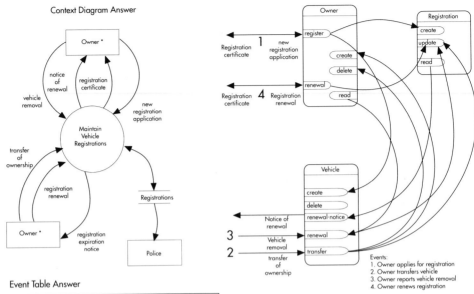

Events:
1. Owner applies for registration
2. Owner transfers vehicle
3. Owner reports vehicle removal
4. Owner renews registration

Event Table Answer

No.	Event	Detection	System Outputs
1	Owner applies for registration	new registration application	registration certificate
2	Owner transfers vehicle	transfer of ownership	registration certificate
3	Owner reports vehicle removal	vehicle removal	none
4	Owner renews registration	registration renewal	registration certificate
5	Time to notify owner that renewal is due	time	notice of renewal
6	Registration expires	time	registration expiration notice

Event \ Entity Relationship	Owner applies for registration	Owner transfers vehicle	Owner reports vehicle removal	Owner renews registration	Time to notify owner that renewal is due	Registration expires
Owner	c,m	c,d,m	m,d	r	r	r
Vehicle	c	m	m,d	r	r	r
Registration <Owner> registers <Vehicle>	c	c,d	d	u	r	u

Entity Relationship Diagram

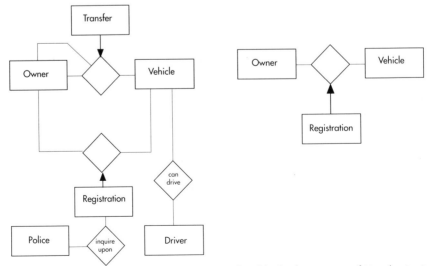

Figure 8.17　DMV worked example (OIN) (reproduced by kind permission of Yourdon Inc.).

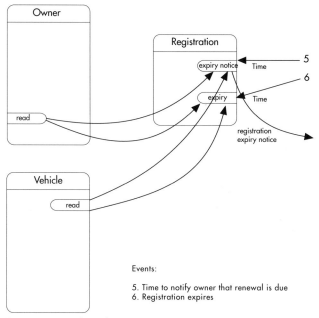

Events:

5. Time to notify owner that renewal is due
6. Registration expires

Event message thread

1. New registration connects to Owner registration and Vehicle.create and Registration.create and produces registration certificate.

2. Transfer of ownership connects to Vehicle.transfer which connects to Owner.new and Owner.delete and then connects to Registration.update.

3. Vehicle removal connects with Vehicle.removal and then Owner.read and thence to Registration.update.

4. Registration renewal connects to Owner.renewal and thence to Registration.update and produces Registration certificate.

5. Time triggers Registration.expiry notice which accesses from Owner.read and Vehicle.read and produces Registration expiry notice.

6. Time triggers Registration.expiry which accesses Owner.read and Vehicle.read.

Entity State Transition Diagram
Answer

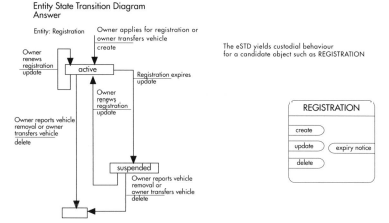

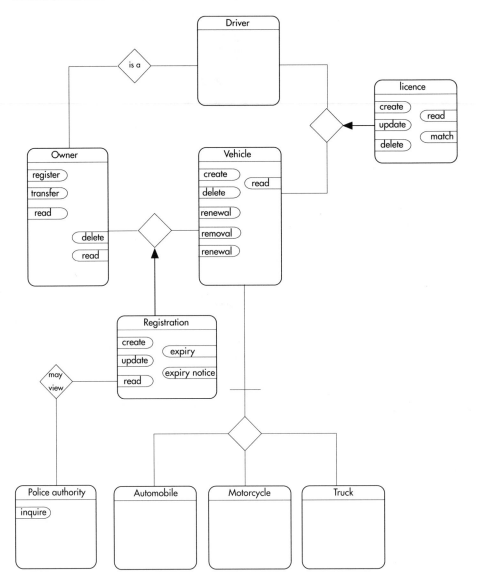

Figure 8.18   DMV worked example (ORD).

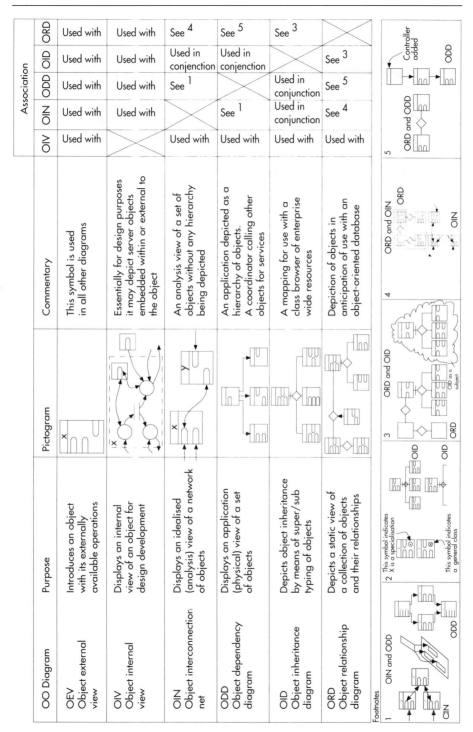

OO Diagram	Purpose	Pictogram	Commentary	Association OIV	OIN	ODD	OID	ORD
OEV Object external view	Introduces an object with its externally available operations		This symbol is used in all other diagrams	Used with	Used with	Used with	Used with	Used with
OIV Object internal view	Displays an internal view of an object for design development		Essentially for design purposes it may depict server objects embedded within or external to the object		Used with	Used with	Used with	Used with
OIN Object interconnection net	Displays an idealised (analysis) view of a network of objects		An analysis view of a set of objects without any hierarchy being depicted	Used with		See [1]	Used in conjunction	See [4]
ODD Object dependency diagram	Displays an application (physical) view of a set of objects		An application depicted as a hierarchy of objects. A coordinator calling other objects for services	Used with	See [1]		Used in conjunction	See [5]
OID Object inheritance diagram	Depicts object inheritance by means of super/sub typing of objects		A mapping for use with a class browser of enterprise wide resources	Used with	Used in conjunction	Used in conjunction		See [3]
ORD Object relationship diagram	Depicts a static view of a collection of objects and their relationships		Depiction of objects in anticipation of use with an object-oriented database	Used with	See [4]	See [5]	See [3]	

Footnotes

1   OIN and ODD   OIN   ODD

2   This symbol indicates X is a specialisation / This symbol indicates a general class

3   OID   OID   ORD

4   ORD and OID   OID as a subject

5   ORD and OIN   ORD   OIN

ORD and ODD   Controller added   ODD

Table 8.1 The relationship between the diagram types

CHAPTER 9

Modelling human activity systems with objects

Let's not confuse the meal with the menu
(Anon)

This chapter outlines the idea behind using the object-oriented notation for expressing human activity systems in terms of objects and operations. This activity may be preliminary activity prior to some subsequent automation of the system on a computer. The notation is not altered in any appreciable way.

The essential idea

A system can be expressed in purely essential terms. This is the focus of the analysis model. It leaves the physical realisation options open for as long as possible. The system being analysed could be automated by placement on appropriate machinery or it could remain a human activity system or an organised mix of the two. Most developers will be keen to model the major physical options as they are perceived, with a view to showing these to the client to elicit a decision and to make sure the client is fully cognisant with the options available.

For the purposes of this chapter, a human activity system will be an organisational unit that performs a role in an organisation and is made up of people performing roles as operators upon messages from externally perceived units. This will serve as another application for the use of the notation and possibly may be a helpful analogy to further understand the thinking behind the notation.

The object view

An object view of a system is fully independent of whether it is mechanised or not. Our objects can be recognised at the early stages by developing an entity relationship diagram, which shows all the concepts that have to be recognised and dealt with.

The object context allows the placement of an arbitrary boundary around the system situation as it is perceived, so that one can recognise the items that are externalities.

The event list becomes the source for recognising the relevant messages that will affect the object context. The responses that are made to each event (message) will be the core of the system. They will in this case be modelled as if we had a collection of organisational units (objects) that attended to messages by means of people (operators) who were well trained.

Each object will have visible operators displayed and this means that in a human activity system there is a counter (like in a shop) that will enable our operators to receive the messages directly from the public, i.e. public services. This is, of course, the external view of an object (OEV). Here an 'operator' is a facility that has the capacity to perform an operation.

There may be operators that work in the background of the object and do not directly provide public services. They may provide various housekeeping functions that are private to the object. These would not be shown as visible services. The communications to these objects takes place by means of messages, i.e. dialogues coupled directly to the object's operations. These messages may take the physical manifestation of notes or business forms, teletype messages or telephone inquiries.

The internal view

Upon 'looking inside' the object we shall consider that such views inside are restricted to those who have a direct interest. We shall recognise that similar rules apply to human activity systems.

Every publicly available operator will be visible as 'working' and will have message flows of the various types inbound to it. It will also access a store, representing memory. This is analogous to using a filing cabinet or a storage carousel. There may be extra operators who are present for maintenance of the object's well-being. They may operate upon the store, or memory; they may not be offering a public service.

Any operator may communicate with another object by initiating a dialogue with that object's operator. In physical terms this may be a telex or even a telephone call. The object that is providing these services may be another collection of human activities or may be a hardware device.

The style of protocol for either would be:

> Object + (instance) + Operation + {argument}.

For a human activity system:

> *Object* is needed as a target for the message.
> *Instance* is needed if a particular (specific) department is required.
> *Operation (Service)* is the particular publicly available operator that is required.
> *Argument* is the set of parameters (extra pieces) of information (e.g. date item is required by, number of units) needed for the operator to work effectively.

For a hardware device (system) that is needed:

> *Object* is the class of device.
> *Instance* is the particular (specific) device.
> *Service* will be some specific 'button' denoting the service offered.
> *Argument* is the set of values required to make the selection effective (e.g. size or number of copies, etc.).

The OIN and OIV in human activity systems

For a complete visualisation of what is happening in a human activity system one would ideally use a combination of diagrams such as the OIN – the connection net to show how the various departments (objects) would interrelate; the OIV – the object internal view – shows an expansion of an object department (as if for audit); the ODD – the object dependency diagram – shows a hierarchy, and this type of diagram would augment the views of a system depicted by the interconnection net. All these three diagrams can directly express a human activity system. The object inheritance diagram (OID) is optional, but may be helpful where there may be classes of behaviour that are useful to recognise.

A worked example

This particular example is a Catering system that may also be perceived as a Fast-food outlet. It is all based upon a Menu that is offered to the public. The offering is in the form of a menu, which invites individual selections. Each selection, whether it is a Hamburger, Cheeseburger, Vegeburger or Chickenburger, will require specific ingredients:

```
Hamburger    = Beef Patty +(onion)+(relish)+2{bun}2+(lettuce)
Cheeseburger = Hamburger + Cheese
Chickenburger= Chicken Patty+ (lettuce) +Mayonnaise+ 2 {bun}2
Vegeburger   = Vegetable Patty + (lettuce) + 2{bun}2
```

Any of the above requires these ingredients to be stocked and it shall be expected that it will have at least the following structure:

```
Stocked_ingredient= @Commodity type + description
                                    + units of order
                                    + units of issue
                                    + recorder level + stock
```

It shall be assumed that a supplier will be involved in the reorder chain of events with a supply of ingredients being provided for given orders. The consumer will also pay his/her selection by the tabulation total.

External events

The following external events are perceived:

> Consumer selects item(s) from the menu
> Consumer pays for item(s)
> Time to reorder ingredients from the Supplier
> Supplier provides ordered ingredients.

The systems context

The systems context perceived as an object will look something like that in Fig. 9.1. At the topmost level our catering system is perceived as an object with two externalities, Consumer and Supplier. The principal flows are shown: Selection, Settlement, Tab and Order and Order Replenishment, their structures being:

```
Selection            = Menu_item_ref + Quantity
                       + (option)
Settlement           = Amount tendered + time
                       + date
Tabluation           = {Menu-item ref + quantity}
                       + total
Order                = Order-ref
                       + ingredient_ref
                       + quantity_required
                       + today's date
Order replenishment  = Delivery-number
                       + Your_order + quantity
                       + date
```

The data model (ERD)

So far we have described the boundary to the problem area; we now need to recognise the concepts needed and the entity relationship diagram (ERD) is ideal for exploring the concepts needed.

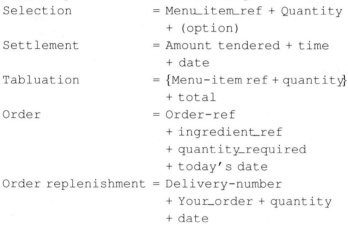

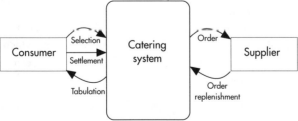

Figure 9.1   The system boundary.

The ERD can be used to express facts about the system as we perceive it (Fig. 9.2):

> A Menu comprises of menu items.
> Each Item will be a superclass of specialised items, such as Hamburger, Cheeseburger, Vegeburger or Chickenburger.
> Each item will be made from Ingredients.
> Ingredients are supplied by a supplier on an order.
> A Consumer may view a menu.
> A Consumer may select an item.
> A Consumer settles their item tab.

So far the ERD does not show us work. It shows only the concepts and how they are associated. From the ERD there is enough detail to outline how these concepts may be interrelated in the form of a network. In Fig. 9.3 an outline sketch of the objects described as clouds is shown along with its linkage to the outside world. Menu and Menu Item have been collapsed in one object – Menu item – because of the close coupling of the two and because it is acting as an assembly structure. This takes the form of external stimuli and responses. It also shows potential intercommunication between the various objects. As it stands it needs further expansions.

Developing the object network

If we return to the event list we can start to unravel how the inbound flows and the events are linked:

1. Consumer selects item(s) from the menu. Now here we are going to accept the selection as our message from the outside and we shall create an operation called select. It will also communicate by sending a message to Tab and the operation associated with billing.
2. Consumer pays for item(s). The message is the settlement and there will be an operation to update the object Tab with the value of the settlement.
3. Time to reorder ingredients from the Supplier. Time is a pseudo-agent, which stimulates an operation that should look at the ingredients stock and check the level. If it has impinged upon the reorder level it will message an order object to generate an order to the supplier.
4. Supplier provides ordered ingredients. This event is associated with the stimulus from the supplier in the form of the order replenishment, which will expect an operation to accept the replenishment subject to its being correct. It will thence message the order object to cancel the appropriate outstanding order.

This form and style of processing is shown in Fig. 9.4, where we can see the inside of these cloud objects.

There are some additional operations required to make the system viable, for

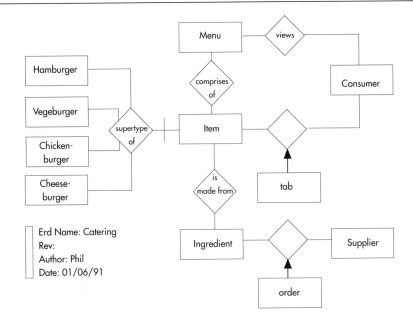

Figure 9.2   The entity model depicting the food items.

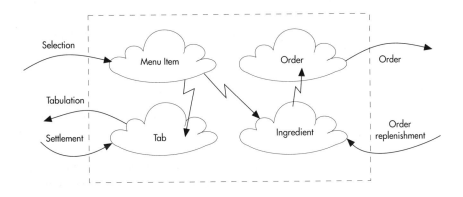

Figure 9.3   The concept linkages.

example we will need an operation `Menu item.make` to continuously monitor the state of the current menu item `Stock`. Where more items are required it would message the operation `Ingredient.make` and receive appropriate delivery. This is an operation that will be needed to make menu item a self-contained unit.

In addition, there may well be extra custodial operations that are required to create an `Menu item,` `change menu items` and `delete menu items` as and when

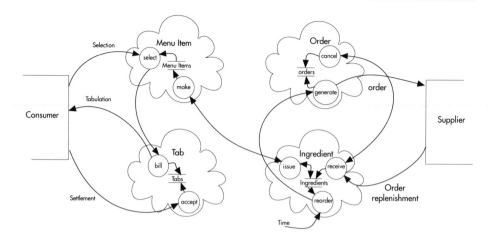

Figure 9.4   The concept linkages showing also the internals.

needed. Custodial activities are those activities that are not specific to one application but are needed in all applications to maintain the object. These custodial activities can be ascertained by undertaking a life-cycle for the object (see Fig. 5.5). Suffice it for now that what are really essential are the fundamental activities.

We should now have a look at the object interconnection net (OIN) (Fig. 9.5). We should be aware that this model would be supplemented with appropriate textual definitions and internal views (Fig. 9.6) of the objects to supplement the view used where necessary. It is then a theoretical and essential view of the objects and it relies on the appropriate technology to realise it at a later stage.

The internal view

Inside each object the operations act as operators, and each of these is equivalent to a job function. The actual manning may involve one person undertaking many roles (functions: operations).

At a later stage it will have to be recognised that a hierarchical (organisational) view of the system will be required for it to be effectively managed. This is usually accomplished by means of an object dependency diagram (ODD). This is easily derived from the OIN by perceiving the network space as one plane and the manager (coordinator) object acting in a vertical plane upon each of the objects. The ODD for this system is depicted in Fig. 9.7. This viewpoint is implementational and there may be additional rearrangements required but it is a good starting point. (Note the previous discussion on ODDs and OINs (see pp. 89–93), and see Fig. 8.16.) Additional operations may be required to enable management to exercise some effectiveness like for example, operations check and report.

If we look inside the manager coordinator object (Fig. 9.8) we see a collection of

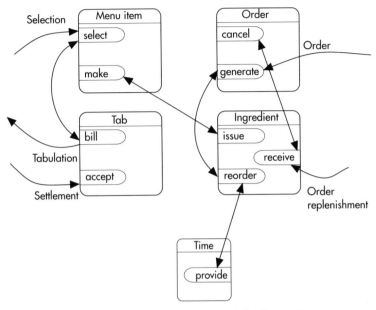

Figure 9.5   An object interconnection network for the catering system.

objects with flows from central operations Report and Check to the appropriately named 'buttons' of the objects: Menu Item, Ingredient, Tabulation and Order.

If we refocus our view and remind ourselves that this is a human activity system, then we can make some predictions from the model. We have identified all the items needed to service each concept area. The actual demand upon the system is modelled in terms of message arrival rates and we can calculate how the manning of the system should be arranged. The diagrams OIN, OIV assist in allowing modelling of those particular parts of the system.

For completeness we have to define all of the operations required of the appropriate operations:

Menu item	Tab
select	bill
make	accept
check	check
report	report

Order	Ingredient
cancel	issue
generate	reorder
check	check
report	report

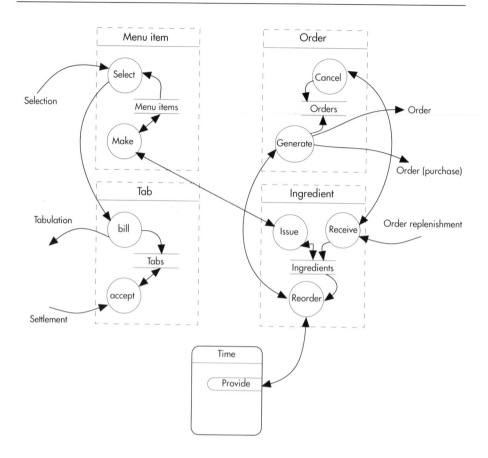

Figure 9.6   A joint external and internal view of objects.

The operation specifications

Rather than go through all of the specifications I will define four of the operations with pre- and post-condition specifications:

```
Menu item.select
```
   Pre-condition
   A selection occurs AND
      commodity-ref matches Menu-item AND
      `Menu item.stock` ⩾ quantity
   Post-condition
   Selected item is presented AND
   `tab.bill` is messaged

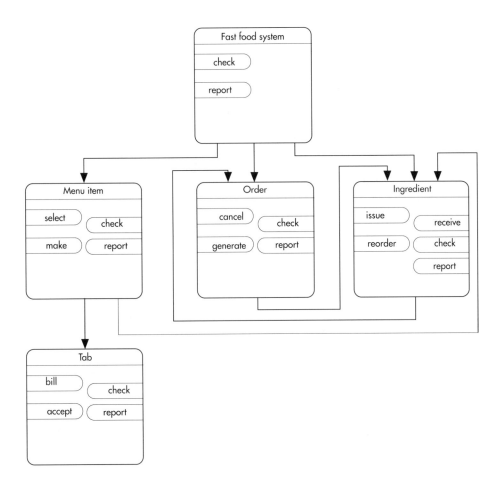

Figure 9.7 An object dependency diagram for the catering system.

Menu item.make
   Pre-condition
   any Menu item stock < reorder level AND
   Ingredient.issue is messaged
   Post-condition
   Menu item – stock is incremented by 1

Tab.bill
   Pre-condition
   A message from Menu item occurs
   Post-condition

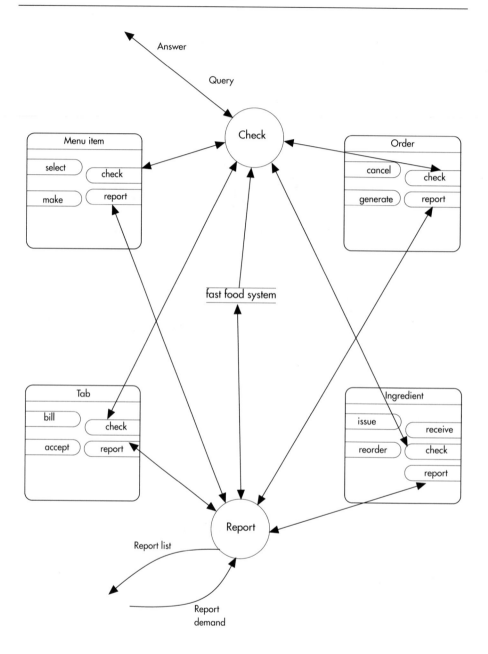

Figure 9.8   An internal view of the fast food system.

A tabulation is emitted AND
a Tabulation is stored

`Ingredient.issue`
   Pre-condition
   A message from `Menu item.make` occurs AND
   required ingredients are present
   Post-condition
   Ingredients are supplied AND
   Ingredients stock is decremented by 1

Inheritance

So we can model the majority of activities so far with ease. However, what about inheritance? How can we model that and where is it relevant?

   The ideal in a business system is that you have flexibility to provide services without undue cost. So, for instance, if a new product line is envisaged, how can it be made with the minimum cost? An inheritance structure allows abstraction of general class categories that cover the basic characteristics. Then a series of more specialised units at the next layer down allows inheritance of the most basic characteristics.

> New product = Class (basic character which is common to the product range) + Specialisation.

By looking at our products in terms of generalised classes and specialisms we have a flexible structure with which to operate. In the specific example we are working with, the Menu item is a class structure where we have specialised items such as Beefburgers, etc. This part of the ERD may be refined further so that we have a more effective structure (Fig. 9.9). This ERD supertype structure can become the basis for a full object inheritance diagram (OID), which is displayed in Fig. 9.10.

The OID in human activity systems

You should notice that the OID is organised so that it shows the publicly available operations for each object. We have focused our attention on the Menu item, which will hold the basic details associated with the item and its particular options. The next layer is a series of objects that are specialisations of the Menu item, these being Redmeat burger, Chickenburger and Vegeburger. The Redmeat burger is further refined by two specialised types: the Beefburger and the Cheeseburger. You will notice that the objects Redmeat burger and Cheeseburger have the same operation name (*make*). This means that the Beefburger will automatically inherit the operation *make* from the object Redmeat burger. However the object Cheeseburger will override the operation *make* in the object Redmeat burger and will use its own version of *make*.

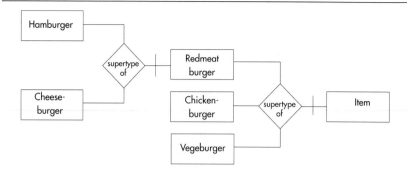

Figure 9.9   An ERD for a subset of the fast food system.

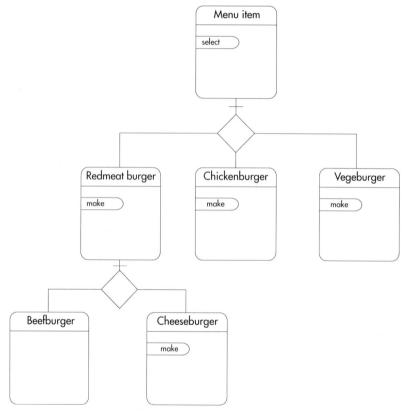

Figure 9.10   An object inheritance diagram for the fast food system.

It may also be an idea to show what actually happens with objects under inheritance. Communications need only be directed at the specific object. It will automatically collect all the inherited objects and it is as if all of these inherited objects are 'glued' alongside one another. To show more completely what is happening, we can view the inside of the objects (with the OIV). It seems as if the objects are placed alongside one another and are joined by a common memory. This is depicted in Fig. 9.11 for the situation of the Vegeburger and what it inherits. It is as if the two objects are joined over their store.

What about where there is inheritance and one of the objects operation is overridden, such as in the case of a Cheeseburger (Fig. 9.12)? Here you will see that the objects are joined together and the interim object, Redmeat burger, from which we are inheriting data only, will show a store and its operation make is not present because we already have the particular one we want from the object Cheeseburger.

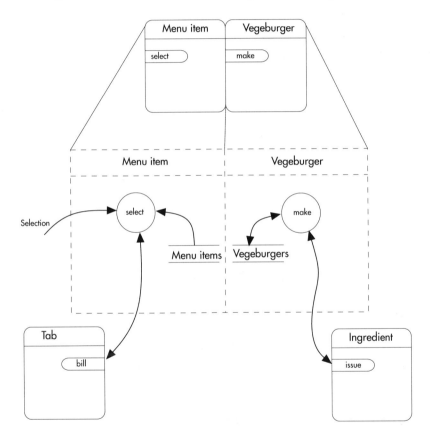

Figure 9.11   How inheritance works.

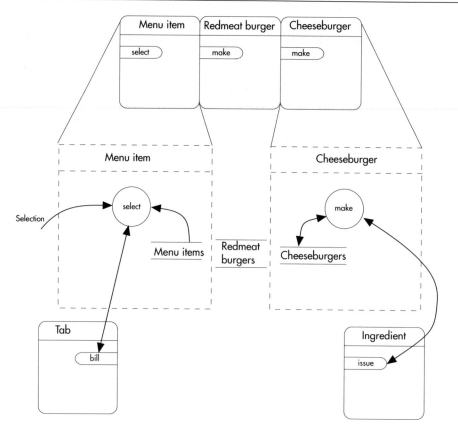

Figure 9.12   How inheritance works (another internal view).

Conclusion

You should be able to perceive that an object model can represent human activity systems in their own right prior to some automation activity. As it happens the human activity system can be a good analogy for the object models as a whole.

References and further reading

Graham, I. (1991) *Object-Oriented Methods*. Wokingham, UK: Addison-Wesley.

CHAPTER 10

The documentation of objects and their operations

The first law of ecology: Everything is connected to everything else
The second law of ecology: Everything must go somewhere
The third law of ecology: Nature knows best
(Faber's *The book of laws*)

The object diagrams require a family of textual definitions to assist in refining an understanding of what is being introduced. The diagrams along with their textual items, would probably be viewed together in some computer-aided software environment (CASE) tool. This chapter ensures understanding of the concepts behind the documentation.

The concept

The graphic diagrams can accomplish a visualisation of the object and operations but they require some form of textual specification to formally tie down the meaning.

Throughout the period of using structured models, there were many attempts to have a graphic-based notation that attempted to eliminate textual specification; they all failed!

In other disciplines, such as engineering, the drawings accomplish much but require textual specification as an annexe, for example the bill of material and dimensions and performance information.

In this chapter we shall look at the specific requirements for the definition of the object and associated operations. The majority of the chapter will be devoted to a frame-based approach, as is available with many current CASE tools. However, these same principles may be used in the form of a project-dictionary based approach, which, although cumbersome, may still be effective. The documentation should also include checking that the object and its operation are a consistent set of behaviour. To ensure this, a message thread is introduced.

The idea behind all this is to ensure that we have a complete set of documentation that can enable us to predict behaviour of the system as accurately as possible and demonstrate the idealised behaviour.

Example background

To make things a little more comprehensible an example drawn from a hospital situation is used. This hospital situation will be described with a view to the subsequent definition.

This hospital situation requires a system to look after the administration records, that is admittance of a patient, the examination of the patient and the appropriate scheduling of the patient and the checking of the credit-worthiness of the patient. The object interconnection net (OIN) (Fig. 10.1) shows just the objects Patient, Credit and Schedule. There would, of course, be many more objects involved but we shall restrict our attention to this area for explanation purposes.

Patient object defined by object external and object internal views

An expansion of the object Patient is also given in Fig. 10.2, showing all the operations that are publicly available. This is depicted here to explain how the external and internal views of object Patient should correspond.

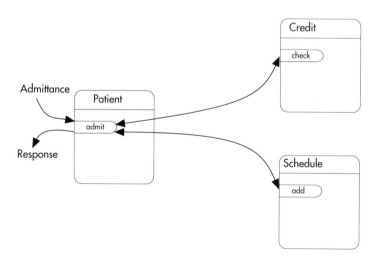

Figure 10.1 Patient credit and schedule objects linked by a thread.

Background to text frames

The preferred style to represent the definition text is by means of a frame that binds all the appropriate material into an easily understandable form for those people to actually perform their checking for completeness and consistency. The idea of the frame emanates from the workings of Bartlett (1932) on memory schemas in a pre-automated computer context. Bartlett considered the idea of cells based on concepts, and the presentation of slots that held the actual values. If there were some updating undertaken the viewer would only be aware of the values in the slots and not the precise mechanisms of production. This idea is often used in the representation of knowledge in expert systems. All we are doing is using these frames to represent textual information in a fashion that has the greatest cognitive economy for its users.

Object frames

Object-oriented textual definition comes in two major parts: the object itself and the associated operations specifications. An example of the suggested frames is shown in Fig. 10.3, which shows an object frame with suggested slots on the left, and on the right the suggested frame for an operation specification.

The minimum set of slots for the objects are as follows:

Object

A unique identifying name for the object. Ideally, this should be drawn from the subject area being investigated. It is quoted in the singular case because it is a class.

Description

This is a freeform slot to describe the nature of the object to aid readability as to what the object is representing.

Inheritance

This is a slot to represent those objects from which this object directly inherits (i.e. the immediate objects). Note that we are, conceptually, allowing multiple inheritance to occur, that is more than one object from which it may inherit. It should therefore be a scrolls slot (i.e. being able to scroll down or up through a list).

Attributes

These are the data items that are associated with this object. At the very least we should expect all items to be elemental with a definition of the units of measure and range of values expected for the item.

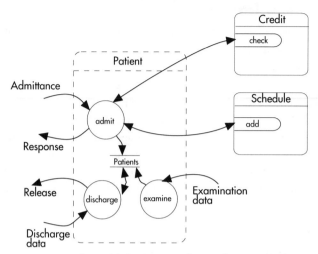

Figure 10.2   An internal view of patient (OIV).

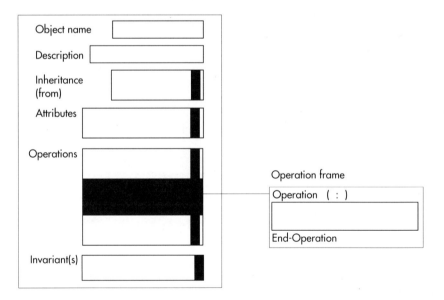

Figure 10.3   Object and operation frame.

Operations

These are the items that perform the work (i.e. a transformation) and they are only being introduced in these slots. The typical items that I would expect here are the name of the operation and an indication as to whether it is a class-sensitive or an instance-sensitive operation. Additionally, it is imperative to define whether the operation is publicly available or whether it is an operation private to the workings of the object. The definition of the transformation is prescribed in an operation frame, which we will meet shortly (see p. 118). There should be a link from the operation introduction to the operation specification frame.

Invariant

This is an option slot, which is useful to have in order to define all the assertions that are held to be true upon using this object. This slot can also be used for insertion of production rules related to accessing or updating the object.

Operation frame

The operation frame is where the specification of the transformation is undertaken.

This has an identifier for the operation followed by an interface definition, which takes the form of open brackets followed by the inbound message name(s), each separated by a comma, followed by a colon then the response message(s) each separated by a comma, followed by a closed bracket.

Operation specifications

The body of the specification can be in your own house style, which may be structured-language based or pre- and post-condition based. It is, however, recommended that the operation specification refer to any server objects that are used in the transformation. In a structured approach, process specifications were written for primitive processes, i.e. those that could be decomposed no further. In an operation specification we will often use another operation to perform some fragment of behaviour. This is because we have effectively factored the transformations to the concepts they are servicing. The specification must be explicitly terminated by an 'end_specification'.

If you are using a structured language to prescribe the operations you will no doubt use the following constructions:

```
For < each > <imperative action >

For < modifier > < threshold >, < limit >, ( < increment > )

Case<data item> :{<literal value> : <imperative action (s) > }

IF <condition> Then<imperative action (s) > (Else <imperative
action (s) > )

Repeat < Imperative action (s) > Until < condition >

Do < imperative action (s) > While < condition >.
```

Where an imperative action is a set of statements that express assignments or calculations; modifier, threshold, limit and increment will be data variables; conditions will mean comparisons that are made between data items and other data items or literals; literal value means a specific instance value that a data item may take on such as '66' or an 'MTY' or 'Closed'.

If you are to use another object's operation, there is a way it should be prescribed for ease of reading:

```
< object > . < operation > '(' < message(s) > ':
' < response(s) > '')'
```

This list is not exhaustive and it is probable that your own organisation will have an augmented list of allowable functions. All I suggest is that consistency is observed.

The intention behind structured language is that it is readable by being similar to natural language and, additionally, that it can be developed into a pseudocode easily and thence to a source language.

Pre- and post-condition style specification

If you are using pre- and post-condition specification there is also a grammar that assists in its prescription. The assumptions are that the operation has only discrete states, the pre-condition (i.e. the logical assertions that are true before the operation 'fires') and the post-condition (i.e. those assertions that are true after the operation has 'fired'. Pre- and post-conditions are paired, so a given set of desired pre-conditions are matched against the corresponding desired post-conditions. If you wish to express more pairs of pre- and post-conditions you are totally free to do so, your only restriction is that they are orthogonal (non-overlapping) sets of behaviour:

```
'Pre-condition-' < integer >
{< stimulus > 'occurs' < logical conjunction >
{< data item | literal > < comparison > < data item | literal >
(< message > < object > '.' < operation > '('post-condi-
tion)')}}

'Post-condition-' < integer >
{< response > 'occurs' < logical conjunction >
{< data item | literal > < comparison > < data item | literal >
(< calculation assignment >)
(< message > < object > '.' < operation > '('pre-condi-
tion)'}}
```

where stimulus and response may be data items that are the messages to and from the operation.

Logical conjunctions are 'and, 'or', 'not' and 'not or'. A calculation assignment, as an example, is:

```
fuel_budget = (distance/Mpg) * 1.10
```

The italicised pre- and post-conditions are those associated with a server object's operation that is being used.

There is one minor set that does not strictly fit with the object and is referred to in the operation, and that is the messages and responses. These are usually structures, are part of the project specification and will probably from a complex structure, and for this we use the project dictionary grammar.

To demonstrate what this all looks like we define an object frame for patient and define an operation admit and shall also define server object operations `Credit.check` and `Schedule.add`.

The object frame Patient will include the following slots and values:

> Name is Patient. It is a class name and our restriction is to ensure that this name is unique.
>
> Description: this will be inserted with some definition of Patient, 'A Client within the care of our medical system'.
>
> Inheritance: in this case it is nil because there are no Objects from which this directly inherits.
>
> Attributes: these are the data items that are held within the concept Patient. These will include an identifier for each Patient:

```
Patient_number and Surname,
Forename, Date_of_birth,
Year_of_birth,
Credit_ref,
Last_operation_date,
Location_of_operation,
```

> Operations: these are the services that the object is offering. In this case the following operations are available: Admit, Discharge and Examine. Each of these operations is instance-based, because they are going to operate only individual patient instances. The other type of operation is the class-based instance, which operates at the class level in Patient.

The last slot that should be defined is the Invariant, which means all the assertions that are held true upon using this object or any of its operations. In this case we shall quote that there shall be at least one occurrence of Patient and no more than 1250, and that all the instances of Patient are active. The implications from this are that one does not have to 'initialise' the object Patient with the first occurrence and that inactive Patients (those archived) are held elsewhere.

The object frame for the Patient is depicted in Fig. 10.4.

An example of operation specification

The operation frame requires that we have an operation specification for each operation (Admit, Discharge and Examine). However, I shall define one operation, Admit, and use that as an example of style:

Operation `Patient.Admit`(admittance : response)
Pre-condition
  `an admittance occurs AND`
  `Patient_year_of_birth > 1921 AND`
  `Patient_year_of_birth < 1980 AND`
  `Credit_ref Credit.check (` *postcondition* `)`
Post-condition
  `a Patient instance exists in Patient AND`
  `a Response = 'accepted' AND Occurs AND`
  `Patient-detail Schedule.add (` *precondition* `)`

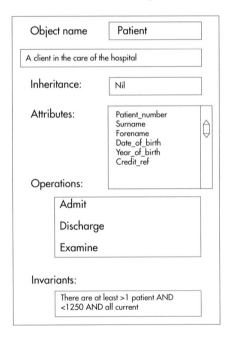

Figure 10.4 Object frame for patient.

This operation specification is quite straightforward as a set of assertions. However, you will see from Figs 10.1 and 10.2 that server operations are participating with this operation `Patient.admit` To fully explain what is occurring, we shall have a quick look at the other operation specifications (`Credit.check` and `Schedule.add`) participating in this relationship.

Server operations:

> Operation `Credit.check` (message : response)
> Pre-condition
> `a message occurs AND`
> `credit_card_ref matches credit_number AND`
> `credit_card_expiry_date > current_date AND`
> `credit_Card-ref is not = 'stolen'`
> Post-condition
> `response = 'valid'`
>
> Operation `Schedule.add(Patient_detail: List)`
> Pre-condition
> `a Patient_detail occurs AND`
> `Schedule_date(date) = 'open' AND`
> `Physician_date(date) = 'open'`
> `etcetera . . . . .`
> Post-condition
> `a Schedule(date) is updated with Patient-detail AND`
> `a List occurs.`

When we require a service to be performed by another operation we expect that the other operation performs its activity with the minimum of fuss. What we are actually doing is delegating (or subcontracting) work.

Redefinition of pre- and post-assertions

When we 'use' another operation as a server from the pre-condition side of the requester we only quote the 'message' that the server operation is sensitive to, then quote the server `Object.operation` and then state the post-condition from the server operation. We could quote all the pre-conditions necessary for the server operation to 'fire' but what we would be doing is like 'keeping a dog and barking ourself'. Plainly it is the result that we are interested in, so it is the post-condition from the server that attracts our attention.

When we use a server operation on the post-condition side of the requester we have a similar situation, although when we refer to server operation here we shall quote the respective message along with the `Object.operation` and its pre-condition. Again we are delegating work. We are only interested in our part of the pre-condition being upheld. The server operation may have additional pre-conditions that it uses to enforce the quality of responses that are private to it. It will also produce its only post-condition when all its pre-conditions are met. This is its own business.

The above specification, for `Patient.add` can be augmented by an additional pair of pre- and post-conditions to cater for the complementary situation that will occur where the above pre-condition fails and an appropriate post-condition is constructed to define this.

Project dictionary components

The majority of the object and operation components have got a 'home' for their definition. However, there is a class of components that still have to be defined – the messages and the appropriate response. As an example we shall have to define the structure for admittance and response, both of which are messages directed at `Object.operation` admit.

The definition of each is:

```
Admittance = Surname + Forename + Date_of_birth +
    Credit_reference + Gender + etcetera
Response = ['Accepted' | 'Rejected' | '']
```

Note this is the same language that we would use for defining data dictionary terms as per DeMarco (1978). The grammar is straightforward and easy to recall (Table 10.1).

Balancing diagrams and text

Text and diagrams should balance completely. In this section I shall define exactly how they are interrelated.

Table 10.1 Data dictionary grammar

Fragment	Explanation
`Group_item =`	A group item introduced
`'+'`	Joins a pair of data items
`'[..|..]'`	Selection of one from a list separated by the '|' symbol. For example ['male'	'female']
`'(..)'`	Optional data item e.g. Suite = Jelly + (cream)
`'{..}'`	Indicates a repetition group such as the fact that a patient may have a history
`Patient_name + {history}`	This means there may be many occurrences of history from zero to infinity. An integer prefix and postfix to the symbol can further define the limits

Each object external view (OEV) will have a corresponding object frame; this is obligatory.

Each OEV will have an object internal view (OIV). Each operation visible in the OIV will have an operation specification. Each message and response to and from operations will have:

1. Been introduced in the operation specification.
2. Will be defined in the project dictionary.

Any OIV may have an associated eSTD. All actions quoted on the eSTD shall match operations named in the object. This is the normal balancing required.

Any OIV may have a control operation. It shall be assumed that a control STD will exist and be visible. Its actions, where referring to enables, disables and trigger, shall match the names of `Object.operations` that currently exist. All raises and lowers of flags shall refer to items in the project dictionary. All signals shall refer to messages that are defined in the project dictionary.

An OEV shall correspond to objects appearing in the object dependency diagram (ODD), object inheritance diagram (OID), object inheritance network (OIN) or even the object relationship diagram (ORD).

The number of operations visible in any one OEV, wherever it appears, is at the discretion of the author. The definitive definition of how many operations constitute the complete object is accommodated in the object frame. Similarly the operation's specification is the complete specification for an object's operation.

The message thread is the way of demonstrating complete behaviour. As an example, I shall refer to the thread exhibited in Fig. 10.1. The principle behind a message thread is that one would start with an event and trace the event through to a message (flow) through to an operation and thence to any participant server operations through to the alteration in the object's status (Table 10.2).

Table 10.2 Event message threads

Event	Message	Response
Patient is admitted	Flow:admittance	Operation:admit using Credit.check using Schedule.add Patient instance created Response flow emitted
Patient discharge	Flow:discharge data	Operation:discharge Release flow emitted
Patient examination	Flow:examination data	Operation:examine Patient attribute altered

Conclusions

Documentation is necessary and should show balance between the graphics and the textual specification. The aim of our definitions is for both user and developer agreement. The frame approach certainly aides comprehension and subsequent development of the specification through the stages from analysis to design and implementation.

References and further reading

Bartlett, F.C. (1932) *Remembering*. Cambridge, UK: Cambridge University Press.
DeMarco, T. (1978) *Structured Systems Specification*. New York, NY: Yourdon Press.
Meyer, B. (1988) *Object-Oriented Software Construction*. Hemel Hempstead, UK: Prentice Hall.

CHAPTER 11

Object-oriented databases

The Ecological Law
Nobody owns anything and all anyone has is the use of his presumed possessions
(Philip Wylie, in *The New York Times*, February 1, 1970)

This chapter describes how object-oriented databases should work and it describes the concepts behind them such as normalisation of behaviour and the object relationship diagram (ORD). At the time of writing, object-oriented database management systems (OODBMs) are very sparse and do not encompass all the behaviour that should be reasonably expected from them in object-oriented terms.

Background

In the early 1970s the ideas of the database became described in modelling terms. Codd (1970) proposed a relational model based on set theoretic terminology. There were alternatives that, in turn, were based on a network resolution of the data sets. In both cases a theoretic model determined the direction of the technology of the database.

The key principle that was underlying a database was *data independence*, which meant that data was to be placed in one location and all applications that were to use that data would be provided with the appropriate views to assist. This has many administrative and developmental advantages.

The database was defined by means of a schema that had a language to assist in that definition: data definition language (DDL). This DDL would be 'compiled' into a schema (database definition). Work was performed in conjunction with the database by means of the data manipulation language (DML). The DML provides the navigation from set to set and the criteria for selection and update. The DML was usually implemented as calls that an application may make in a high level language. Superb administrative control could be applied to the view-ability of the sets for control purposes.

Data independence

To reach data independence there must be principles of efficiently placing that data. The concept of the attribute (the elemental data item) and the entity (collection of attributes of which one will be an unique identifier) came into its own.

To effectively visualise one's options with an evolving database, data modelling became an excellent tool. Chen (1976), amongst other data modelling notations, formulated an extremely friendly notation that we have already seen: the entity relationship diagram (ERD). This notation allows people to model choices of arrangement of data, whilst retaining a concept level view of the data.

On a more mathematical basis Codd (1970) formulated his normal forms, which are tests for effective placement of data.

A set should adhere to:

> *First normal form*: if, and only if, it has no repeating data items.
> *Second normal form*: if the set has a compound key, all data items depending directly upon the compound key.
> *Third normal form*: if all the non-key data items depend directly on the single identifying key for the group.

There are higher normal forms (as with inflation) and I do not propose to go into them, suffice that the first, second and third normal forms allow effective placement of the data for accessing.

So far we have not said anything about processing behaviour other than that it is associated with the DML, which itself lies with an application program.

Database concepts have worked effectively, but now with ideas based on object-oriented concepts suggest that there is the opportunity to take the ideas much further for the databases to become object-oriented databases.

What an OODBMS should do

An object-oriented database is an architecture that presents as its major items class objects and their interrelationships and it uses an object model as its foundation.

An object-oriented database should be a representation of a network of class-objects, which in themselves are encapsulations of state, data and processing as a single unit. Each record, or tuple, in this database shall represent an instance. The tuple becomes a template for describing its structure. All instances that share the same set of data items and methods are grouped within a class.

These classes may be interconnected to one another as a network. Any class may display subclasses. Any subclasses may have more than one parent (or super-) class.

The ORD graphic tool

The ORD should define all the relevant class-objects and should introduce the available operations. Additionally the object frame should be sufficient to define all the data items (attributes) and the their domains, and the operation frame should define the behaviour of each of the operations. All of these contribute to the specification definition for the object-oriented database's structure and behaviour.

The object-oriented concept applied to a database

Concepts are placed in one location together with all their requisite behaviour. In essence the definition that we have for our class-based object is still the same and the definition we have for an operation is still the same – it is a procedure (or even a transformation). This is not the first time that a theoretical description has preceded the realisation of a databases technology.

In current DDL terms it should be possible to derive a schema directly from the ORD and the appropriate object frames. The DML is located as an operation or subset of an operation.

An application would be equivalent to a collection of class objects represented by an ORD together with the text frames. Additionally, the relationship between class objects shall also be represented in terms of the mapping of one class object to the other participant class objects. An object base administrator would then allow generation of this object database set (ORD plus frames) as an application.

This could then be available for prototyping to ensure the completeness of the object base in both user and developer's perceptions. Any additional accoutrements specific to the realisation would be additional software layers added during the implementational phases.

So far, for the conventional databases, we have described what should occur with data, i.e. it should be located in one place. The normalisation rules assist in this aim. With our object database we have a similar set of rules that occur with behaviour. When we locate all the processing, state behaviour and data in one place we are, in fact, normalising the behaviour as well, albeit subconsciously.

I propose that there is an analogue of data normalisation rules for behaviour, and that they have a similar type of nature.

For behaviour, the item that is being normalised is the processing that is referring to an operation:

> *Behavioural first normal form*: if and only if it has no repeating pieces of processing within the operation. This is very similar to factoring out repeated behaviour to a subroutine (Fig. 11.1) or more exactly to another class.
>
>   The idea of good cohesion for each object, and therefore reduced coupling, is necessary. The converse is true, where bad cohesion exists there will be bad coupling. Coupling is equivalent to the ideas of emitting messages and cohesion where the object is a good candidate!
>
> *Behavioural second normal form*: if the set of processing, all the operations, relate specifically to items only in a specific class. That is to say that the operation will operate only over a domain defined by the class.
>
> *Behavioural third normal form*: if all the processing of the operations is directly related to a specific specialisations of a class.

A piece of behaviour may refer only to a specialisation of a class. This behaviour may be deemed to be an exception. This exceptional behaviour should be placed in a subclass as a specific operation.

What is actually happening is that one is factoring the behaviour of the appropriate operation site. Within a DFD we were seduced into putting as much as possible of the processing into a single process. Here we are attempting to place the processing in a factored-out form, to the concept (class object).

Do relational concepts still apply?

For the majority of concepts associated with relational sets they still apply. However, there is a family of operators, such as Joins, Projects and Selects, that have severe consequences and hence restrictions placed upon their use.

Each of the above sets has a virtual existence that persists only for the run time (session). On this basis a join between two sets (relations) creates a third new relation.

Figure 11.2 shows two relations, X and Y, that are being joined. Clearly a join of two 'create' operations will be meaningless. Joining two previously used 'update' operations will only update parts of the new class object. However, a delete operation will have been resident in each original object. Other non-custodial operations (those not attending to the maintenance of the class object) can still be effective though they will only operate over their original domains.

Only those operations whose domain is still relevant in this new 'joined' set can be used safely. Those operations that are custodial actions cannot be used safely.

The Project operator 'projects' a suitable subset of the domains for some specific use. The project operator 'destroys' some domains that may be relevant to certain

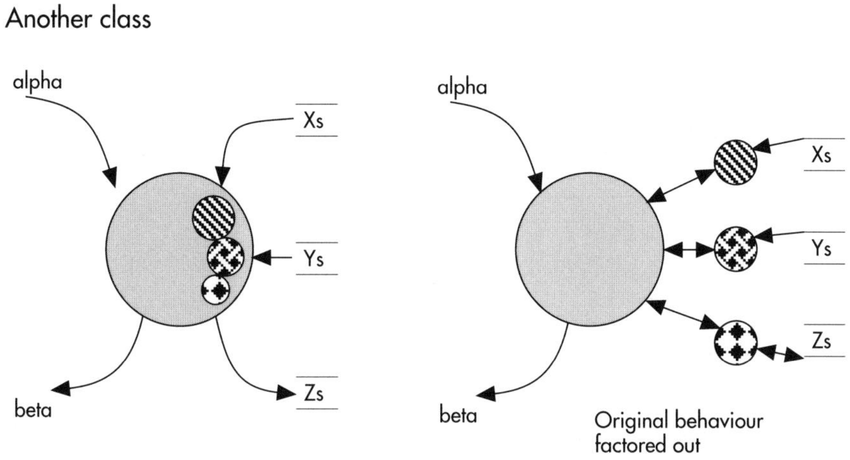

Another class

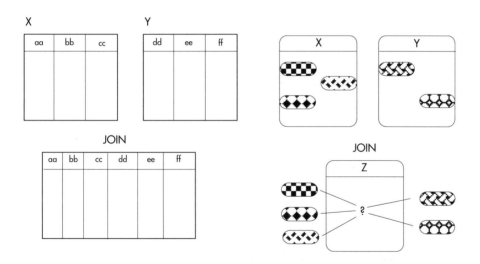

Figure 11.1   Factoring of processing.

Figure 11.2   The join operation for relations and objects.

operations. Custodial actions such as a 'create' are catered for by means of the 'project' (this is creating a class object). Deletions simply remove an occurrence and so can operate safely (Figs 11.3 and 11.4).

As this operation may alter the domain of working for the operations, only those operations whose full domain of behaviour is still relevant can be used safely. Custodial actions (i.e. create, update and delete) cannot be used safely.

The third major relational operator is the Select. This operator selects specific

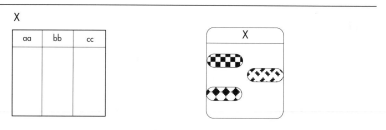

Figure 11.3   The project operation for a relation object.

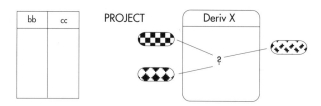

Figure 11.4   The project operation for an object.

occurrences (instances) of an object. This, in object terms, is 'safe' because it does not destroy the structure of the Class object (Fig. 11.5).

Both custodial and fundamental activities can be used safely and no operations would be 'affected'. The only restriction is that the selection should remove all the occurrences of a set, otherwise the 'invariant' for the object will not hold.

Each class object should be refined to have its data at least at the stage of third normal form. Additionally, its operations should be defined so that they conform to the behavioural third normal form.

An object-oriented database should be easily specified from the ORD, which should also introduce all the operations that are available for each class object. The relationships between class objects should be defined and these will easily be mapped to the object-oriented database technology in the form of cross-references or pointer

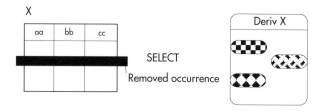

Figure 11.5   The select operation for relations and objects.

chains. Associative relationships indicate information that is to be stored about a relationship (i.e. a connection between objects, which in turn is an object). Super- and subtype objects indicate specialisation of classes. Either way, its actual realisation should be transparent to the user of the object-oriented database. This is all equivalent to the DDL for conventional databases. All of this should be available from the object relationship diagram (ORD).

The object text frame should supply the textual definition material. In addition to normal text frame, there should be a frame to define the relationship between the class objects. The equivalent of the DML is distributed over the operations available for each class object and the availability of a query language facility to navigate between the various class objects.

What state is the object-oriented database technology currently at?

At the time of writing there are not many OODBMS in existence. IRIS, a Hewlett Packard prototype, is currently layered into an object manager and an IRIS storage manager. The means of interacting with IRIS is via object SQL, which uses SQL grammar with an object emphasis.

This object SQL requires some adaptations such as:

1. Users manipulate object types as opposed to tables.
2. Objects can be referenced by an identifier.
3. User-defined operations (functions) and IRIS service functions may appear in *where* and *select* language clauses.

The object SQL appears English-like and is hence very readable and also, within the syntax, there are features to allow the cascading of messages:

```
Create Type Dossier
  (name Charstring required,
  subject_title Hospital administration)
Create Type Document subtype of Dossier
  (Document_title BioRhythm);
```

Actual navigation through various object classes is allowed by means of the SQL-*like* query language.

```
Select Document_title (Alpha_rhythm)
  For each Document
    where Value > Reference_threshold
    /* list off names */
```

Gemstone QL:OPAL is a system based on Smalltalk and shares many of its features.

The user of this system is encouraged to recognise a classification structure (OID) and with its full definition prescribed by something approaching an object Frame. As an example, a Dossier is a collection of documents and may be defined in the following style:

```
Object subclass: 'Dossier'
  instance variables: # ('Title' 'Text' 'Originator')
```

The specific operations available for this class object may then be introduced.

```
method: Create
title: aString
'' A method which creates an instance of a Dossier''
title := aString.
%
method: Create
Title
'' A method to create the dossier's title''
^title
%
```

An access operation (method) to select special dossier titles may look something like:

```
method: SetOfDossiers
findDossiersEntitled: aString
"Using a method inherited "select" to return Dossiers
entitled aString"
^self select:{:i|:i.name = aString }
%
```

The syntax and grammar look very Smalltalk-*like*.

It would seem useful that in specification for either of the object-oriented databases that an ORD is used as the references along with the object and operation text frames.

Example

As an example, it may be useful to look at a theoretical office automation, which stores and allows editing and display of the various items in an office environment.

In this Office automation scenario we have the requirement to recognise and store all the various types of office 'object' possible and have an appropriate environment to express the definition of the various objects and their operations (Fig. 11.6).

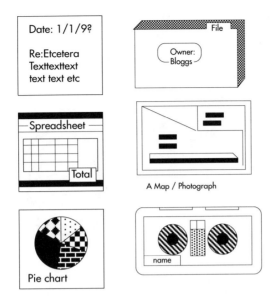

Figure 11.6 Office objects.

In this system the various types of units recognised are:

1. The dossier.
2. The Office-unit.
3. Text document unit.
4. The spreadsheet.
5. The statistical graphic.
6. The graphic image (bit mapped).
7. The voice memo (acoustic image).
8. The business graphic.

As you will no doubt notice, there is a principal supertype in the form of the Office item, and it may have several 'specialisations'.

To define this system more fully we have an environmental mode, which depicts the system boundary and the associated external event list. This is depicted in Fig. 11.7.

From the subject area knowledge we would develop an entity relationship diagram (ERD). The subject centre, the office item, is a supertype with all the various specialisms sited below. The office item itself will be associated with a Dossier. The Agent (user) is introduced, as is a subject link to allow the cross-referencing of various office items together to facilitate searches. All the major entities are described in the ERD diagram shown in Fig. 11.8.

When one is satisfied that all the entities and the relationships are complete as possible, one can set out to define all the relevant attributes for each of the entities.

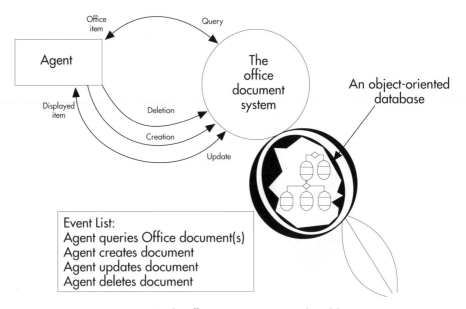

Figure 11.7   The office system environmental model view.

Office item:
    Reference number
    Description
    Date of creation
    Time of creation
    Author
    Last modified date
    File
        Office item type
        Identifier
        Number of lines
        Number of data items
        Associated Template name
    BitGraphic
        Office item type
        Identifier
        BPI
        Size
        [Colour | Monochrome]
    Text document
        Office item type
        Identifier

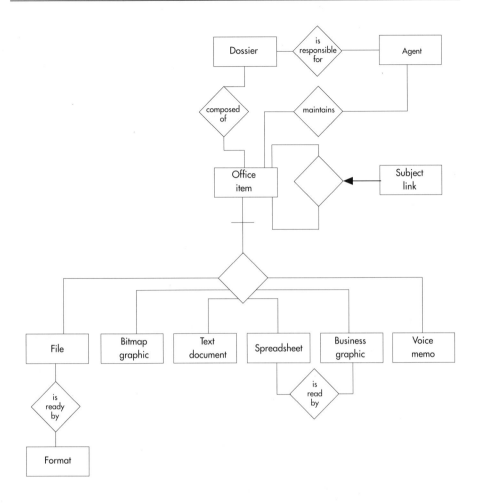

Figure 11.8   The office system entity relationship diagram.

    Number of words
    Number of pages
  Spreadsheet
    Office item type
    Identifier
    Title
    Columns
    Rows
  Business graphic
    Office item type

        Identifier
        Array dimensions
        Origin
     Voice memo
        Office item type
        Identifier
        Audio_title
        Audio_message
        Audio_message_meter
   Dossier
     Dossier_identifier
     Dossier_owner
     Dossier_creation_date
     Dossier_item_count
   Agent
     Agent name
     Agent location
     Agent security level
   Subject_link
     Subject
     Number of references
     Reference_number as anchor
     {Next Reference number }.
   Template
     Template number
     Format instructions
     File reference.

Now that the data items have been identified for each entity we can also define each of the relationships (Table 11.1):

Providing we are happy with the overall data contents we may now proceed to draw up an ORD to show the various class objects. To complete this activity fully we should have identified each operation that is required by each class object.

This activity of operation identification may be achieved by asking oneself what are

Table 11.1 Relationships within an entity relationship diagram

Relationship	Description
Composed of	Links 1 Dossier to *n* of Office item
Is responsible for	Links 1 Agent to *n* of Dossier
Maintains	Links 1 Agent to *n* of Office item

the services that each class object should provide, whilst considering the overall objective of the system. The only restrictions are to ensure operations are placed where they may usefully achieve a good encapsulation for the object.

A good hint is to think of:

> *Custodial activities*: those related to creation, deletion and general maintenance.
>
> *Fundamental activities*: those related to the main purpose of the system.
>
> *Control activities*: those related with good general control and audit principles.

If one is at a loss to define what the desired time sequence behaviour should be for an entity, an entity state transition diagram (eSTD) is the ideal vehicle for exploring that behaviour (Table 11.2). Table 11.3 is a supertype object. Table 11.4 shows class objects that inherit data and operations from the Office item class object.

Operation specifications may be written in the conventional style even independent of the particular technology. So, for example, the operation specifications for the Voice memo may be written in pre- and post-condition specification style (Table 11.5).

Table 11.2 Entity state transition diagram—custodial operations

Object	Operation	Justification
Dossier	Create	Custodial activity
	Include	Custodial activity
	Remove	Custodial activity
	List	Useful control activity
	Status	Useful control
	Delete	Custodial activity
	Locate	Fundamental purpose

Table 11.3 Entity state transition—custodial operations

Object	Operation	Justification
Office item	Create	Custodial
	Delete	Custodial
	Update	Fundamental
	Display	Fundamental
	Tour	Fundamental
	List	Fundamental
	Organise	Custodial

Table 11.4 Class objects that inherit data and operations from the Office item class object

Object	Operation	Justification
File	Edit	All files may potentially need editing
	Attach	This allows attachment of a template
Template	Edit	Editing a style template
	Attach	Attachment to a file
BitGraphic	Edit	Edit a bitmap
Text document	Search	Normal requirement to search for a string
	Format	Format of a document
Spreadsheet	Edit	Normal requirement to edit a spreadsheet
	Copy	Copy an image and rename
	Graphic	Give a graphical rendering of a spreadsheet
	Calculate	A toggle switch to allow or inhibit calculation
Business Graphic	Edit	Allowing editing a spreadsheet locally
	Attach	Attach a spreadsheet source or the graphics
Voice Memo	Play	Play the recording audially
	ff	Fast forward
	rw	Rewind
	Record	Allow the acceptance of a recording

The rest of these class objects have an attachment to other objects based on the ORD (Table 11.6). All of these items have visibility in the form depicted in Fig. 11.9. Any one of these class objects may be expanded into an object internal view should you wish it.

An internal view of class object Spreadsheet is shown in Fig. 11.10. The visible operations are shown and the linkage from the operation 'graphic' to the server `object.operation` 'attach' which allows the representation of a spreadsheet in business graphic form.

The class object Spreadsheet inherits from the class object Office item, and the relationship between an object and what it inherits is displayed in Fig. 11.11. Essentially it is as if the 'office item' is 'glued alongside' the spreadsheet and they are sharing a common piece of storage with all the inherited operations being available for use.

The relationships (for the OODBMs) are imported from the ERD definitions and become references between the various class objects. The cardinality of the relationship is still important for physical placement reasons.

Conclusions

This chapter has introduced object-oriented databases and the appropriate concepts that go with them. Normalisation has been associated with data but here we have introduced

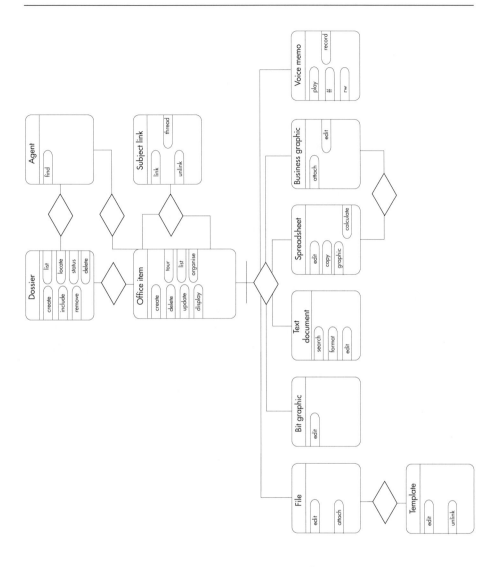

Figure 11.9   The office system object relationship diagram.

behavioural normalisation where the behaviour should be best placed for object purposes. The ORD is the major means of depiction of the object-oriented database. The office document system was really to demonstrate that the object-oriented database can accommodate comfortably mixed modes of information (objects in their true sense). Appropriate behaviour being inherited where ever is useful.

Table 11.5   Pre- and post-condition specification style for the specifications of Voice memo

Operation	Specification
play	Pre-condition a message occurs and a non-empty audio_message Post-condition an audio-message is reproduced
ff	Pre-condition a message occurs and audio_message is not at end Post-condition an audio_message_meter is fast forwarded
rw	Pre-condition a message occurs and a non-empty audio_message Post-condition an audio_message_meter is rewound
record	Pre-condition a message occurs and a non_empty audio_message Post-condition an audio_message is played and audio_message_meter is incremented

Table 11.6   Class object attachments to other objects based on the ORD

Object	Operation	Justification
Agent	Find	Find a dossier and start session
Subject-link	Link	Allows a linkage from one office item to another
	Unlink	Removal of an existing link
	Thread	'Thread through' a linkage showing all associated documents

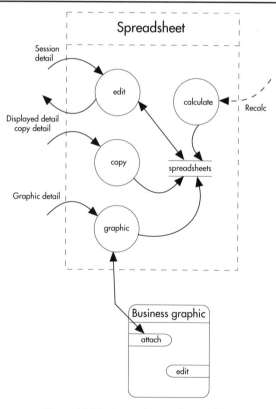

Figure 11.10   Internal view of spreadsheet.

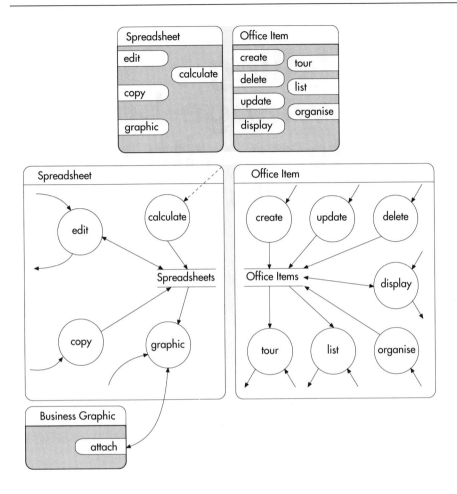

Figure 11.11 Internal view of spreadsheet.

References and further reading

Blair, G., Gallagher, J., Hutchison, D. and Shepherd, D. (1991) *Object-Oriented Languages, Systems and Applications*, pp. 166–202. London, UK: Pitman.

Chen, P. (1976) 'The entity relationship model towards a unified view of data.' *ACM Trans. on Database Systems*, **1**(1), 9–36.

Codd, E. (1970) 'A relational model of data for large shared data banks.' *Comm. of the ACM*, **13**(6), 377–87.

Dittrich, K. (1990) 'Object-oriented database systems: the next miles of the marathon. *Information Systems*, **15**(1), 161–7.

Kim, W. (1991) 'Object-oriented database systems: strengths and weaknesses. *JOOP*, July/August, 21–9.

CHAPTER 12

Modelling knowledge-based systems with object orientation

Eddington's Theory
The number of different hypotheses erected to explain a given biological phenomenon is inversely proportional to the available knowledge

(Quoted in *Murphy's Law*)

This chapter addresses knowledge-based systems and outlines how and where an object-oriented representation may assist with both the understanding and consequences of what is being presented. It is *not* intended to go into great depth on knowledge-based systems (KBS) *per se*. Should you require more detail on this subject please consult one of the books cited in the bibliography. This chapter shows also the diagram types and frames that are useful for an object-oriented representation and there is an example of a KBS representation towards the end of the chapter.

What are knowledge-based systems?

Knowledge-based systems are those systems that represent closely a specialist domain of human knowledge. This may be represented in the form of either many production rules (if . . . then . . .) or by means of frames, which may be similar to those introduced already in this book.

The primary use of this type of system is to obtain from a machine a logical result based upon quickly chaining forward from antecedent (the IF part) to consequent (the THEN part) through a plethora of rules to derive a certain result. Alternatively this may be done by deducing results from certain pieces of evidence, expressed in a frame – a diagnosis. Humans are accomplished experts in specialist fields and are capable of resolving this forward chaining apparently intuitively and with a high degree of speed and accuracy.

An example of this genre of system may be related to a hardware manufacturer who has a vast range of components that have complex dependency rules associated with whether they are mutually compatible or not. A customer engineer will want to list off the model type with the options and make sure that he or she does not make a choice that is not viable. In addition, with a particular option there may also be other components that should also be included. To express this situation you can imagine that the rules will be expressed in the form:

```
Rule A31:
  IF Device_class = 'A31' AND
   Option-2 is selected
  THEN a Gizmo_67 AND
   a Hyperlead are required
Rule A32:
  If Device_class = 'A32' AND
   Option-2 is selected
  THEN a Gizmo_89 AND
   a Hyperlead AND
   a Thermal-Isolator are required
```

This type of application essentially requires facts about the system and all of its significant subsets; this is essentially a data capture exercise.

After the rules have been defined and loaded into some appropriate storage mechanism (working memory) the next ingredient is the inference engine. The 'inference engine' is a virtual machine optimised to chain through access to the rules/frames in a forward or backward manner and produce results. This device handles all the appropriate chaining forward or backward through the appropriate rule base. So, in a nutshell, the three components for the knowledge-based system are: the rule base (collection of rules), the working memory (storage of the facts) and the inference engine.

There are two major styles of representation: one being production-rule based and the other frame-based.

Production-rule-based

This representation relies upon a series of pages defining all the rules as a set of productions. Each of the rules would be expressed in the form of If ... Then ... statements using logical conjunctions wherever necessary. This is usually coupled to a piece of equipment that digests and interprets these rules. This becomes the rule base for usage in conjunction with working memory and the inference engine. Some computer source languages (e.g. Smalltalk) have a sufficient grammatical repertoire to accommodate rules expressed in this form as a specific logic class.

Frame-based

This style of representation was originally formulated by Bartlett (1932) to model human knowledge representation in the form of a schema with various slots. These present the values to the user, without his/her actually seeing the mechanism of presentation. Many of these slots may have default values so that the omission to assign a slot value will result in a safe value being used. Many of these slots may have an automatic mechanism attached to them to allow updates whenever a related value changes, so it may be presenting the most up-to-date values. This automatic feature is often called a demon, and presents limited visibility – an object-oriented concept. So far we have introduced the ideas of frames for our definition of the textual components related to a class object. One will still have to formulate rules related with the slots and their associations, but the viewer only sees what is relevant to his/her context of use.

Figure 12.1 shows an object inheritance diagram (OID) used to depict the overall inheritance structure. The text frames that may be used to define the employee rely on a template to define structure. Because we have subtypes Engineer and Accountant we will have template definitions for these. When an instance of an employee 'Smith' appears, the system immediately recognises the fact that Smith is an Engineer. So, upon looking at the display of Smith's details, it is as if the template of Engineer and Employee are concatenated. For example, the Equipment types that this engineer Smith may work on are displayed accordingly. If any fields have rules attached, this will condition the emission of the appropriate details.

Thus a frame-based representation is friendly to the users in as much as they only see what is helpful for them to use and refer to. All distracting details are removed from view.

What is object-oriented about KBS?

One of the concepts mentioned in Chapter 1 was the idea of encapsulation of the concept's memory, processing and state behaviour into one unit with a protocol to allow communication with it. In a knowledge-based system another type of processing is undertaken – the rule inference. Additionally we have another type of memory, that of the rules to be stored. This, to our object-oriented view, is just another piece of memory to be managed. We would still use this class-object by means of messages directed at specific services to query the class-object and receive the appropriate results. Additionally there will also be custodial services to allow updates to the memory (data and rules). Additionally we have the concept of limited visibility which means we show only what is helpful for users to perceive for their effective usage of this class-object.

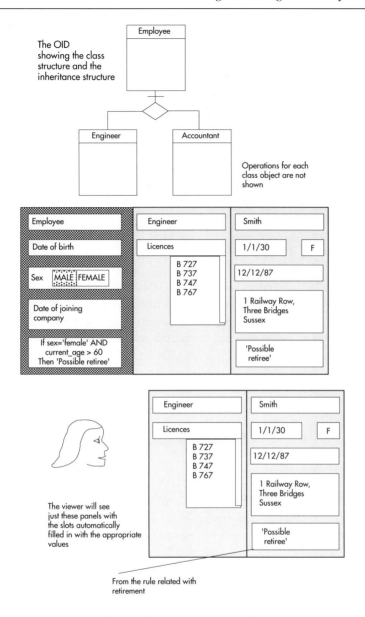

Figure 12.1   Employee object inheritance.

Many systems currently being developed will probably have knowledge-based components alongside object-oriented databases, and possibly alongside control systems. Clearly if we are talking object-oriented it is desirable that the notation encapsulate each of these types within one notation with the minimum of fuss and distinction.

Figure 12.2 shows a generic class_object that is associated with a knowledge-based system. Externally it looks no different from other class_objects shown. The services (operations) offered, however, give some clues as to its vocation (e.g. create rule, update rule and delete rule). The other services (operations) may be quite common (e.g. query, update working memory (wm)). One test of a modelling notation is whether you can model the detail behaviour further. Thus expanding the class_object into an object internal view (OIV), shows the storage as two store types joined together (working memory and rule base). The operations introduced externally are depicted one for one with the inside view. The query operation, however, has two dialogue flows with another class_object (inference engine). This is how the role of the inference engine's behaviour may be explained. Alternatively you may choose not to show the 'inference engine', that is your choice.

Can it help?

Having seen (from Fig. 12.2) that there is no difference in the representation of external view of an object and that there is very little difference in the notation for an internal view of an object, it is useful to represent the object being discussed by its external view with messages (queries) directed at specific operations. The operations, as we

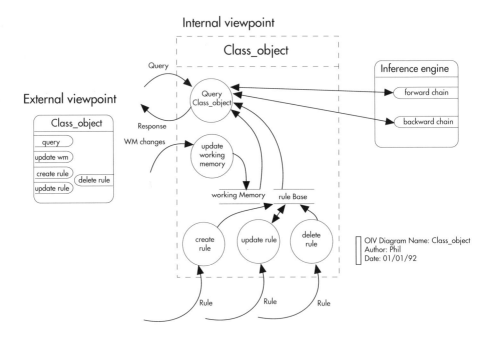

Figure 12.2   Internal view of a knowledge-based object.

saw, are essentially, from the user's point of view, no different from so-called normal objects.

I believe this notation is useful for representing objects in any type of system, of which a knowledge-based system is but one instance. It is additionally useful that we have one notation to express how we perceive the various objects. In knowledge-based applications they too may avail themselves of predefined objects and an inheritance structure to reduce the effort to build.

Importance of inheritance

We have already talked of the concept of inheritance (see Chapters 1 and 3). It is the characteristics whereby a class may automatically place alongside and make available for a subclass all the items of data and operations. This saves redefinition at the subclass level (i.e. a specialisation). In the case of knowledge-based systems we also want that definition to include rules being inherited. If we introduce rules at the class level we expect these rules to be inherited by the subclass (i.e. the specialisation).

We shall offer examples from the animal kingdom. For example, feline as a specialisation inherits mammalian characteristics, and that in turn inherits animal characteristics

What about the exceptions?

Exceptions are not a problem because we can override rules and data that may be inherited. A specialisation may override certain data items and rules. In the case shown below, of Manx cat as a specialisation of a feline, we have chosen to override the standard appendage 'tail' with 'no tail'.

A frame is equivalent to an object. A 'kind-of' indicates specialisation. The specialised group inherits from the general group. A specialised group may override a characteristic by an explicit statement (in the source language 'flex'):

>   frame animal
>
>   frame mammal is a kind of animal;
>   default skin is fur and
>   default habitat is the land and
>   default motions are { walk and swim } .
>
>   frame feline is a kind of mammal
>   default motions are { jump, crawl}
>   default appendage is a tail.
>
>   frame manx is a kind of feline
>   over-ride appendage with 'no tail'.

frame bird is a kind of animal;
   default skin is feather and
   default habitat is a tree and
   default motions are { fly } .

frame fish is a kind of animal;
   default skin is scale and
   default habitat is the water and
   default motions are { swim } .

The principal means of representation of inheritance is the OID, which introduces the class-objects and their supertype and subtype relationships. It is also useful to point out that multiple inheritance is allowed (i.e. a subclass may inherit from two or more classes). Each class-object introduced will have an object frame, which prescribes the more complete behaviour.

The object frame for knowledge-based systems

In Chapter 11 we defined what should be textually defined for our class-object. In knowledge-based systems we are going to elaborate upon this structure. The slots that were defined for the class_object were name, description, attributes (data items), supertypes (which class objects this object inherits from), an invariant and an introduction to the operations that are available. What is missing for knowledge-based systems is the provision of a slot for identifying and defining rules.

Additionally each attribute should have the provision for a default value and where any automatic (demonic) activity is required upon a change of value.

An example of a knowledge-based system

How a knowledge-based system is explored and documented using object concepts will be shown using a scenario for managing and assigning work in the consulting business. The first step is one of marking out all the relevant concepts; the entity relationship diagram is the vehicle for this type of representation. The key concepts in this scenario are:

Consultant: the human resource whose services are sold.
Ergonomist and Analyst: these are specialisations of consultant.
Requirement: this is a demand for a specialised service.
Schedule: this is a time-ordered list of planned activities.
Location: this a specific place where the scheduled activity should be undertaken.
Assignment: this is the assignment of a consultant to undertake a requirement which is scheduled.

This is expressed in an entity relationship diagram (ERD) (Fig. 12.3). The further elaborations required are that the assignment is an associative entity because it is dependent upon the interrelationship of Requirement, Schedule and Consultant. The consultant entity is related to analyst and ergonomist by means of the supertype/subtype relationship, which really introduces inheritance of data that will take place between the representations of Analyst and Ergonomist and that of the consultant. Lastly the Location is linked to the schedule by the fact that a scheduled activity will take place at some location.

ERD as a source

The ERD becomes an ideal way to stimulate questions as to what are the rules associated with each concept (entity) that is being represented. For example, there may be rules associated with the class Consultant, perhaps minimum duration and general types of assignment, and there may be rules more specifically associated with the Analyst. At the bottom-most levels there may be rules associated with a specific consultant, reflecting each analyst's particular preferences of type assignment and preferred locations.

There may be rules associated with the Schedule as to what becomes a viable mix of types of assignments and ensuring that a certain resource profile is not exceeded.

The ERD may be tentatively expanded into an object relationship diagram (ORD) by literally exchanging entity symbols for object symbols (Fig. 12.4). However, we must collect behaviour for each entity before it becomes an object.

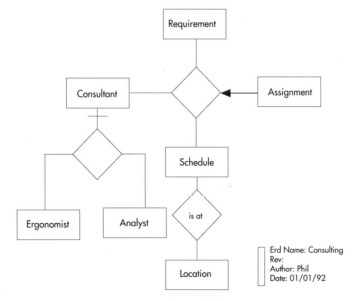

Figure 12.3 An ERD for consulting.

The custodial operations are the easiest to identify. These are the activities that create and delete occurrences of the class_object. Additionally we must have a mechanism to look after the rules so there will be custodial activities associated with the creation and removal of rules.

The next activity is to insert the fundamental operations, which are associated with the purpose of the system. These are the activities related with updating and querying the class_objects; they are named accordingly. The class_objects work just as before; a message will be directed at an operation and it will pass arguments to that operation, which will in turn respond as prescribed in the operation specification. The only differences are where the operation is using a rule base in conjunction with working memory (stored data). Conventional operations would not be using the rule base. The

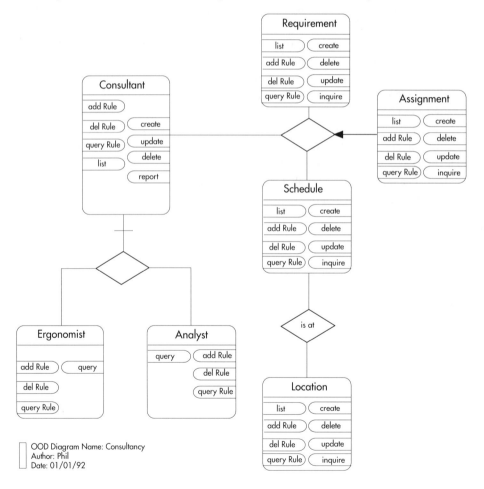

Figure 12.4   An ORD for consulting.

detail behaviour can be expanded by means of looking at the object internal view (OIV) and the object frame (Fig. 12.5).

As mentioned earlier, the object frame may be expanded, compared to what we have seen before; additional slots will cater for rules. There will be a slot to define rules for the class and there will be an object frame slot pattern to insert instance-based information (related with specific occurrences); there may also be rules that are specific to a instance.

Remember that our objectives with this notation are to allow a representation of the situation in modelling terms so it can be visualised, manipulated and additionally act as a reference point for development in the form of a solution technology.

At the time of writing the object-oriented notation expressed above, particularly in the form of the ORD and the object frame, assist towards the aim of representation of objects and the modelling thereof. The OIV may certainly be used, but it is not strictly speaking necessary in knowledge-based applications.

The other diagram types, like the ODD and the OIN may certainly be used, but each has a specific context of use. The ODD is optimised towards showing an implementation structure, and if rules are relevant they may certainly be embedded into the object. If the operations are rule-based queries they are, for all intents and purposes, no different from other operations.

The OIN is optimised to depict an implementation-free network of cooperating objects. If rules are relevant to any of the objects they may be depicted in the same manner as outlined above. Remember that, essentially, we wish to define systems

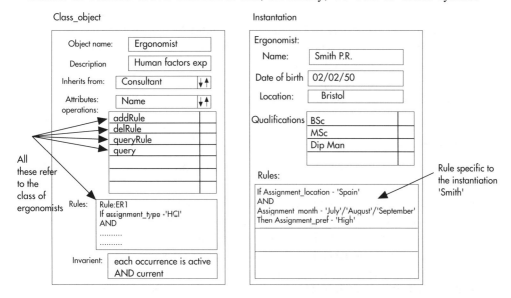

Figure 12.5 Object frame for ergonomist.

without undue distinction between their types, so the notation is intended to be as general as possible in its application.

Knowledge-based object-oriented programming languages?

Are there such things as knowledge-based object-oriented programming languages? There are some knowledge-based development languages that do have object character, for example LISP (LISt Processing) and CLOS. These do have the rule base structure and exhibit object-like characteristics, such as the 'object' concept and a rule expression mechanism, and additionally the characteristic of inheritance.

Prolog has 'grown' some object characteristics, such as the concept of the object and inheritance mechanisms to become Prolog^{++} as offered by LPA associates.

However, one interesting direction is exhibited in the Digitalk release of Smalltalk (an object-oriented programming language (OOPL) in the conventional sense). This has extensions in the form of methods (operations) that use Prolog to formulate rules and appropriate queries. This seems to be an ideal direction for the development of object-oriented languages where they will see no real distinction between knowledge-based systems and so-called conventional applications.

Knowledge bases and databases

It will be apparent to the reader that there is no difference between the knowledge-based representation and a databased representation. Both may be easily represented by means of the ORD. The only real distinction lies in the fact that the knowledge-based system requires rules to be represented. This extension is easily handled in the object frame. It is a more reasonable conclusion that our ideas about knowledge bases and object-oriented databases should be merged and rules viewed as a more general definition of how the object should respond.

Operations and rules

Throughout this chapter, rules have been considered as distinct from operations. It has been the intention that developers have freedom to describe the operations in either a pre- and post-condition (declarative) form or in structured language (procedural) form. However, there is the need to define rules that apply to a specific object, and the most effective form is in declarative form. These rules would be capable of being 'used' from an operation or a query language. Additionally, rules need not have the same degree of visibility as given to operations and if a developer has used a pre- and post-condition style of operation specification, he/she may see rules as similar in form. The developer then has the freedom to see rules as a very granular form of pre-conditions, which live separately. Alternatively, the developer also has the freedom not to make any distinction between the two, and to see them as extensions to declarative operation specifications.

Conclusions

This chapter has been about knowledge-based systems and object-oriented systems development. Objects that exhibit knowledge-based behaviour can easily be recognised by and recorded by means of the ERD. The ERD, in turn, may be developed into an ORD by the addition of the suitable services that each object will offer. The definition of the object is by means of the object frame, with the addition of the slots for rule definition. It does not seem necessary to expand the object, in this context, into an OIV but you may do so if you find it useful.

Object-oriented databases and knowledge-based systems have a high degree of similarity as far as representation is concerned, and it is my belief that they should be viewed as very similar.

References and further reading

Bartlett, F.C. (1932) *Remembering*. Cambridge, UK: Cambridge University Press.

Keller, R. (1987) *Expert Systems Technology – Development and Application*. New York, NY: Yourdon Press.

Miller, J., Potter, W., Kochut, K., Keskin, A. and Ucar, E. (1991) 'The active KDL object-oriented database system and its application to simulation support.' *JOOP*, July/August, 1991.

Minsky, M. (1984) *The Society of Mind*. London, UK: Picador.

Winston, H. (1984) *Artificial Intelligence*. Reading, MA: Addison-Wesley.

CHAPTER 13

Object-oriented programming languages

Brook's Law
Whenever a system becomes completely defined, some damn fool discovers something that either abolishes the system or expands it beyond recognition

(Fred Brooks)

This chapter focuses attention upon what constitutes an object-oriented programming language (OOPL) and what criteria distinguish an OOPL from a conventional computer source language. Many benefits are promised from an object-oriented programming language and this chapter outlines specifically what they are. There is a brief description as to a selection of OOPLs and what features they offer.

A brief genealogy of OOPLs is also given, which describes their various origins. Smalltalk is the basis of an example OOPL and an explanation of how it is used and how it works is given.

What is it, in an OOPL that makes it effort-saving, and are there any performance drawbacks of which a user/developer should be aware of?

The origins of OOPLs

The first object-oriented language was Simula, which introduced the notion of classes and general inheritance into a programming language in 1966 (Dahl and Nygaard, 1966). The language was based upon a language for expressing discrete event simulation. Simula, in its general form, was very Algol-like in its structure. It also had a form of flexible behaviour based on overloading and was based upon process, rather than data.

The idea of simulation and its relevance to computer systems is important. All computer solutions are simulations of some mental model of a projected system. It is also ideal that our language reflects that mental model as much as possible.

Since that date many OOPLs have been developed. The principal one that is worth discussing is Smalltalk, which came out of the work of Alan Kay, Adele Goldberg, Daniel Ingalls and many others from Xerox Parc in the 1970s. The principal paradigm behind Smalltalk was a world of objects and messages that are interchanged. Within Smalltalk, everything is an object, even items such as Number are decomposed into subclasses of Float, Fraction and Integer. Storage of data is represented in a Collection subclass, which in turn has many subclasses in its own right, such as Bag, Indexed collection and Set. Many other OOPLs have sprouted up over the last six to seven years, such as Eiffel and various extensions to languages such as C, namely C++ and Objective C; even Pascal has an object-oriented extension – Objective-Pascal.

What constitutes an OOPL?

Languages may have various gradations of objectness and thus the flavour of 'objectness', and this can be presented in a language. These flavours are object-based, class-based and object-oriented.

Object-based is the facility of the language to cater for encapsulation and present an object identity.

Class-based is the facility within the language to offer an object based unit and offer a set abstraction.

Object-oriented is the facility of the language to offer class-based units and inheritance and self-recursion. So, as we see, object-oriented offers the highest degree of object character.

At this point, I believe it would be in order to offer definition as to what an OOPL is:

> **An OOPL is a programming language, the principal construct of which is the object, which shall encapsulate all the services and data as one unit and shall avail itself of inheritance of both data and services.**

Meyer (1988) suggests that an object-oriented development is just another form of modularisation where the units are much more self-contained and based upon more sensible units. His modules should exhibit five key principles:

1. Each module should map to a unit within the language.
2. Every module should communicate with as few others as possible.
3. Should any communication occur between modules then the coupling should be as 'thin' as possible.
4. All interfaces will be explicit.
5. Each unit will exhibit information hiding.

Expanding on each of the statements.

1. This means that each of the units (modules) correspond directly to units within the OOPL itself.
2. This refers to the linkage to other modules and the idea is that the modules are as self contained as possible. Whilst not forbidding communication to other modules it is attempting to restrict the variety.

3. Any communication that takes place between units will involve as few 'tokens' as possible. The principles here are similar to those related to coupling in hierarchical program structures.
4. All interfaces will be explicitly defined and displayed so that they invite as much usership as possible.
5. Each unit that is available for use will only exhibit what is available rather than the precise mechanism.

Many of the principles stated above are common to those that already exist in program structures. Certainly the ideas related to cohesion are equivalent to the self-containedness of the units. Coupling is the interdependence of one unit upon another and this is expressed in the exchange of tokens. Ideally as few tokens as possible should be exchanged. The concept of fan-in from structure charts is really an expression of reuse, which we are encouraging.

Cox (1986) suggests that the level of reuse of units in software today has been primarily focused at the function. This is analogous to the situation in the electronic industry where reuse units at the level of the transistor are helpful but possibly we should be thinking of the integrated circuit or at some higher order device (see Fig. 2.1 concerning granularity of reuse units).

Another way to discuss the issue is to look at what the options are in lumped terms. Remember that the key issue is what and how much the lumped units (modules) should contain. The essence of this trade-off is that we also have the choice as to where we place items (modules) in bigger lumps (i.e. more cohesion) or with smaller lumps and lots of communication going on between them (coupling).

The 'lumps' shown are graphic metaphors – units for intended processing. There are three distinct lumps shown X and Y and iXY with iYX (Fig. 13.1). X and Y are single units, which may be connected to by bridging unit (interface), called iXY and iYX, depending on your direction of use.

The costs of each are cognitive costs (i.e. the mental effort to develop and maintain the unit (lump)). The options are easy to evaluate in qualitative terms. We shall

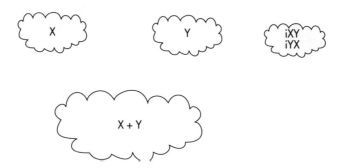

Figure 13.1   Integrate or split?

consider that the key cost is this cognitive effort cost (mental effort for a developer and maintainer). Note that the size of a unit and its associated has a diseconomy in relation to scale as found by Nanus and Farr (1964).

Cost = K*(size)**1.5 where K is a constant

This formula has the same form as that found by Boehm (1981) namely:

Effort = A*(KDSI)**B

where KDSI = thousands of lines of code and A and B are constants.

We have then in principle two options:

Option 1
keeping X and Y as separate units
costX + cost iXY + costY + costiYX
if X and Y do not have any linkage then:
costiXY & costiYX = 0

Option 2
integrating X and Y into a single unit
The cost here has the cost (X+Y).
Due to diseconomies to scale cost (X+Y) > costX + costY

However, there is another dimension, that of the interface costs: costiXY and costiYX which is linked to the effort related to attending to coupling (Fig. 13.2). So when do we integrate and when not? Integrate (X+Y) when:

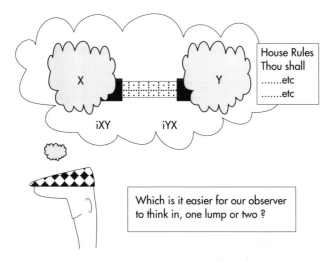

Figure 13.2 A single lump or two simpler lumps?

$$\text{cost}(X+Y) < \text{costX} + \text{costY} + \text{costiXY} + \text{costiYX}.$$

note typically `costiXY` & `costiYX = 0` if they are unrelated.

Keep separate when:

$$\text{costX} + \text{costY} + \text{costiXY} + \text{costiYX} =< \text{cost}(X+Y)$$

The tendency is to keep the units as compact (cohesive) as possible (i.e. granular) because it potentially makes them more reusable. This additionally becomes more attractive if the interfacing costs are made as small as possible and and object-oriented environment makes the effort to send messages between objects as easy as possible.

Additionally, inheritance encourages us to consider as a unit specialisations of more general classes, which reduce further the effort to develop.

Key concepts of the object paradigm

Encapsulation

The first key concept is that of encapsulation, which provides a boundary around the unit hiding the complexity. This elaborates on the ideas of limited visibility and information hiding. Additionally we ideally want to keep (as much as possible) a conceptual view of our units, and do not want to be distracted by the specific implementation code. The encapsulated unit is communicated to by means of a 'tight interface' in the form of a message. The messages will take the general form of:

Class + (instance) + service + {argument}

The class is the specific object class, the instance is the specific occurrence. The service (or method) is the specific function required of the object. The arguments are the parameters that are sent to the object. The exact style and organisation of the variable is deliberately not visible to the 'user' (or caller) of the object, who will only 'see' the encapsulation and the offered services and shall know the 'addressing protocol' for the object.

The unit building block

The second major concept is that this unit should be based on data, and more often than not this is based on the class. We have already elaborated upon the rationale behind basing the unit on data but, in a nutshell, it is a less volatile unit than basing the unit upon a process.

Inheritance

The next key concept is the inheritance mechanism. This allows the specialisation of a class (i.e. a subclass) to inherit data values (or, if you like, have automatic access to data held) at the class level. Services too may be inherited. A message directed at a subclass will be redirected to the class, making it appear as if all the data and services of both the class and subclass are held in one unit. This feature allows a tremendous amount of flexibility in developing systems, where we are being encouraged to recognise the general and the specific and only add extra behaviour where necessary.

Some languages offer a feature called genericity, which is the capability to define a module's behaviour based upon parameters. This allows generic messages to interpreted and the appropriate behaviour template being accessed is the response from a specific type unit. This feature can simulate inheritance.

Polymorphism

The next key feature that is needed is polymorphism, which is the ability to send the same message to many different objects (each sharing the same ancestry) and having each object respond in its own specific manner. This is, in principle, the same as operator overloading. Two separate objects may have operations that share the same name. However, when the message is sent to the object its operation responds with the specific behaviour of the specific operation.

For example, in the field of Container operations we may have an object Container, which may have subtypes such as Tankers, Refrigerated units and Vans. All these container units will have a load operation. Each specialisation of a container has its own particular load operation. For example, for a Refrigerated unit a desired temperature setting will have to be included. For a Tanker we will need to identify the chemical being transported to test for any safety exclusions. For a Van unit we will need to know specific details, such as units of measure and how many occurrences. The objects are best arranged in the following fashion:

Object	Operation (method)
Container	
Van	load
Refrigerated_unit	load
Tanker	load

Messages to update the load situation of each type do not specifically have to mention that they are directed to a Van or a Tanker or a Refrigerated unit. They need only pass a message:

Container + (instance) + load + { parameters specific to the subtype }

The polymorphism mechanism sorts out the message automatically, on the basis of the instance (unique identifier) and, what subtype the message is being directed at and the appropriate 'load' operation is presented, ready for use, with the appropriate template for receiving the appropriate arguments. For example, for a Tanker the arguments will be chemical-reference and the volume, and for a Refrigerated unit they will be the temperature setting and weight of foodstuff.

There are various subclassifications of polymorphism, such as *ad hoc* and universal. *Ad hoc* polymorphism is actually the overloading of operator symbols. Another subtype is coercion, where the operation works on a variety of messages. The other genre of polymorphism is called universal polymorphism, which has parametric and inclusion as subtypes. Parametric polymorphism allows the substitution of arguments from a variety of sources. Inclusion polymorphism is, in fact, inheritance.

This concept of polymorphism brings additional effectiveness in development effort and exception behaviour.

Dynamic binding

The last feature is dynamic binding, where the physical behaviour is taken on at the last possible instant. This is the mechanism for implementing polymorphism. In other development cultures it is called 'late binding'.

The five optional components that make an OOPL are:

1. Encapsulation of data and methods.
2. Units based on data.
3. An inheritance mechanism (or subtyping mechanism).
4. Polymorphism.
5. Dynamic (or late) binding, which is an implementation mechanism.

Some so-called OOPLs have these characteristics, some do not. There are also some features that should be incorporated in an OOPL from function-based languages:

Concurrency

This characteristic allows units to exhibit execution at the same time. It is not strictly a feature of OOPLs but is available in other language types. However, an object-oriented architecture assists providing facility for message passing. Additionally there is the clustering of objects with frequent intercommunication.

Garbage collection

This is important because object-oriented systems tend to use a tremendous amount of storage and so there must be an efficient means of removing superfluous storage as quickly as possible. Automatic garbage collection is the reclamation of storage that has recently been recognised as being no longer needed. OOPLs such as Smalltalk, Clos and Eiffel have these facilities.

Persistence

This characteristic is the capability of the object-oriented system to be able to keep a 'file structure' beyond the duration of the session (i.e. files stored off-line). It is imperative that an OOPL has this feature if it is going to provide effective information system management. OOPLs such as Simula and Smalltalk do not offer an explicit solution to this problem.

An example of an OOPL: Smalltalk

Smalltalk is being introduced as an example of an OOPL that exhibits most of the characteristics that we have discussed. Smalltalk's origins, as mentioned before, emanate from Xerox Parc in the 1970s. It uses the paradigm of a 'world of objects' and 'message passing' in a perfectly communicating 'ether'.

The main building blocks are the class, which accommodates all the variables, and the method, which is the OOPL term for an operation. Any class can have any number of subclasses. When a class and subclass structure is constructed it is automatically setting up an inheritance structure ready for use.

The language constructions are made up of objects held at a very granular level. All the message-passing happens according to a well established protocol. The message contains a selector and a series of arguments, or may be more elaborate and contain both keyword message selectors and arguments.

There are three types of message: the unary, where a message contains solely a 'selector'; binary messages, which contain a selector and an argument and a keyword message expression, which contains keyword selectors and arguments (Fig. 13.3).

In the examples above, the first message is directly equivalent to an assignment of the colour black to the item Turtle, which in this instance is a drawing device.

The second example contains a selector. In this case, '−' is a minus operator that will be applied to Balance with its argument 'withdrawal'.

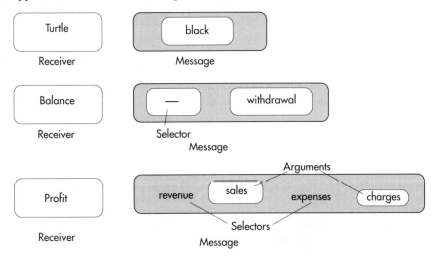

Figure 13.3 Messages and receivers.

The last example depicts a message with its keyword selectors and arguments. Profit is being derived from the revenue keyword and its argument 'sales' and the expenses argument 'charges'. We cannot see the detailed mechanism of executing the calculation that is being accomplished within 'Profit'. Should we wish to delve into the exact mechanism that is where we would do it. This is an example of limited visibility.

Smalltalk has a comprehensive class structure. The top of the class structure is the Object, and all other classes are arranged as subclasses of it. To look at one subclass such as 'Collection' we have all the subclasses that can be used to place information for various styles of storage.

```
Object
 Collection
    Bag
    Indexed Collection
       Array
       String
    Set
       Dictionary
       SymbolSet
```

This structure reflects the various styles and types of storage. A `Bag` is an unordered collection with a family of methods that are appropriate to an unordered collection. An `IndexedCollection` allows the random ordering but this time has an index to assist with access. `String` allows a family of specialised methods for dealing with strings as a subset of the `IndexedCollection` class.

To express and allow access and maintenance to the class structure, Smalltalk has a Class browser that is a comprehensive repository of all the classes and subclasses available for use (Fig. 13.4).

The class browser is an essential ingredient in the effective development of Smalltalk solutions. It becomes a source of ready-made components and can become augmented by means of extra subclasses and methods that can be added to the browser.

To illustrate the usage of Smalltalk and to demonstrate inheritance and polymorphism, I wish to use an example drawn from the Digitalk Smalltalk tutorial. It uses, by means of illustration, a subset of the animal world and their various behaviours (Fig. 13.5).

Animal is the base class that we will work with, the subclasses being Bird and Mammal. The Bird has two subclasses: Parrot and Penguin; the Mammal has two subclasses: Dog and Whale.

The variables are arranged in such a way that Animal will have all the base class variables such as name, habitat, topSpeed, colour and diet. Bird will have variables such as flying and wing-span.

Mammal may have no specific variables and may be viewed as if it is a placer, anticipating possible development of this class at some later time.

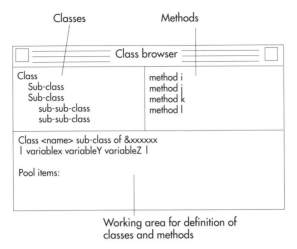

Figure 13.4   A Smalltalk class browser.

The Parrot will have a variable such as vocabulary; the Dog will also have a variable: barksAlot.

Inheritance supplies all the additional variables for the subclasses such as:

> *Parrot*: vocabulary, name, habitat, topSpeed, colour and diet.
> *Penguin*: name, habitat, topSpeed, colour and diet.
> *Dog*: barksAlot, name, habitat, topSpeed, colour and diet.
> *Whale*: name, habitat, topSpeed, colour and diet.

The methods in Smalltalk are of two types – class or instance-based. The class-based methods are those methods that are sensitive to messages sent to the class itself. Instance-based methods are those that are sensitive to the instance of the class.

From Fig. 13.5, showing class structure, we can see various methods placed with the appropriate classes. Method 'talk' is in three locations: Animal, Parrot and Dog. This means that Penguin and Whale will inherit the method 'talk' from the animal superclass. The method 'talk' for Parrot will be specfic to the utterances from a Parrot and its vocabulary. The method 'talk' will be specific to a Dog's utterance in the form of barking. The methods for both Dog and Parrot automatically override that of the animal class.

Let us see some specific methods and comment on them.

Class Animal

Method	Smalltalk source

answer
```
answer:aString
Transcript next putAll:
self class name, '', name, ':' aString
```

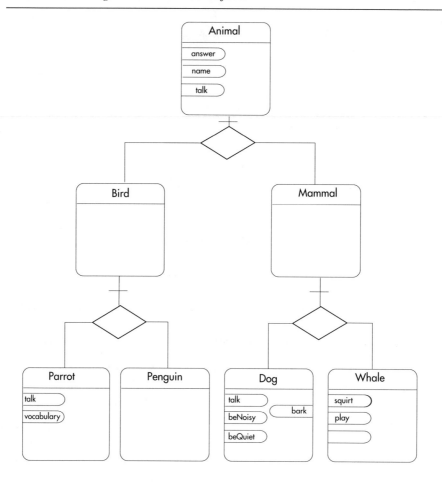

Figure 13.5 An object inheritance diagram for animals.

Class Animal

Method	Smalltalk source
name	`name: aString` `name:=aString`
talk	`self answer: 'I do not speak'`

Class Parrot

Method	Smalltalk source
talk	`self answer: vocabulary`
vocabulary	`vocabulary:=aString`

Class Dog

Method	Smalltalk source

bark	`Terminal bell.`
	`barksAlot`
	      `ifTrue:[self`
	      `answer:'bow wow']`
	      `ifFalse:[self`
	      `answer:Woof']'`

beQuiet	`barksAlot:=false.` `self answer: 'I will not bark any more'`

beNoisy	`barksAlot:=true`
	`self answer: 'I will bark till the cows`
	`come home'`

talk	`barksAlot isNil`
	      `ifTrue: [super talk]`
	      `ifFalse:[self bark]`

Most of the methods are readible and make some sense. The Dog, as you will notice, will only bark when 'barksAlot' is a Boolean variable and has an appropriate value 'true'. Additionally you will see the 'self bark' is one method calling another method. If it has the value 'false' then the Dog's talk utterance will be that inherited from the animal class.

To animate our menagerie we would first create the animals by introducing specific instances of animals and naming them.

Smalltalk	Commentary
`Rover:= Dog new`	Introduce a new instance of Dog 'Rover'.
`Rover name: 'Rover'`	Ensuring it 'knows' its own name.
`Rover beQuiet`	Command be quiet.
`Rover talk`	Rover would respond 'I do not speak'.
`Rover beNoisy`	Command to be noisy.
`Rover talk`	Rover would then utter 'bow wow'.

Now other animals such as the Parrot have the capacity to speak so we can see how we can get it talking.

Smalltalk	Commentary
`Janet:=Parrot new`	Introducing a new instance of parrot called Janet.
`Janet name: 'Janet'`	Ensuring it knows its own name 'Janet'.

Smalltalk	Commentary
`Janet vocabulary:`	
`'Who is a pretty girl then?'`	Learning a repertoire to go into a variable named Vocabulary. The method is also called vocabulary.
`Janet talk`	Janet is given command to talk. Janet then responds: 'Who is a pretty girl then?'

The 'talk' command being sent to the objects Janet and Rover and their separate and distinct responses is an illustration of polymorphism.

Dynamic binding is the capability of a language to have the behaviour of its object determined at the latest possible instant and that is demonstrated by the objects Rover and Janet, which have their behaviour determined during the execution.

OOPLs and their differential features

There is a plethora of object-oriented languages that exist and form a motley set of sources. These languages range from Ada through to Smalltalk (see Fig. 13.6 for a tentative genealogy of some source languages).

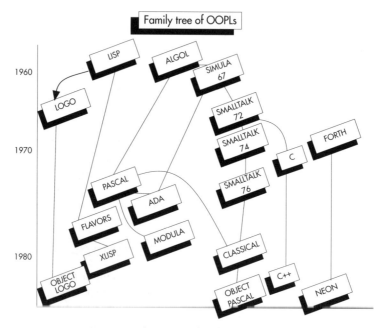

Figure 13.6   OOPLs genealogy (reproduced by kind permission of Yourdon Inc.).

I now intend to show a list outlining the comparative features of each OOPL. The template I shall use will be based upon the following items: binding, inheritance, multiple inheritance, polymorphism, persistence, genericity, object/libraries. I use as a basis a template from Graham (1991).

ADA

Language	Ada
Binding	Early
Inheritance	No
Multiple inheritance	No
Polymorphism	Yes
Persistence	Yes
Genericity	Yes
Concurrency	Possible
Garbage collection	No
Object/libraries	Some, usually in the form of a domain library

C

C is an efficient foundation language and it is augmented by the extensions C^{++} and Objective C.

Language	C++
Binding	Both
Inheritance	Yes
Multiple inheritance	Yes
Polymorphism	Yes
Persistence	No
Concurrency	Yes (some)
Garbage collection	No
Genericity	Yes (Templates have been recently introduced)
Object/libraries	Some, usually in the style of the class browser such as 'objectworks'.

Language	Objective-C
Binding	Both
Inheritance	Yes
Multiple inheritance	Yes
Polymorphism	Yes

Language	Objective-C
Persistence	No
Concurrency	Yes (some)
Garbage collection	Yes
Genericity	No
Object/libraries	Some

Language	Eiffel
Binding	Early
Inheritance	Yes
Multiple inheritance	Yes
Polymorphism	Yes
Persistence	Some
Concurrency	Yes
Garbage collection	Yes
Genericity	Yes
Object/libraries	Some.

Pascal

Extensions to Pascal are offered in two major kinds, Object Pascal and Turbo Pascal. This option offers Pascal practitioners an effective extension to their repertoire.

Language	Object Pascal
Binding	Late
Inheritance	Class based
Multiple inheritance	No
Polymorphism	Yes
Persistence	Some
Concurrency	No
Garbage collection	Yes
Genericity	No
Object/libraries	Some

Language	Turbo Pascal
Binding	Early
Inheritance	Yes
Multiple inheritance	No
Polymorphism	Yes
Persistence	No

Language	Turbo Pascal
Concurrency	Yes
Garbage collection	No
Genericity	No
Object/libraries	No

Language	Simula
Binding	Both
Inheritance	Yes
Multiple inheritance	No
Polymorphism	Yes
Persistence	No
Genericity	No
Object/libraries	No

Language	Smalltalk
Binding	Late
Inheritance	Yes
Multiple inheritance	No
Polymorphism	Yes
Persistence	No
Genericity	No
Object/libraries	Yes – a comprehensive class browser

Can you make an object-oriented solution with a non-OOPL?

Many so-called conventional languages, such as Cobol and Fortran, are based on functions. However, with some 'shoe-horning' they can be modified to become object-based, which assists with making them better units for reuse and better modules.

If you are working from structure charts and conventional languages there are definite advantages to be gained by modifying the chart to use a predominance of Information Clusters, which are encapsulations of function modules around a common subject. This aids both production and maintenance effort.

Conclusions

We have seen the various kinds of objectness that there can be in various source languages. This extends from object-based through class-based to object-oriented. Our definition of an OOPL was:

> A programming language, the principal construct of which is the object, which shall encapsulate all the services and data as one unit and shall avail itself of inheritance of both data and services.

OOPLs have a genealogy based predominantly on Simula and Algol and we can also see that many so-called 'conventional' languages have grown extensions, notably C and C^{++}, Pascal and Object Pascal and even Logo and Object Logo.

OOPLs are useful. Much of their benefit derives from their facility to construct solutions by use of both inheritance and class browsers. The unit of reuse in OOPLs is much greater than that offered by function-based libraries. The OID assists in the form of a graphic mapping of class and subclass to the language units.

Much of the conceptual basis for an OOPL was based on Smalltalk. The other OOPLs were described as a basis for comparison.

References and further reading

Boehm, B. (1981) *Software Engineering Economics*. Englewood Cliffs, NJ: Prentice Hall.

Booch, G. (1987) *Software Engineering with Ada*, (2nd Ed.). Redwood City, CA: Benjamin Cummings.

Budd, T. (1987) *A Little Smalltalk*. Reading, MA: Addison-Wesley.

Cox, B. (1986) *Object-Oriented Programming – An Evolutionary Approach*. Reading, MA: Addison-Wesley.

Dahl, O. and Nygaard, K. (1966) 'Simula, an algol based simulation language.' *Comm. of the ACM*, **9**, 671–8.

Graham, I. (1991) *Object-Oriented Methods*. Wokingham, UK: Addison-Wesley.

Gray, P. and Ramzan, M. (1990) *Smalltalk-80, A Practical Introduction*. London, UK: Pitman.

Lalonde, W. and Pugh, J. (1991) *Inside Smalltalk*, pp. 1–64. Englewood Cliffs, NJ: Prentice Hall.

Meyer, B. (1988) *Object-Oriented Software Construction*, pp. 12–40. Hemel Hempstead, UK: Prentice Hall.

Nanus, B. and Farr, L. (1964), 'Some cost-contributors to large scale programmes', AFIPS, *Proc. SJCC*, **25**, pp. 239–48.

CHAPTER 14

Prototyping and object-oriented development

No experience is ever a complete failure – it can always serve as a good bad example

(Anon)

Prototyping is an effective way to ensure that a candidate solution is correct and, furthermore, it allows the user to participate in the process. The style of prototyping that is being advocated is one of active modelling. We shall describe what we consider to be a useful prototyping process. With the object-oriented representation the form of a theoretical model can easily be animated into an active model for perusal by the client and his/her representatives. There are many prototyping tools for quickly assembling a prototype. The majority of the more effective ones are object-oriented; we shall have a look at some of these tools. We shall also look at the organisation of a prototyping activity.

The prototyping activity

Prototyping is a style of development by which versions, representative of the projected end-product, can be produced easily at an early stage for end-user assurance review and participation.

Prototyping, as a style of development, has been used successfully in other industries for decades and is perceived as a desirable way to proceed in areas where new technology is being used in its infancy.

As an illustration of prototyping from another area of technology I will use the development of the Anglo–French Concorde (supersonic transport).

When the development of the Concorde was agreed there were some several unknown areas in the flight regime. For example, the high speed of supersonic cruise and, of equal importance, the the low speed handling of a slender delta whilst climbing, manoeuvring for landing and manoeuvring subsequent to takeoff. Exploring both of these flight regimes in a full size Concorde would have been both expensive and risky. The most effective answer to the problem was to reconfigure an existing delta aircraft (the Fairey Delta 2) to have the similar ogival (slender delta) shaped wings and become the new BAC 221. This aircraft would then be able to explore the high speed flight regime. The low-speed part of the flight envelope was explored by building a slender delta aircraft (the Handley-Page HP115) out of low-cost components. This delta was not built for high speed, just for the low speed regime (Fig. 14.1).

The conclusions intended to be drawn from this example are that each prototype (BAC 211 and the HP115) is focused to examine a specific class of problems (or unknowns). Neither prototype was intended to become the final product. The knowledge from the prototypes is incorporated into the development of the final product. The costs were contained by using existing items that could be converted or by building highly focused units out of low-cost, easy-to-acquire material. The risks were contained into a much lesser set of variables (i.e. looking at one area only) and expense (should an accident occur).

Why is prototyping useful?

The principles behind prototyping may also be adopted in systems development. According to Connell and Shafer (1989), much of existing development effort is wasted. Typically 20 per cent of the functionality of systems that was developed was not used. Why? Connell and Shafer also point to the high volume of change traffic (requests for changes to a system's functionality). All this suggests that expression of the user/client's needs are not being fully comprehended and that we have not completed the analysis activity correctly. The end user is often 'surprised' by what is delivered.

Connell and Shafer mention that many development shops used structured methods and relied on users participating in many cases with structured methods. However, the users did not fully perceive the consequences of their choices.

The system's problem domain can be partitioned into three principal domains: transformation (the work a system performs), information (a structural map of all the concepts used) and time/sequence (how time may affect the system). Each system that we look at can be assessed against this template to ascertain the predominant domains of the system. This can be helpful in identifying what aspects may be useful to prototype (Fig. 14.2).

For example, a high concentration in transformational events may suggest that a prototyping tool optimised to express algorithms and transformations might usefully be deployed. This sort of emphasis can be expressed by means of the data flow diagram (DFD).

For example, a system that is looking after structures of information and all the events that are associated with updating sets of information or inquiring into individual

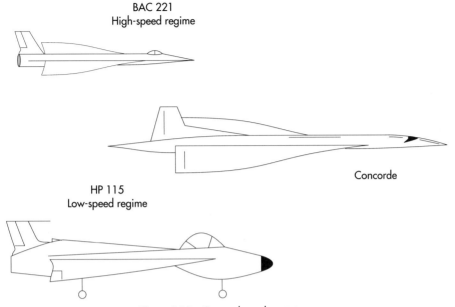

Figure 14.1 Concorde and prototypes.

sets of information of aggregations may well be expressed by means of an entity relationship diagram (ERD).

For example, a system in which time/sequence behaviour is important as the control of some complex plant we would normally use a state transition diagram (STD) to express such behaviour. These types of system would be principally related to discrete control.

Some prototyping tools

It is my intention to introduce a family of prototyping tools that directly map to the structured and object-oriented models. It is important that a set of essential requirements is expressed in either structured or object-oriented form. These models then become the source for the construction of an appropriate prototyping tool. The more visual the prototyping tool the easier and better it is.

The principal idea is that the three major domains may each have a separate tool optimised to express and emphasise that domain whilst de-emphasising the other domains.

For the information 'strong' system

First, let us look at the information structure domain, where we would use an ERD to express how various entities are interrelated (Fig. 14.3).

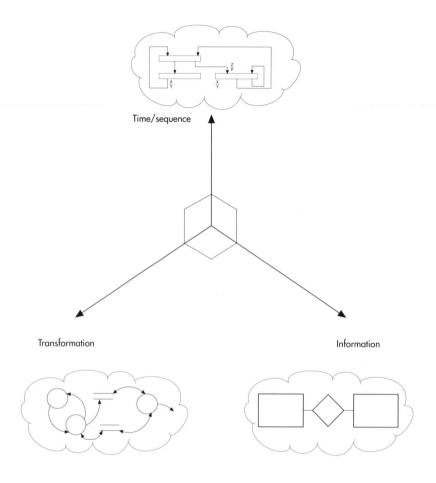

Figure 14.2   The three main viewpoints.

This fragment is taken from an envisaged system to supply tourist information, so we can see Hotel, Town and Attraction as individual entities with supporting text to define the attributes. We must also identify all the viable relationships between the entities.

An ideal prototyping tool here is Double-Helix^{TM}, which is a visual programming facility. It is based on the idea that every entity, which is known in Double-Helix as a relation, will have a special window that will, when opened, show information about the relation (attributes) and will also show templates for updating, accessing or using the relation in any way. Additionally it has a graphic facility, called an Abacus, for performing mathematics on any attributes by means of Mathematical 'tiles', which may be slotted together to express a function. If one is modelling an information-strong system in which there are significant amounts of transactions there is a 'Post' icon that,

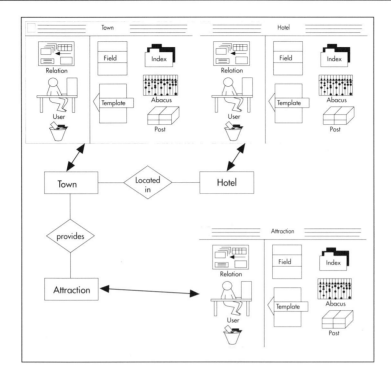

Figure 14.3   ERD as source for Double-Helix.

when opened, depicts a template for updating an entity, the essence being very speedy construction of an animated model of the desired system.

Any linking from one entity to another, hence demonstrating an access path, is performed by means of special 'tiles' within the Abacus. Any user special features connected with the Relation are represented by a user where the pull-down menus are defined and implemented.

Double-Helix has the charm of directly mapping to the ERD and its textual support, i.e. the attribute definitions. Additionally being visually based makes the tool easy to use and develop with. It recognises the criteria of an easy-to-assemble prototyping tool. Of course, this tool may well be effectively used for an end-solution.

By further examination Double-Helix suggests all the behaviour that may well be used to transform an entity into an object. The object-oriented derivative from the ERD is the object relationship diagram, which allows a more complete representation of an information dominant system (Fig. 14.4). Each of the operations depicted for each object will correspond to an access function that will be built in Double-Helix.

A Double-Helix representation may use as source an ERD plus appropriate definitions and an eSTD or, alternatively, if one has constructed an ORD (plus suitable text frames) then that will be suitable source material.

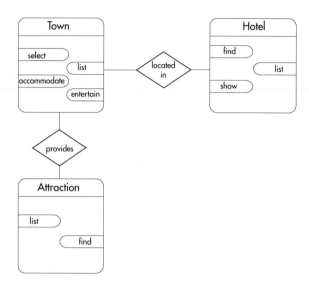

Figure 14.4   An ORD as source for Double-Helix prototyping.

Figure 14.4 shows an ORD with all the fundamental operations or services available. These fundamental services may be implied from discussion with the client user as the most likely activities required upon selecting a given concept. For example, upon selecting a given Town it is most likely that one may require some accommodation, which may be originated from the Town object by means of the 'accommodate' operation. This in turn will link to the Hotel object to list off accommodation meeting perhaps certain criteria. Remember relationships are like the 'trunking' of messages.

For the 'strong' time sequence system

This genre of system has an importance attached to either human–machine interaction or discrete control. Either way the modelling tool that gives us a good representation as to what should happen is the STD. The STD is a friendly tool to use and it 'suffers' little change between both structured and object-oriented representations. As with the previous tool, we ideally require a rapid prototyping tool that maps neatly from the STD to an active model of the system.

One such tool is 'Hypercard', which allows a rapid assembly of what is projected and can be shown to demonstrate animation in such a way that it may 'look and feel' like the projected end product. Hypercard is based on the units of windows, which may have smaller windows placed on them. Any of these windows may be Text or Graphics. 'Radio' buttons may be 'pasted' anywhere on the window area and labelled with whatever functionality is required. The functionality 'underneath' the buttons may be provided by 'Hypertalk' which is a production-rule-based language, somewhat like Pascal (source language), which allows calculations to be performed or transfers of controls or any 'pop-up' window or mini-window to be displayed.

Each of these components maps neatly from the STD. Figure 14.5 depicts a control console facia that we are to actively model.

The states from an STD are modelled by a specific screen window being displayed. 'System awaiting selection' is modelled with the facia at the idle state.

The conditions that are associated with that state are depicted by 'buttons' being displayed and labelled appropriately. Upon the condition 'happening' the button is depressed. This activates the 'Hypertalk' associated with the button (the action(s)) and it may also direct control to another screen window, which is then duly refreshed. Any additional pieces of processing, such as additional mini pop-up windows that may be displayed *ad hoc*, may be added to the Hypertalk. Hypercard has the charm of allowing

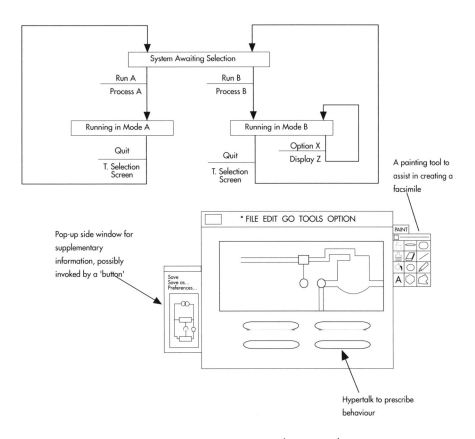

Figure 14.5 Using STDs with Hypercard.

the screen window to be 'painted' (off-line) by means of MacPaint™ to allow appropriate artistry to show a realistic-looking console.

For the transformation 'strong' system

In this domain the key essence is the transformation, i.e. the particular work that the system is intended to perform. This may be specifically some algorithm that must be developed and checked out. The DFD is a good representation of transformations and we can take an isolated area in the DFD (core transformations and store that are related with some key area) and make these the focus of our prototype. Smalltalk, which we met in Chapter 13, is ideal for prototyping an algorithm. It also has the class browser to assist in the assembly of a prototype.

Figure 14.6 is based around an application to deal with the complexities of a viable schedule, say for production purposes. The DFD fragment is isolated into schedule, which, from Chapter 7, is a 'librarian' object. This becomes our base class in Smalltalk.

In the development of our algorithm for minimising time and minimising materials,

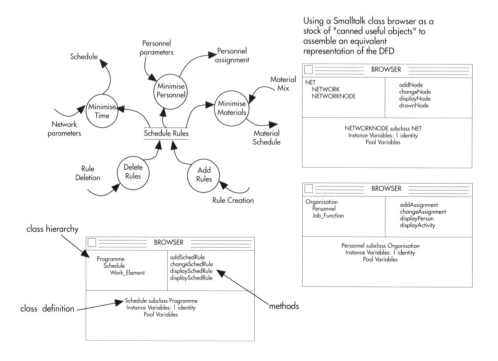

Figure 14.6   The DFD and object-oriented programming.

which may be expressed as Smalltalk methods, we may avail ourselves of the plethora of useful classes in Smalltalk, such as perhaps Net with subclasses Network and NetworkNode. These are ready-to-use in the specific methods where useful.

Smalltalk also has the charm of allowing infinite customisation of the Class browser to allow extra classes to be built in for subsequent prototypes. There are organisations that sell specific classes, such as Dials and Gauges, to be imported to your class browsers.

Rule-based systems

This is a genre of system that cuts across the specific three domains already mentioned. It is often important to prototype this specific area of a system. Rules may be expressed in the form of a set of production rules related with specific classes. The ideal vehicle for expressing the rules is the object inheritance diagram (OID) which readily sets up a class structure to accommodate potential inheritance that may well occur between the classes and subclasses. Whatever the selection of rules relate to, whether complex settlement or administration or transport routing rules, it is essential that they are prototyped to ensure their correctness.

The ideal tool for this purpose is to use an expert system as a prototyper. One such tool, which we met earlier, is Flex. This tool allows the construction of rules in easy to use 'English-like' grammar with production rules. It also uses the concept of classes and subclasses and allows easy-to-use animation to demonstrate whether the rules are correct or otherwise and then to quickly modify.

Do all the prototyping tools have to be object-oriented?

All the prototyping tools mentioned so far have a significant object content. The more important factor is that the prototyping tool is easy to use and visual programming assists towards that aim.

Double-Helix has the concept of the object and a form of encapsulation, but no inheritance to allow a quick animation of the projected system. The lack of inheritance, is not a great handicap in this tool.

Hypercard again is based on the concept of objects and has a form of encapsulation by everything being 'anchored' to a screen window. Inheritance occurs by means of overlays.

Smalltalk conforms to the full definition of an object-oriented-based tool. It also has the capability of importing class members and has a built-in windowing environment to make the prototypes 'look and feel' more like the target system.

Flex has some object-oriented capability based around classes and rules that make it ideal for checking out the correctness of rules. Later versions of Smalltalk have special classes, such as Logic, with subclass Prolog, which allows a comprehensive facility to accomplish rule checking within one language.

Prograph is another visual prototyping tool with a very friendly front end. It is a whole object-oriented programming language (OOPL) environment, which has an equivalent of a browser. Each of the hexagonal symbols is an object class. The division of the hexagon into a left half (a triangle), a right half (rounded boxes) represents the data and the methods associated with an object (Fig. 14.7). By clicking the mouse on the left half of the hexagon we can proceed to define the data. By clicking on the right

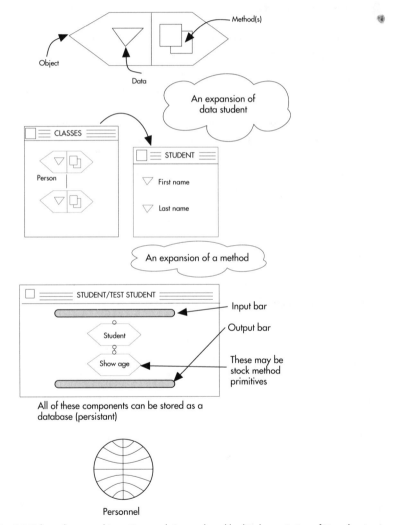

Figure 14.7   An OOPL based on graphics – Prograph (reproduced by kind permission of Yourdon Inc.).

half (methods boxes) we can proceed to define each method. Each method is defined by means of an input bar and then by mouse dragging a line to a cellule, which may represent another object or a standard method. A prototype may be assembled very quickly by this means.

Project management issues

The main worry that many project managers possess is that it appears to be 'just anarchy by another name' or alternatively 'I see no difference between prototyping and on-going maintenance and furthermore I cannot tell where one ends and the other begins'.

This raises the issue of the style of prototyping undertaken. There are two major styles of prototyping: evolutionary and rapid prototyping.

Evolutionary prototyping

This assumes that the solution is prototyped and that it undergoes a series of incremental steps in which the last phases become its realisation as the final system. This is a viable option but it does rely on the fact that the prototyping tool is one that will allow quick assembly and also will yield satisfactory performance in the target environment.

Rapid prototyping

This assumes access to a set of rapid prototyping tools, which are optimised to be easy to learn to use, easy to use, very quick in the assembly of a representation for the user to see and easy to modify in the light of user feedback. The end product from the rapid prototyping activity is the refinement of a specification.

With these distinctions it should be clear that project control should still be exerted and it is not an 'anarchic' activity. It should be organised with all the parties understanding their respective roles.

For effective systems development there should be a systematic assessment of how all the various components of systems development should integrate. Specifically there should be three key components in place: methodology, automated CASE tool set and a set of management procedures (Fig. 11.8).

Methodology

This should define the set of development methods in place, including structured and/or object-oriented, together with the project management methods and change control methods. The method set should be defined formally, as should the linkages between product development, project management and change control.

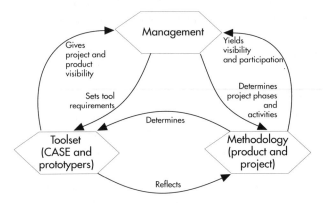

Figure 14.8   The interrelationship of toolset/methodology/management.

Automated CASE tool set

This should define all the CASE tools used both for systems development and project management and should additionally include the rapid prototyping tools (to be) deployed. Of course, any CASE tool set deployed should reflect faithfully the methodological tool set chosen.

Management procedures

This is often a lesser valued component. It should embrace what and how the CASE tool set will undertake, how it will do so and what visibility shall be presented. Additionally there are linkages between management procedures and the methodology, and these will be related to how the project should be undertaken, and what responsibility each of the parties possess. Additionally there should be definitions as to how the project progresses from stage to stage and the mechanism of 'sign-off'.

Organisation of the prototyping activity

The organisation of the prototyping activity is of such importance that if it is not organised, all the benefits will be negated. The prototyping activity also relies on the assumption that there is a set of formally defined requirements from which to work. These may be expressed in the form of a set of structured models (e.g. DFDs, ERDs or STDs) or a set of object-oriented models (e.g. OINs or ORDs). These are to be held as a reference point.

   The prototyping activity comprises selection, segmentation, construction, demonstration, modification and documentation.

Selection

This is the selection of the appropriate prototyping tool for the undertaking. It relates back to considering what the system's principal domain is, e.g. is it transformation dominant, information structure dominant or even time/sequence dominant?

Segmentation

This is the partitioning of the models into 'chunks' that can be easily prototyped. This is usually segmented by picking key subject areas and using these as the basis for units for prototyping.

Construction

This involves the assembling of a prototype of a subject area of the system. Ideally we should be picking 'chunks' that can be easily constructed in two to four days.

Demonstration

This is the 'parading' of a prototype of a section of the user's system. This demonstration should last between one to two hours to allow the prototype to be fully demonstrated. This should allow our developer to collect the full comments from the user.

Modification

This activity is the modification of the prototype to accommodate the user's comments. Providing the segments have been chosen of small size, these modifications will be easily accommodated within one or two days. It is usual that these modifications are paraded at the next scheduled demonstration session along with next development step.

Documentation

The prototype is the documentation. Whatever rapid prototyping tool is used, it will require there to be a full definition of all the data items and the details of the algorithms that have been exercised. This is a 'draggy' activity, but nevertheless it is important for the subsequent development.

Who should be prototyping?

The developer will probably be a systems development person skilled in analysis and developing a rapid prototype, as well as possessing the appropriate set of skills to interact effectively with a user. The user(s) should be selected from the people who are going to actually use the system; the user management are not usually the best people for this activity. The users must commit a regular portion of their time to demonstrating the prototype and their management must also agree to this investment of time. To ensure a completion of the prototyping activity, the user and developer should agree to the segmenting of the logical view of the system (essential model) into useful units for prototyping and into regular slots to meet and demonstrate prototypes. Typically one or two sessions a week are adequate. It is also useful if an upper limit is placed on the number of iterations, or an absolute deadline is set for the prototyping activity. It is best to keep the deadline at no greater horizon than three months.

Rules of play

The user must know what the prototype is, namely it is not the real thing but an active model of the projected system. There have been instances where a rapid prototype has been left in the hands of users who then attempted to use it for real, only to find that it collapsed under the volume of usage. This does not augur well for the relationship between user and developer. The developer and user should be aware of their respective roles. The user should be aware as to what the logical/essential model is and that the 'essence' of the system cannot be altered but its detail and representation can.

Conclusions

Prototyping is an effective way to proceed with development. As long as the prototyping is an organised activity it will be effective. An object-oriented rapid prototyper assists greatly with the rapid construction and modification through the ease of construction and the reuse of components. All the tools mentioned have some object-oriented content. However, both Smalltalk and Prograph assist as the most integrated of the tools. The other tools are optimised to service principally one aspect of the system.

References and further reading

Connell, D. and Shafer, L. (1989) *Structured Rapid Prototyping*. Englewood Cliffs, NJ: Yourdon Press/Prentice Hall.
Gunton, T. (1988) *End-user Focus*. Hemel Hempstead, UK: Prentice Hall.

Prototyping tools mentioned

Double-Helix from Odesta Corporation, Northbrook, Illinois, USA.
Flex from LPA (Logic Programming Associates), London, UK.
Hypercard from Apple Corporation, Palo Alto, California, USA.
Prograph from Gunakara Systems, Nova Scotia, Canada.
Smalltalk from Digitalk Inc., Los Angeles, USA.

CHAPTER 15

Human factors and an object-oriented approach

There's never time to do it right but there is always time to do it over again
(Meskimen's Law)

Computers are unreliable, but humans are even more unreliable
(T. Gilb)

This chapter introduces what good human–computer interface (HCI) practices are and shows how and what components ought be preserved in your repertoire of objects in your development environment. Object-oriented concepts are relevant to the specific area of HCI, such as class structures, inheritance, limited visibility and encapsulation. It also shows how the HCI may be explored and refined using object-oriented concepts and a text-based notation. A suggested ideal design tool is described along with its constituent components.

Human factors and systems development

At the detail level HCI will involve itself with the nature of the task that a user is being invited to undertake and with what are the most effective devices for input and output. The capacities and limitations of each of these devices are evaluated. The work environment for use of the system is also considered to ensure certain minima are covered (Fig. 15.1).

The cognitive effort is also assessed for ease of dealing with the task in hand. The nature of the specific tasks being undertaken by the user can by analysed in terms of criteria for cognitive effort required. New styles of interfaces can be examined for their effectiveness and appropriate recommendations made. The HCI practice will also give recommendations concerning specific software applications and their degree of customer friendliness and will advocate the use of prototyping to ensure the HCI is effective.

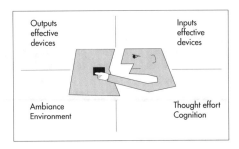

Figure 15.1   The four domains of HCI.

Advocating a user-friendly system

'Customer-friendly' means that the on-line information gives its users the information they require with the minimum of fuss and complication. However, to achieve this end you should be aware of the following areas: the working environment, the nature of the task, the dialogue that you expect your users to adopt, the nature of the computer–user interface itself and, last, the skills needed and the appropriate training. Let us tackle each of these.

The nature of the task can be expressed in terms of using structured diagrams such as data flow diagrams and state transition diagrams. This, in effect, is structuring the functionality of the system. However, we ought to do this as a preliminary stage when delineating which tasks are to be automated and which are to be resident within the user. This stage also serves to identify the productivity gains that should be evident in the new system.

The nature of the computer interface itself is important. We must not expect users to remember cumbersome codes or rituals in order to complete the work-related task. Graphic interfaces are ideal and a plethora of devices can be recommended from different interaction devices to easy-to-use menus (pull-down type) or even icons, which may get the most effective use from the system. In this instance we devise an appropriate panel with cells arranged in the appropriate sequence of the transactions. Should a user become 'lost' (or need help) we should provide context-sensitive help, which gives helpful information rather than a reference in some other manual. For the development of the interface it is recommended that a prototyping approach is adopted, so that the users can participate.

We should be able to identify the skills required from the description of the functionality of the system. Additionally the appropriate training should be given to our operatives to ensure they feel comfortable with the application. HCI should not be looked at as an expense 'featherbedding' the users but as an investment in the form of enlightened self-interest.

As HCI is a developing science, it has not reached the heights of being prescriptive, although it has a very full inventory of 'good bad examples' from which we may learn (Fig. 15.2).

This template is an expansion of Fig. 15.1 and makes recommendations for the four important domains (inputs, outputs, cognition and environment). The WIMP (windows, icons, mouse and pull-down menus) interface is becoming a *de facto* standard, however, we still have to consider the cognitive aspects as extremely important, these being the thought processing that our users will have to undertake to use our system effectively. The people who are to use the system effectively must be able to use it with the least number of 'mental somersaults' (i.e. cognitive economy).

Cognitive aspects of systems

Cognition, as already mentioned, is the mental processing undertaken by humans. The HCI aspect of a system presents stimuli to the user for an effective response. There may well be a plethora of responses that our user may make, but our systems design should present an 'image' in such a way that the user responds as 'naturally' as possible.

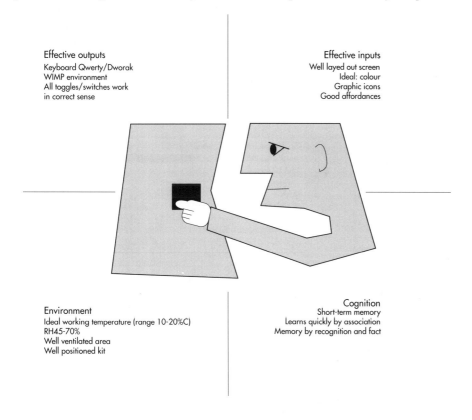

Figure 15.2   The details of the four domains of HCI.

Another important aspect of this is the idea of the task. A task in this case is a 'chunk of work' that the user perceives as a single unit and the functions that are presented to a user should therefore be perceived by the user as 'chunks' of work.

It is also useful for the developers to have a perception of the user's mental image of what is happening. For instance, many users perceive a computer-aided software engineering (CASE) tool in terms of a drawing board. A developer here might use metaphors that are related with the drawing board as ways of describing operation of the system (Fig. 15.3).

Additionally we also have to consider how the user integrates all the various components and also what he/she expects the machine to accomplish. Figure 15.4 shows the expectations that some users may have for a system.

Memory and representation as object-oriented

Memory and knowledge representation in human beings closely resembles that of an object-oriented representation. In Chapter 1, the concepts of Eleanor Rosch and the class structure representation of memory was described. People remember items in a 'natural' class structure for cognitive economy (i.e. they use the least effort to store and remember). People find it easier to remember codes by means of well structured acronyms or mnemonics. Or, alternatively, people can recognise what they are attempting to recall.

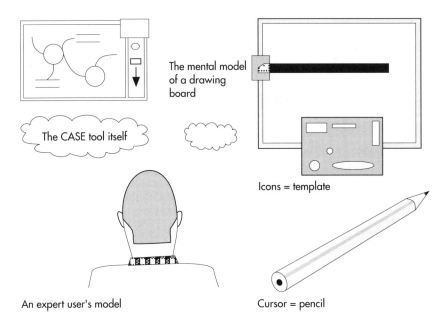

Figure 15.3   A mental model of a user and his/her CASE tool.

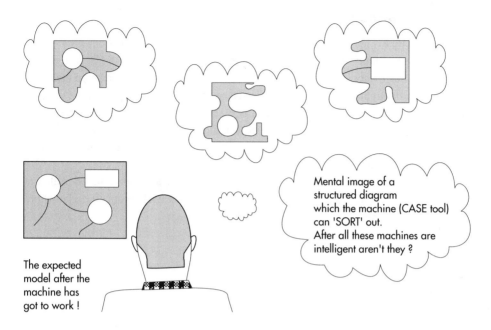

Figure 15.4   The mental images and the user's perception of integration.

All these features should be adopted for use in our application structures for our user's benefit. We should remember that frame structure for memory is also a very good and effective way for modelling and representing knowledge structure and one that users can easily handle.

Object-oriented and human factors

An effective HCI design must avail itself of an easy-to-use presentation of the stimuli upon which our user is to respond. The grouping of items on the screen and the consistent assignment of meaning is important. The user should perceive that his/her view of what constitutes unit tasks should be preserved as unit operations offered to the user. All the items that are to be operated upon should be good affordances. That is, the item should 'suggest' how it should be used. For example, a 'button' on the screen should suggest that it may be pressed and it will undertake the operation labelled on it. A different coloured bar along the top of the screen will suggest pull-down menus from which options may be selected. It is important that the operator does not have to strain his/herself to remember complex or even esoteric abbreviations (e.g. Unix) commands, but is able to recognise appropriate operations from presented lists. The whole message is that the HCI presents itself as friendly and easy-to-use, so that the application becomes a productivity tool not an encumbrance.

An object language

To satisfactorily explore the HCI behaviour of an evolving system it is necessary to be aware of all the 'items' that will be manipulated by the user. The STD is useful to prescribe the macroscopic behaviour but it is useful to recognise and describe the items that are to be manipulated. These 'items' may be more usefully expressed as objects. The definition of the object in this context is essentially no different than the one we have used so far. We are still interested in perceiving our objects with limited visibility, the only exception being that these objects may be extremely granular (e.g. one character at a cursor position).

This object language requires that all the components to communicate with the system are identified as 'objects' upon which our users may wish to operate. The whole language is text based.

Defining terms

Objects

An object is a thing that is deemed to be of importance in the use of the tool being examined (e.g. a document, diagram type or a point or a line or a word). These items are denoted by square brackets surrounding the specific objects. In this case objects may be nested.

Operations

An operation is a means of operating on the object to accomplish some end. In this case we are applying an operation to an object.

Places

These are specific locations of relevance in the application. These may be cursor positions or positions within a file.

So we may express the interaction for, say, an electronic mail system:

Objects

```
[ mailbox]
[ message ] in [ mailbox]
[ message type ] is [ textfile], [bitmap], [voicememo ],
 [spreadsheet]
```

```
[string] in [message]
[clipboard]
```

Places

```
<<end>> of [message]
<<position>> of [message]
<< start>> of [message]
```

Operations

```
open [mailbox]
open [message]
cut [string] from [message] at <<position>> to
 <<position>>
paste [string] from [clipboard] to << position>>
list [message]
close [mailbox]
close [message]
copy [message] <<from position>> to << end position>>
 to [message]
remove [message]
clear [clipboard]
```

With this grammar we have declared all the 'objects' that we need to perceive. In this electronic mail system we can send messages to mailboxes and the messages may be of subtypes textfile, bitmap, voicememo and spreadsheet. The grammar for operating on any of these objects is the same. The user of this notation need not concern him/herself with the actual physical routines for opening a message. If it is a text message it will be presented on the screen; if it is a voicememo then it will be presented to the audio system and 'played'; if it is a bitmap graphic then it will be presented as a graphic image.

This expression of operation is useful for describing how the system will work without getting into technical 'quicksands' and whilst retaining a user's understanding of what is going on.

As a further example of how it is used, we shall use a CASE tool. All the items on a CASE tool are introduced. We should consider the user's 'mental model' of the system and express all the items in terms of the model. In this CASE instance the most popular mental model is that of the drawing board upon which diagrams will be affixed.

Of course, as it is mechanised it is expected that the connection rules behind the symbols and connectors will be observed.

Objects

```
[Diagram] of [Diagram type]
[Diagram type] is [DFD], [ERD], [STD]
[Diagram type] of [Diagram Component]
[Diagram component] is [edge], [point], [label], [network],
[ string ] [free space]
[ String] is [alphanumeric]
[Icon] of type [symbol], [connector], [comment]
[Command_bar] type [ delete], [copy], [reroute], [move]
```

Operations

```
Navigate [ location]
Move [ Diagram component ]
Move and Size [ Diagram component ]
Copy [Diagram component]
Delete [Diagram component]
Reroute [ edge]
Text [string]
Size [Diagram component]
Mouse_operation [button1|button2|button3]
where button1 = selection
      button2 = cancel
      button3 = associate
```

Places

```
Reference points
<< insertion point >>
<< replacement region >>
(location of drawing pointed by the mouse, location on a
command bar)
```

The means of communicating with the system (in this instance with a WIMP environment) is the following:

[Object (designated by mouse in drawing area space) + Operation (selected by the mouse (insertion point + mouse select button) from the command bar object).]

This textual notation allows expression as to how one will effectively use a system. It is also useful for training someone to use a system as description text within the training materials.

Addenda to the prototyping chapter

Following Chapter 14 on prototyping, the HCI aspects of a system are amongst the most sensitive and it is my recommendation that one should prototype the system with a representative set of end-users to ensure that designer's and user's idea of being able to use the system are as congruent as possible.

The well-tooled HCI

For effective development of 'tools' that others use we need to have some family of constructor sets from which we may build any likely interface. To accomplish this there are, in essence, seven generic tool components: compositor, display editor, input configuration, interaction definer, session editor, linkage editor and run tool. Each of these components has a well defined role in the construction of an interface for an application.

Compositor

This is a tool for configuring the desired output. It is essentially a tool for configuring the 'shape' of the output. As an example we have chosen an instrument gauge (Fig. 15.5). We lay it out on the display surface and relate it to any 'buttons' to be put on the screen. This tool allows the layout of the various symbols, with their various constraints, and other items to be arranged in an effective manner.

Display editor

This tool allows us to modify the shape of the tool being used (Fig. 15.6). An object inheritance diagram may give a whole class family of objects from which we can start with and, upon finishing this activity, we may file a new subclass as symbols for subsequent use.

Input configuration

This is the textual definition to commit the appropriate devices that we are to use to the specific application. In this case we are going to use a mouse to communicate with the screen, so we have to define what operations are associated with what mouse buttons (Fig. 15.7).

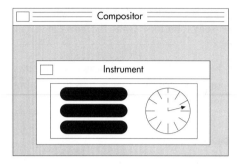

Figure 15.5   A compositor.

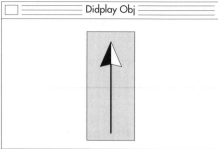

Figure 15.6   Display definitions.

Interaction definer

This defines the sequence of using the particular application. The diagram is actually an STD and the states are control states, which are equivalent to visible states of the application. The conditions correspond to 'buttons' on the screen. The actions are operations that will perform work (Fig. 15.8).

Session object editor

This is a definition of all the object components that are to be used in this application. It is in essence a catalogue of all the pertinent items (Fig. 15.9).

Linkage editor

This provides an interface between the underlying application and the presentation of session to the user (Fig. 15.10).

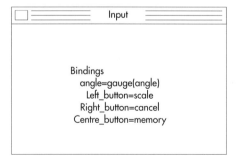

Figure 15.7   Input definitions.

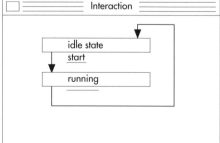

Figure 15.8   Interaction.

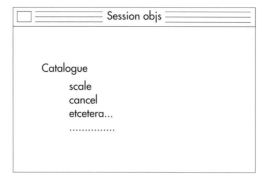

Figure 15.9   Session objects.

Run tool

This is the actual means of commissioning the application. It can be implemented in the form of a command language or, more effectively, by a more elegant interface with buttons (Fig. 15.11). The above set of seven items constitutes an effective tool for designing an interface for an application. In some tools some of these component items are merged into one, but nevertheless, one at least needs the functionality of these items.

Conclusions

HCI is the means of making an application effective; ignore it at your peril! HCI has been made easier to understand by use of object-oriented concepts. Expression of class structures for data, operations and rules is made easier to understand and use. Prototyping tools, such as Smalltalk, Hypercard and Prograph, all have an augmented role to play in representing interfaces from class structures of 'ready-to-go' units.

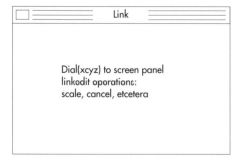

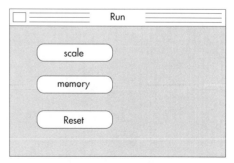

Figure 15.10   Linkages.

Figure 15.11   Run time environment.

The STD is a useful graphic tool for expression of the general style of interaction but to express the fine detail of interaction, the introduced object language will allow more accurate description. The well tooled environment outlines the tool components that should be available for expressing an interface to an application.

References and further reading

Laurel, B. (1990) *The Art of Computer Interface Design.* Reading, MA: Addison-Wesley.

Norman, D. (1988) *The Design of Everyday Things.* New York, NY: Doubleday.

Preece, J. and Keller, L. (1990) *Human Computer Interface.* Hemel Hempstead, UK: Prentice Hall.

Verplank, W. (1989) *'CHI' 89 Tutorial Notes: Graphical Invention for User Interfaces.* San Francisco, CA: ID Two.

CHAPTER 16

Object-oriented implementational units

Fifteenth Law of Systemantics
A complex system that works is invariably found to have evolved from a simple system that works

(John Gall)

This chapter deals with the various implementation models that should be used in the development of applications solutions, such as the processor model, the architecture model and the code organisation model. Each model is optimised to give a particular viewpoint. Issues such as processor choice are reviewed and modelled with the object-oriented notation. The software architecture and detailed design issues such as tasks, concurrency, performance and priorities are also discussed. Finally, code organisation models are discussed.

The organisation of the implementation models

Our approach is to model options and play them through until we are sure that we are undertaking the right design options. A model contains a representation of the objects concerned, plus their textual definitions, and where necessary the internal views of the objects concerned. There may well be additional viewpoints that serve the aim of providing a clear definition of what is to be undertaken.

The object-oriented design activity is made a more productive process than the structured design process because reuse of the design of units is undertaken at the outset.

It is intended that the implementational phases directly abut the preceding essential (logical) phases. These phases are useful to recognise for structured modelling, object modelling and the integration of the two. However, there are three distinct phases that are perceived: processor model, software architecture and code organisation.

Processor model

The processor model is optimised to start from the essential model and to visualise various processor choices. Processors in this context mean devices that will undertake the work prescribed in the logical model. Whether we are using structured or object-oriented technology, it is important that we recognise this stage. There are two 'types' of processor: hardware (which is in most cases devices like computers) and liveware (which is the human processors that will be undertaking some of the work). All interaction of humans and the system are prescribed at this stage (using state transition diagrams (STDs), etc.). With any choice made at this point, it is the ideal point at which to commence prototyping. It is at this stage that we may evaluate various candidate solutions on the basis of some figure of merit, such as reliability, ease of construction, ease of maintenance and cost. In an object-oriented context the development of this set of models is facilitated.

Software architecture model

The software architecture model is optimised to allow exploration and representation of software issues. The starting point of this model is a completed processor model with a partitioning of the major processing regions. Again, whether we are using structured or object-oriented technology, it is important that we recognise this stage. The principal concerns we may have at this juncture may be to identify tasks (units to be scheduled) and what they will realistically contain. The design issues, such as the physical realisation of the database technology, is undertaken in this phase. At its most granular level all the primitive units that have to be defined will be defined. It is at this stage that an accurate estimation may be made of effort to construct. In an object-oriented context the development of this model is again facilitated.

Code organisation model

The code organisation model is optimised to allow exploration and development of the groupings of code. The starting point is a family of models. This is a completed set of software architecture models. The code organisation model serves to allow review and consideration as to other code organisation structures. Whether we are using structured or object-oriented technology, it is important that we recognise this stage prior to final commitment of the technology. The optimisation that takes place here is to make an effective grouping of modules. Remember that modules are self-contained units, of which objects are better organised units, and their intercommunication, which will also take into consideration ease of realisation (including coding and testing) of the units. In an object-oriented context we ought not to forget that objects are 'modules', which are more 'self-contained' and that concepts of cohesion and coupling are naturally covered in the earlier developmental steps. It is more appropriate to look into each model for the specifics of object-oriented design for each of these phases.

The processor model as an object-oriented development step

Returning to the processor model, and considering the object-oriented activities involved, it is the first stage in which one can start to recognise the physical processors.

The previous object-oriented development steps will have been to construct an object model that was based on the 'essence' (Fig. 16.1). This previous model is the 'essential model' where the model was optimised to assist in the depiction of the logical requirement.

In the processor model itself, we can recognise three styles of implementation upon hardware:

1. All the processing is assigned to one processor.
2. The processing is assigned to a processor and there are multiple copies of the system in existence which will have to interrelate.
3. Asymmetric distribution, where portions of the essential processing are assigned to one processor type and another portion to another different processor type.

Of course, option 1. does not distort the essential model at all, as all the processing can be mapped to one singular unit. Options 2. and 3., however, may potentially alter the essential model when mapped to the processors.

In option 1. the whole of the object model relating to the application may be discretely placed on one processor. As our original context diagram can be said to be placed on a 'virtual machine' here we are assigning the whole application to a realisation of that machine. The only elaboration that may be useful is the prototyping (compare with Chapter 14) of critical areas such as the possible development of the HCI components (see Chapter 15). This activity will, of course, be relevant to the other cases of distribution.

In option 2. the object model may be placed again as if it is on one processor with a form of communication to the other 'copies' of the system. Here, the drawback is the integrity of the data. In essence, the data that is to be persistent with time must be classified as each of the following:

1. Data unique to the whole system. For example, transactions must be unique to exert control over their contents and their integrity. This is, of course, a single copy and a single place of update.
2. Data that is unique to a region, such as transport tariffs, local transport operators,

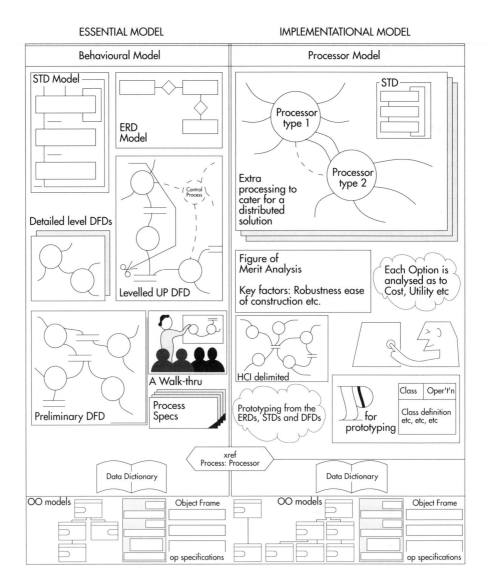

Figure 16.1   Behavioural and processor models.

route structure and local timetables. This is, of course, single-copy with a local site responsibility for update.

3. Data that is 'public', in the sense that it is maintained at one node and 'broadcast' to other nodes, which will then only read the information set. This is, of course, multiple-copy and update responsibility is held at one site.

Controlling the quality of this information type is the principal concern of the 'guardians of data', who may avail themselves of various service 'transducer objects' to make access and communication between the machines as transparent as possible.

In option 3. the situation includes the splitting the processing over different types of machine asymmetrically (i.e. a separation is being made across the processing unevenly). In this case I am referring to completely different technology types, not the case where distribution over various models can be viewed as transparent.

Few will choose this third option; it is usually a constraint placed upon the developers. Ideally one attempts to separate processing into two domains by cutting over the least interconnections (i.e. least weight cut). In a structured solution this is represented by a data flow diagram (DFD), which is cut over a flow. Any cut across an essential flow has the consequence of having to preserve that interconnection in the implementation solution.

An object-oriented solution makes a distributed solution easier to represent. The object dependency diagram (ODD) may be reconfigured, where there is a separation of processing, to present a 'client–server' relationship, where the client is placed on one machine and the server is placed on the other. We have already seen client–server relationships in the form collaboration between objects.

The communications between the two are in the characteristic form of:

$$\text{Object} + (\text{instance}) + \text{service} + \{\text{arguments}\}$$

The arguments are the specific data items related to the access of the server held units. Figure 16.2 shows the segmentation of an ODD over processors.

The other representation style, in the form of the object interconnection net (OIN), is again easier to separate into the two domains and to visualise the consequences of the choices of placement. A cut may be made wherever it is useful and the objects placed on whatever processors and wherever they may be deemed necessary. This gives the designer a lot of freedom. Again a 'transducer' style object may maintain connections between the two object regions (Fig. 16.3). The objects W, X, Y and Z are depicted with their collaborative connections and their flows with the environment. For operational reasons, constraints apply, i.e. two different types of processor are required. Z will be placed on one processor and W, X and Y on the other. To visualise fully the consequences of this choice, a cut along the scissors line shows that it will make an

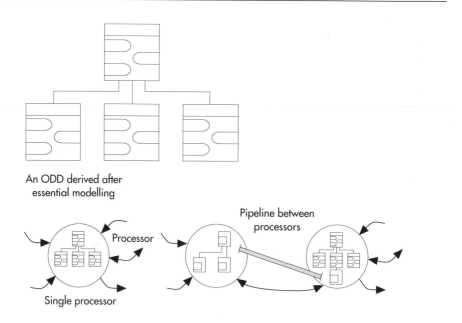

An ODD derived after
essential modelling

Pipeline between
processors

Processor

Single processor

Figure 16.2   Processor models and the ODD.

incision over a dialogue flow between Z.a and X.b. Our processor model should not distort our ideal model as represented by the OIN. To assist in arresting an incipient distortion, a 'transducer object' is used to provide a transparent link between the two processors.

In all the processor models, with all of their components, is important that it is recognised as a key step in the development of an object-oriented solution.

Software architecture model

The software architecture model follows the processor model directly, and is focused to allow recognition of all the software components that have to be used. This will include units to be built and units to be 'drawn' from the infrastructure to be used yet again. Ideally, with object-oriented solutions we will intend to recognise the behaviour required and then to 'draw' upon the infrastructure to reuse existing units.

An effective object-oriented design will attempt to consider all the resources that constitute a task as objects wherever possible. The specific issues that we wish to recognise are task grouping, threading and concurrency. The types of object-oriented diagrams used are predominantly the ODD and the OID, along with the object frames and operation frames to accommodate the text. In situations where an object-oriented database is to be used, it will be necessary to formulate an object-oriented database schema. The ORD, together with the text frames for the objects and the operations, is

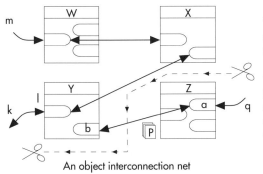

The situation is for the OIN to be placed onto two separate processors whilst retaining the same aggregate behaviour

The cut separates W, X and Y from Z. Each portion is then placed upon a separate processor.
At point P an incission has been made over a dialogue flow Z.a and Y.b

An object interconnection net

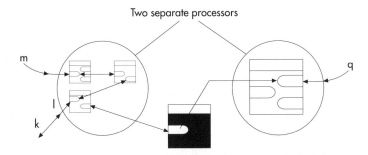

Two separate processors

Transducer object to provide the links

Figure 16.3   Processor models and the OIN.

focused towards this purpose. The ORD provides the relationships and the object frame provides the detail source for development of the object-oriented database management system (OODB) schema. The operation frames provide the source for the access routines.

Tasks

A task is a unit of scheduling, and our attempt here is to recognise that our execution units will be based as near as possible upon collections of objects that can form an efficient execution structure. The application itself becomes the 'binding force' for organising the unit. In ADA, one of the language units is the task. It is itself divided into a task specification, which defines the interface between it and other units, and the task body, which comprises the executable component. Figure 16.4 shows an Ada representation using Booch's notation (Booch, 1991).

The external view of an object may also depict an object as a task because the same rules of limited visibility may be used. This time the external view (OEV) depicts a task. The collection of units (objects) that comprise that task may be embedded into the object in the same way as it would be depicted in a internal view of the object (OIV).

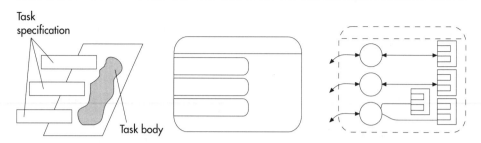

An Ada task using Booch's symbol   An OEV representing a task and its internal view

Figure 16.4   Ada units and OEVs as packages.

Threading

A thread is a unique sequence of execution that can be recognised in the implementation structure. The thread will be associated with the real world and will be represented by an event; there may be many instances of threads. The thread will be interpreted if an object's operation is in a receptive state. It, in turn, will communicate (send a message) to other objects' operations. In the previous object-oriented model at this level of detail (essential model) we did not recognise individual 'instances' and any potential contention. This situation is modelled by means of a table (the events and the threads) in conjunction with a series of STDs representing each of the contending devices.

Figure 16.5 shows a series of STDs in series to illustrate how the thread is, in effect, executed.

The application that demands the resource will encounter a condition that requires the use of an external resource. The transition associated with this condition may communicate to another resource by means of a 'signal'; this signal is a control linkage, and acts as if it is a message. The signal is a condition to the called resource and, in turn, it may require a further resource, which is, in this case, the end of the thread. It will complete its activity and, upon completion, will signal back to the requestor of the resource. This behaviour is repeated, as shown in the STDs until it returns to the application.

The above description is a model of what is occurring for resources. What should also be recognised is that the requestor of the resource (the application) will also refer to specific instances. Each resource call will require instance information.

Concurrency

Concurrency is where we can present a view of many machines that have to cooperate and look as if they are working in parallel. To handle this situation we construct object-oriented resources, which cater specifically for handling cooperation.

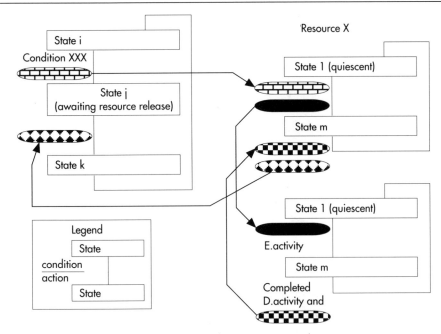

Figure 16.5 An STD depicting resources sharing.

The conventional ways of dealing with this situation is by means of a monitor, a guardian or even a semaphore. Each of these may be modelled with the object-oriented notation.

Figure 16.6 shows a model depicting how a 'rendezvous' may be effectively modelled.

Dynamic allocation of resources

This is the activity associated with dynamically allocating processing to match demand. A specific scenario may be where a system is managing a plant that is susceptible to a wide range of demand for services. The depiction of objects in the case of execution is by means of the ODD. It is in effect a client–supplier model, the client being the application calling upon the supplier objects to fulfil their obligations, as defined by their 'public' operation specifications.

The client object may have behaviour within it that will monitor demand and, based upon demand, it will launch an object whose role may be to control pieces of plant. As the demand may be extremely variable it is wasteful of resources to just cater for the highest number. It is much more ideal that the client application senses demand and 'spawns' off a controlling object whenever one is needed. The diagram on the left of Fig. 16.7 shows the client–supplier relationship as in an ODD. The diagram in the centre depicts an extension to the notation to show multiple instances of an object.

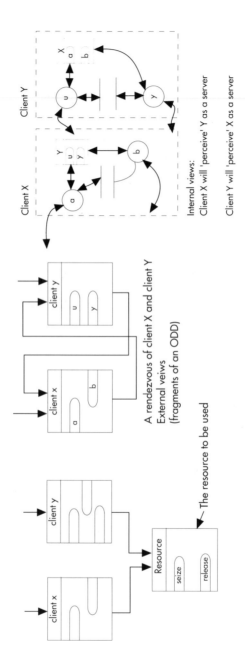

Figure 16.6 A model of a 'rendezvous'.

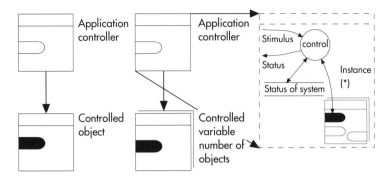

Figure 16.7 Client-server models.

This means that the controlling object will be controlling a variable number of objects. The diagram on the far right depicts an internal view of the controlling object (OIV). The controlling operation may be decomposed to show a controller operation, which in turn may have an STD to depict the discrete behaviour, and there may be another operation which may monitor demand and attend to system status.

Object-oriented databases

The ORD, along with the associated object and operation frame, is the desired style to depict a projected object-oriented database system. The issues that ought be recognised at this stage are to do with detailed placement of the classes, security, volumes and specific access paths and the implementation of business rules relating to each class in use.

Figure 16.8 is related with market trading. An ORD is used as the specification vehicle at an earlier stage, with the appropriate set of object and operation frames. At this stage one will have selected an appropriate specific object-oriented database management system (OODB) technology upon which to place this application.

The following items should be gathered from the ORD for detailed schema specification:

1. Object name and the operations that are placed with it. The ORD should have been examined and tested against the third behavioural normal form to ensure optimal placement of the operations. Any additional custodial operations should have been identified within an eSTD (life-cycle model; see Fig. 5.5). In the case of Seller the operations identified have been create, delete, modify and sale.
2. Each object will have an object frame and the appropriate slots filled out, such as name, description, inheritance, attributes, operations and rules. In the case of Seller the attributes will be defined for each item together with the size and format. For example:

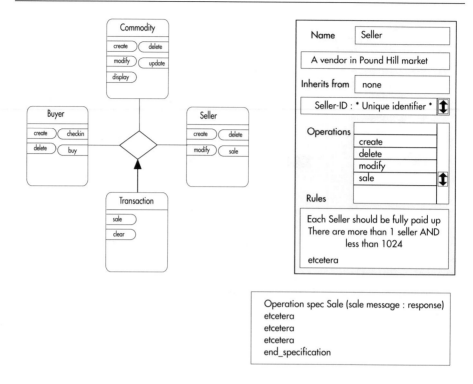

Figure 16.8　An ORD with text frame.

Seller-Id:	*unique identifier for the market*
	size: 4 integer.
	Restrictions: Seller-Id
	> 0 and < 1024.
Seller-name:	*seller company name*
	size: 30 characters.
Seller-address:	*seller address*
	size: 4 {30 characters }.
Seller-telephone:	*telephone number*
	size: 9 integers.
Seller-fax:	*seller facsimile number*
	size: 9 integers.

3.　Each object shall have a definition as to all the rules that should apply to using this object. This is to assist with formulation of accesses to this object and shall cover all invariants relevant to the object.

4.　Each operation will have been defined in either structured language or pre- and post-condition form. Each operation will have been defined as to its sensitivity to a class or instance. In the full implementation there will be an appropriate object-oriented programme language (OOPL) source that may be accessed for examination.

5. Security should be defined in the following modes:

(a) Visibility of the attribute values for an instance;

(b) Accessibility of operations. For example, creation and deletion of sellers would, ideally be, secure as to who should be allowed to undertake these actions.

The remaining operations will have to be defined as to where they may be accessed from. This may well be a specific windows application. Rule maintenance will involve appropriate security to allow adjustment of any of the rules (including alteration of Invariants).

Code organisation model

The code implementation model is solely an organisation chart of the code units that are involved in the implementation of a solution. These are based primarily on ODDs and with reference to OIDs. The appropriate text frames (object and operation) are expected to have been filled out to facilitate the production and assembly of code. It is assumed that an OOPL is being used where the majority of the concepts related to inheritance, polymorphism and dynamic binding are available. It is also assumed that an appropriate OOPL development environment is available with a class browser.

With object-oriented solutions it is intended that the solutions are 'assembled' (as if from a Lego™ kit) with as many existing components as possible. The ODD then becomes an organisation chart depicting the client–supplier relationships amongst all the projected units. The class browser facility from within the development environment is shown to be invaluable.

It is probable that many developers will avail themselves of a Windows environment for the application itself. The Windows environment is usually object-oriented and resources will be arranged in a class structure, of which a new instance of a window type will be 'launched' (created), which in turn will be specific to the application. Appropriate menu bar resources will be altered so that the new application is capable of being run from this environment.

All the units developed should have good cohesion (group identity) and coupling (see Fig. 13.1), to assist with effective development.

Conclusions

This chapter introduces a different emphasis to our object models developed so far. Real-world constraints apply and one must develop the object-oriented solution within these. The notation itself has only introduced one extra piece to the notation – the multiple instance object. None of the major diagram types (the ODD, the ORD and the OIN) have changed, nor have the frames (the object and operation frames). Many applications will be implemented into a Windows environment, which is in itself object-oriented; this facilitates further the job of implementing a solution.

References and further reading

Booch, G. (1991) *Object-Oriented Design*. Redwood City, CA: Benjamin Cummings.
Coad, P. and Yourdon, E. (1991) *Object-Oriented Design*. Englewod Cliffs, NJ: Yourdon Press/ Prentice Hall.

CHAPTER 17

CASE tools for effective development

The good workman is known by his tools
(Fred Brooks)

This chapter deals with computer-aided software environment (CASE) tools and what they should provide within an object-oriented context. It outlines an ideal CASE environment for object-oriented development, with some suggested CASE tool products. It introduces the idea of metamodels as an expression vehicle for 'objects' to be used in a CASE tool.

It also introduces a formal definition for the object internal view (OIV), object dependency diagram (ODD), object inheritance diagram (OID), object relationship diagram (ORD) and object interconnection network (OIN), in metamodel form, together with the appropriate final definitions for the object and operation frames. This outlines appropriate suggestions for effective development using objects including the quantification of effort and prototyping.

CASE tools – what are they?

A CASE tool should provide an environment that facilitates the development of the system solution. Specifically, we are allowing the representation of the logical models, as object interconnection models together with the appropriate object and operation frames. These may be developed step-by-step into a possible software solution, whilst providing traceability. To be effective these tools will be interactive, which implies being on-line.

CASE tools – some history

CASE tools are essentially a product of the mid-1980s, the degree of sophistication ranging from being solely a drawing tool to being a tool that balances and checks the models and will generate outline source code. The early CASE tools generated in some users the idea that there was artificial intelligence in the CASE tool, and so the user could develop models and the machine would straighten it all out because 'the machine is intelligent'. Alas, it came to be recognised that all users must have a fair grounding in methods before attempting to tackle a CASE tool, but then it became an effective development tool. A tool is an instrument that assists its user in the accomplishment of a given task. The tool should reduce the effort required or improve the quality of the end-product.

What do they do and how effective are they?

According to Boehm (1981), the evidence appears to suggest that the most sensitive cost-drivers are MODP and TOOL. Cost-drivers are single factors that can be extracted and identified and which have a measurable effect on a project. MODP means modern development practices such as object-oriented methods, structured methods or even no methods. TOOL means degree of sophistication of the tools employed.

The possible contents of cost-drivers TOOL and MODP are shown in Table 17.1. There are many other cost-drivers, ranging from time constraints to personnel capabilities, but these two (TOOL and MODP) are amongst the most sensitive. In addition, these drivers work in a multiplicative fashion, so a very high setting of MODP and TOOL will have a compound effect on development.

In marketing idiom this has produced a positioning of two key 'flavours' of CASE: upper and lower.

Upper CASE, from a simplified view, is that CASE type that attends to the systems analysis and structural design models. Hence, the 'upper' refers to the upper reaches of the development cycle. Examples of CASE tools that focus upon this area are 3SL's Cradle and Instrumatic's Teamwork.

Lower CASE is that CASE type that attends to the phases following analysis and structural design, which typically involve code structures and testing facilities. Examples of CASE tools that focus on this area are HP's Softbench and Softlab's Maestro.

Table 17.1   The contents of cost-drivers TOOL and MODP

| Cost-driver | Setting | | | | | |
	VL	L	N	H	VH	XH
MODP	1.7	1.5	1.0	0.81	0.65	0.51
TOOL	1.8	1.6	1.0	0.85	0.64	0.53

The coefficients in the cells ought not be taken literally. For more detail see Boehm (1981), chapter 27.

The two instances of CASE types should be linked, and some CASE tools offered allow this form of integration, for example Cradle and HP Softbench.

With the advent of a paradigm change in the way we can build systems, namely object-oriented development, CASE tools should offer an appropriate environment to allow representation of the problem area in the so-called upper CASE area. There should also be a seamless join to the activities in the so-called lower CASE tool area. Additionally the CASE environment should allow interactive traversing of all enterprise objects, with appropriate assistance, to encourage reuse.

Object-orientation and CASE – how should they work?

First, we should state how and what the CASE tool should accomplish and the milieu into which it will be installed. At the time of writing a CASE tool is a tool, and even with the high degree of sophistication of various CASEs, it requires much more to make it effective. It requires a sound methodology to be in place and a management procedure that reaps the most benefits from the methodology (see Fig. 14.8). This means that standards and procedures such as 'walk-throughs' gain as much effectiveness as possible. When a CASE tool enters the milieu it must integrate effectively with these two areas. So the CASE tool set means a collection of tools that will reduce the effort in developing solutions. The CASE tool set will literally be a set that is a collection of tools to effectively present modelling through to design, with access to rapid prototypers and thence to the guardianship of code with comprehensive libraries. This set should be determined by the methodologies selected and the CASE tool presentation of notation should have a high degree of correspondence to the methodology selected. The last thing a serious developer wants is a user to have to perform mental somersaults between methodology and tool; it is just not ergonomically sound. In more scientific terms the mental map of the user ought not be distorted by notational changes.

Specifically addressing object-oriented development, a CASE tool set should reflect the object-oriented notation selected, i.e. the full set of symbols and text frames.

The full set of symbols is, in essence, made up from the external object symbol and its OIV and arrangements of these symbols in the following diagram families: OIN, ORD, ODD and OID. Any object will have an object text frame for its textual expansion and any operation listed may in turn have an expansion of its operation in the form of an operation specification. Access to class browsing is represented diagrammatically by means of the OID. An idealised version of part of a CASE tool of this type is shown in Fig. 17.1.

The above is the basic core of the object-oriented notation. However, for those developers electing to go for a synthetic approach (i.e. synthesising objects from the structured material) we would additionally have a representation of the data flow diagram (DFD), the entity relationship diagram (ERD) and the state transition diagram

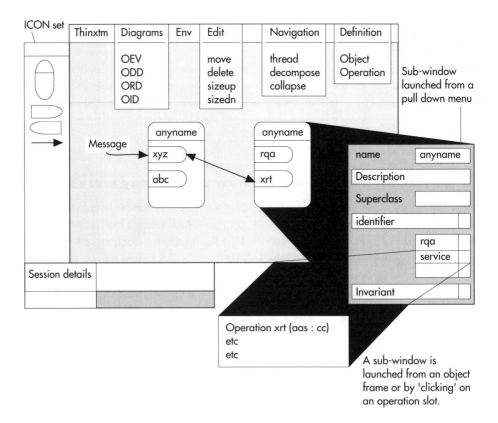

Figure 17.1   An idealised window-based CASE tool.

(STD) with appropriate textual specification. There are many good representations of the structured method on a CASE tool but, for effective object-oriented development with the synthetic method, the two regimes ought to coexist on the same CASE tool with as near as possible a seamless join between the two.

An agent to help

It would be useful when developing in a synthetic mode, to have assistance in the form of an 'agent', who may act in the role of an expert object-oriented developer with knowledge of the rules (heuristics) to derive certain objects from the structured material at the press of a button. I envisage the following scenario: An ERD will have been developed with all of its attributes and will have been developed as far as 3NF (third normal form). Provided naming conventions and practices have been observed, and if there was an eSTD for this entity, then a skeleton object with custodial services can directly be implied. For DFDs there are certain configurations that can be directly implied, such as controller/coordinator objects and librarian objects. There are many other heuristics that could be applied (see Chapter 7). It is envisaged that this 'agent' could provide assistance where invited to by responding to these heuristics expressed as a set of production rules.

Object-oriented programming language development environment

The solution language will probably be an object-oriented programming language (OOPL) if you are to make use of all the benefits of objects. This raises the question as to where the OOPL development should be located. Many CASE vendors perceive the arbitrary grouping of upper CASE tools, servicing the analysis and design phases, and lower CASE servicing the code development phases. Plainly, effective development requires that these two 'flavours' of CASE tool should effectively be one CASE tool.

My advocacy is for OOPL development to be placed as part of an integrated CASE tool set. An effective OOPL development environment should involve the use of a class browser with appropriate working windows and it should appear as if it is connected to its upstream development counterparts. Ideally, this will be implemented on a workstation to make effective use of all the multiwindowing capability. Figure 17.2 shows the sort of items that would be accessible, such as the models from earlier

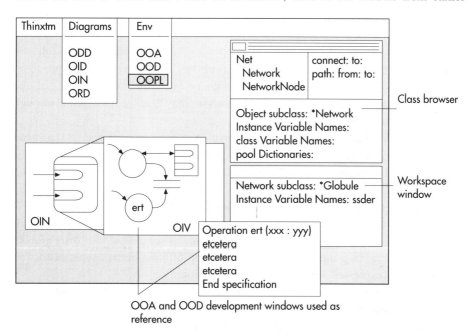

Figure 17.2   An idealised CASE tool showing model and code development.

development phases with the appropriate textual definition such as an operation specification.

Object-oriented notation and customisation

Many existing CASE tools were designed for accommodating the structured methods. The advent of object-oriented design and analysis has suggested to many CASE tool vendors that they pick a 'winning' notation and implement it on their CASE tool. This ploy involves much risk to the vendor and it is not an effective strategy because there are so many object-oriented notations in existence. The ideal CASE tool, then, has the capability to customise the graphic and textual notation. In other words, one can implement one's own choice of notation on the tool. If the notation was held in truly object-oriented form itself then 'we' would have true flexibility.

Metamodels – what are they and how do they work?

To define the rules for each of the symbols and their interconnection we must have some means of expressing them, preferably by graphics and as a model. This is, in effect, a model of models, i.e. a Metamodel. By means of an illustration to explain what a metamodel is, suppose that we had the opportunity to sell it as a tool for representing electrical circuits on a screen.

First, we must identify all the items in purely object terms and express how they may be interconnected. Figure 17.3 shows a notation that involves the globule symbol and a connector that looks like a 'lightning strike'. The situation, amongst all the components, can easily be expressed by means of the ERD (data model; bottom right. Fig. 17.3). (Note that a '1' within a circle indicates the 'anchorpoint' of the relationship. This indicates the entity from which we may read the relationship through to the other entities.)

Each 'globule' is a concept for which information must be held, such as its shape and probably some identifying attribute, plus some non-identifying attributes. The connector itself is a concept for which we hold information, such as its identity, which globule instances it connects from and to and the shape of the connector. The relationship between connectors and globules is expressed by means of the ERD relationship symbol. In Fig. 17.3 it is shown as reflexive, which means that all connectors must connect a globule to another globule. If we choose to restrict globule connection so that they must only connect between different globules that restriction would then be expressed in the relationship definition.

Second, and returning to the electrical example, we would now define all the symbols and how they may be interconnected. The ERD would then be drawn with appropriate definitions as to shape and rules for each of the components and their viable interconnection (electrically). In many cases the components may be arranged into class and subclass structures, which reflect incipient inheritance required.

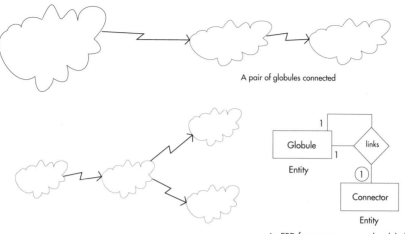

A pair of globules connected

An ERD fragment to express the globule

Figure 17.3   A metamodel for globules.

In this case all the appropriate symbols are identified along with their interconnection rules (Fig. 17.4). All the electrical symbols on a circuit diagram have two components:

1. The shape and text, which defines the component.
2. The interconnection to other symbols along with its identifier (Tables 17.2 and 17.3).

The ERD then allows the modelling of how the various conceptual components ought be interconnected and which characteristics each should have. The ERD gives us a view as to what class of symbols there should be and the specialisations and interconnections allowed. In the case of electrical circuits, the connectors run from terminal to terminal and are solely binary links.

The ERD as a metamodel is essential for this definition phase if one wishes to customise a CASE tool.

Introducing the object-oriented notation of a customisable tool

To assist someone who wishes to implement the notation outlined in this book, we have defined the following metamodels to describe all the notation.

The symbols have their usual abbreviations and each of the symbols, their definition and connectivity to other symbols will be described in the form of an ERD. An asterisk in the entity means this entity is redefined (expanded) in another ERD.

The core symbol is the object external view (OEV), which is made up from the object symbol and a series of operations that may be left- or right-handed. The

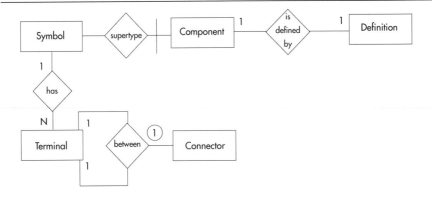

Figure 17.4   A metamodel of electrical circuit items.

Table 17.2   Electrical circuit components and their equivalent entities

Entity	Description
Component	Electrical symbol as a supertype (i.e. general class). The general supertype details are held for a symbol such as its location
Symbol	This is a specialisation (i.e. subtype). The specific specialised symbol shape is defined in this item
Terminal	This is a connection point particular to the symbol (subtype of component)
Connector	This is an undirected arc, which will connect a symbol to a symbol. It may have an identity and a label for display in the diagram

Table 17.3   Electrical component inter-relationships

Relationship	Description
Supertype	Introduces a general/specialisation
Connects	Allows a viable connection between terminals
is_defined_by	Allows a link between textual definition and the component symbol, such as value and units

operations also have another split, which may be control or data. The object symbol is linked to a text frame defined by the object frame (Fig. 17.5).

Associated with any OEV is an OIV. The internal view is accessible from any OEV. The major entities are the flow, of which there are two types (data and control) and the operation, of which there are two types (data and control). Location points are to allow a flow to originate or terminate outside the operation symbol and without attachment to any other component. The OEV (with asterisk) is a server object which may be connected to an operation by means of a flow (Fig. 17.6).

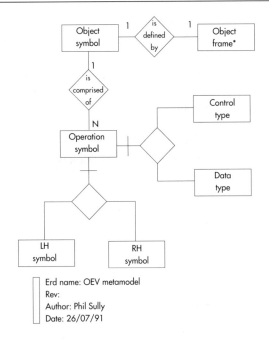

Figure 17.5   An OEV metamodel.

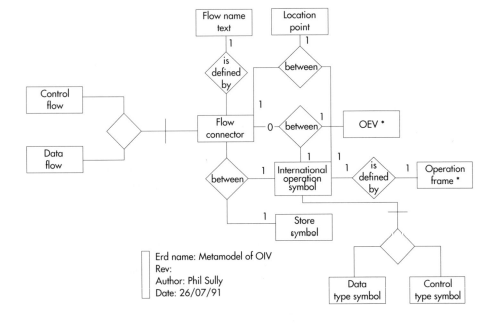

Figure 17.6   An OIV metamodel.

To display the arrangement of objects for execution we have the ODD. This diagram type is a collection of OEVs connected by directed arcs. The only restriction is the location of the connection points (Fig. 17.7).

To give a graphical representation of class relationships (as in a class browser), the object inheritance diagram (OID) depicts inheritance. It is a collection of OEVs connected by means of supertype symbols. The only restriction is the location of the connection points (Fig. 17.8).

To assist in the analysis phases we may depict objects without recourse to a hierarchy. To accomplish this we use the OIN. This definition is in essence a collection

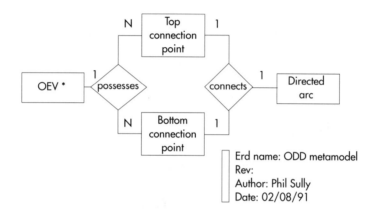

Figure 17.7   An ODD metamodel.

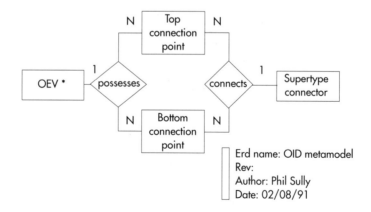

Figure 17.8   An OID metamodel.

of OEVs and the flow connectors that are attachable to the operation symbol (Fig. 17.9).

To assist in the definition of storage resources in anticipation of an object-oriented database we have the ORD. This diagram is a collection of OEVs that are interconnected by relationship symbols (Fig. 17.10).

The graphics take us so far but text has to be defined comprehensively somewhere. We suggest a frame. The object frame (OF) links with all the other concepts we have introduced. Additionally the operations (OP) have to be defined graphically (Fig. 17.11).

The above is not a complete set of definitions because one should define the accessibility from diagram type to diagram type. This is represented by Table 17.4.

Object-oriented CASE tools as examples

There are CASE tools that already have some object-oriented notation available for use, e.g. Teamwork and Software through Pictures. The tool OOA offered by Object International offers a graphics-based notation together with an appropriate Browser feature to encourage browsing for predefined units. However, the notations presented may not suit a particular development shop. Not many CASE tools allow their users to introduce new notations with ease. There are two exceptions that are worth a mention.

Table 17.4 The accessibility between the object components

Document type	Access from	Access to
ODD	OEV	OIV
ODD	OEV	OF
	Operation	OP
OID	OEV	OIV
	OEV	OF
	Operation	OP
OIN	OEV	OIV
	OEV	OF
	Operation	OP
	OEV	OID
ORD	OEV	OIV
	OEV	OF
	Operation	OP
	OEV	OID
OF	OF	OEV
OP	OP	OEV

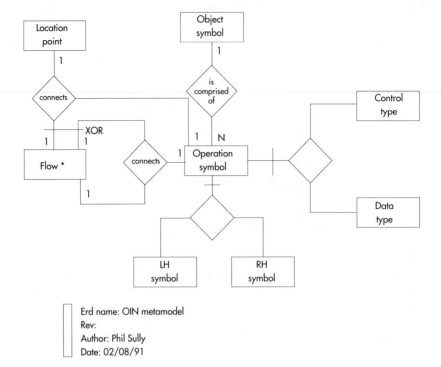

Figure 17.9   An OIN metamodel.

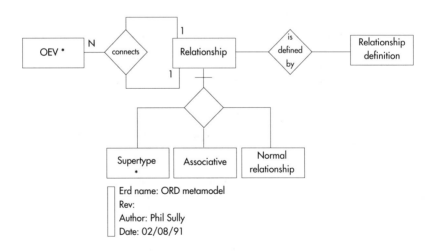

Figure 17.10   An ORD metamodel.

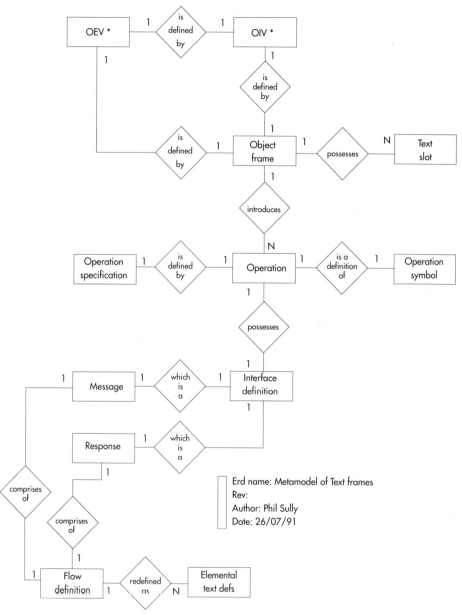

Figure 17.11   A metamodel of the text frames.

The first is the Analyst Designer Tool Kit (ADT), which is marketed by Yourdon in North America and Europe. It has a facility that is sold alongside the normal ADT; it is called RULE Tool, which allows comprehensive definition of new symbols and allows editing of the symbols in object form and in an easy-to-use style. It allows definition of all the symbol connection points and the styles of connection rules and it has the facility to define appropriate icons for display on an icon drum for use in the customised product.

The second tool is 'objectmaker', which is extremely adaptable. It is offered on a 'construct any notation and make a tool' basis. It has graphical editors to allow appropriate construction of the shapes and connectors. The rules associated with viable connections between the symbols are defined in a Prolog form definition language, which allows easy access and subsequent adjustment.

Conclusions

CASE tools are a necessary accoutrement for the development of object-oriented solutions. The graphic editing features are assumed as absolutely necessary and matching the notation chosen. To encourage as much reuse as possible, the CASE tool must have access to libraries of classes that are 'ready to go'.

The most ideal CASE tool will be one that allows customisation of the graphic symbols used. This raises the question about modelling notations, which in turn offers the opportunity to show true object-oriented representation of notations in the form the metamodel expressed as an ERD. The metamodel, for a notation, becomes documentation for its implementation on a CASE tool. the metamodel definitions have been given for the notation introduced in this book.

References and further reading

Boehm, B. (1981) *Software Engineering Economics*. Englewood Cliffs, NJ: Prentice Hall.
Bouldin, B. (1988) *Agents of Change*. Englewood Cliffs, NJ: Yourdon Press/Prentice Hall.
Gilb, T. (1988) *Principles of Software Engineering Management*, S. Finzi (Ed.). Wokingham, UK: Addison-Wesley.

CHAPTER 18

Object-oriented development and the project manager

The first law of scientific motivation
What's in it for me?
          (Isaac Asimov, 1968)

This chapter deals with some of the project management issues such as the segmentation of the development effort, estimation and prototyping. It also raises the issues for resolution related with evolving appropriate development environments and the appropriate supporting infrastructure. Who should supply what deliverables and how do you foster reuse?

The project management issues – Boehm's cost-drivers

There are fifteen cost-drivers (effort modifiers) and two are extremely sensitive and relevant, TOOL (level of tooling) and MODP (modern development practices). Both of these cost-drivers can contribute dramatically to reduction of development effort. Many of Boehm's ideas were based on developers using some systematic style of construction.

The other cost-drivers, such as language experience, schedule constraints, turn-around time, storage constraints and timing constraints are important in their own right but are not altered significantly by an object-oriented development.

However, complexity (called CPLX in Boehm's nomenclature) is affected because we have a style of development that allows a form of development that arrests many of the problems associated with complexity and scale. Additionally, Boehm pointed out the diseconomies of scale with software size.

$$\text{Effort} = A * (\text{KDSI})^{**}B$$

where A and B are coefficients of around 2.5 and 1.2, respectively, and KDSI is the number of thousands of source lines to develop. This formula is simplified (see Boehm, 1981 for more details).

Nanus and Farr (cited by Brooks, 1975) have also found a similar relationship, differing only in the coefficients used. The essential message is this diseconomy with scale. In an object-oriented development the whole perception of scale is different. The economies arrive from three major directions.

First, the average size of the individual operations is generally much smaller than the equivalent module in a structured solution. Coad and Yourdon (1991) give an example for the developers of their object-oriented analysis tool where they talk of an average of seven lines of Smalltalk code. This contributes to the appropriate economies from small scale.

Second, the economy comes from a completely different approach to system building. It is as if, for applications, one is assembling a system from prefabricated parts. These prefabricated parts are lodged in a class browser facility and are available for viewing by the developers.

Third, the additional economy comes from a different level of reuse. Cox (1986) recognised this phenomenon and used the analogy from the electrical industry, where at one time the unit of reuse was the transistor, a highly granular unit, and more recently the unit of reuse is the integrated circuit chip (ICC).

All this inderlines the importance attached to an appropriate infrastructure, which encourages reuse with a meaningful support structure to the individual application development teams.

Boehm's spiral model of development

This model makes tackling complexity easier. However, we must also consider the development 'life-cycle', which, in most of this book, has been presented as linear for reasons of explication. A linear view is too simplistic, we must now consider the what developers actually adopt and find useful. This view of the life-cycle is spiralesque. Figure 18.1 shows Boehm's 'spiral' model.

Each cycle of the spiral begins with a definition of the performance and functionality. The various implementation options are followed in turn by the constraints. The next is the analysis of the risks. This in turn is followed by prototyping a subset of the system, thence to the determination of what functionality should follow and what the next project steps are.

The spiral is 'unwound' by iteration through this cycle of:

> Determination of objectives, alternatives and constraints.
> Evaluation of alternatives and resolution of risks.
> Development, verification and determination of the next level product.
> Plan the subsequent phases.

Gradually, after many iterations, a product 'evolves' in a stepwise fashion. This whole style of development may benefit from an object-oriented development style where the

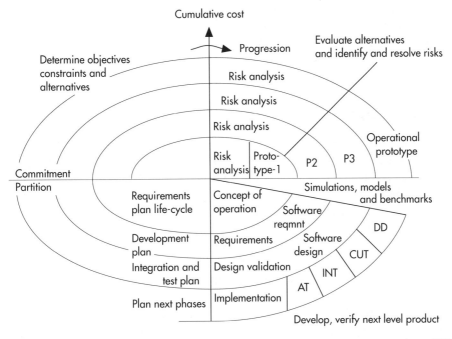

Figure 18.1   Boehm's spiral model of development. AT, acceptance test; INT, integrate and test; CUT, code and unit test; DD, detailed design; P2, prototype 2; P3, prototype 3.

evolution actually takes the form of 'prototypes' that are growing by accretion of new linkages to other objects. The development of a product is facilitated by this style. The problem that remains is one of organising the project to accommodate this style. However, this can be resolved by a suitable pilot project to provide the information.

Control

Control of the development of an object-oriented product is to some extent facilitated by this whole approach. It is assumed that a project manager will be knowledgeable about the object-oriented style of development, whether he or she is using a synthetic or a mutually shaped approach. The segmentation of the project into phases is still recommended, whether one is using Boehm's spiral model, an extension of the Yourdon sequence or a *mélange* of both.

The key difference between a structured approach and an object-oriented is that one should consider all the enterprise concepts that are likely to be involved and then set the definition for the specific application. It is to be recommended that the essence of the specification is presented in terms that the users will fully comprehend; these are checkpoint stages. Prototyping to ensure completeness of a specification should be 'controlled' in the style mentioned in the prototyping chapter. An object-oriented solution, as we have seen, is potentially more easy to extend. This will possibly encourage 'change traffic'. Within normal bounds and appropriate configuration control, the extension of applications to accomplish new opportunities that have been suggested by the objects should not be looked upon as a bane but as a confirmation of the benefits of an object-oriented approach.

Segmentation of work items

Part of the recipe for a successful project's implementation is the identification and control of the various work elements. The usual means for these items to be recognised and developed is the work breakdown structure (WBS). The WBS is a hierarchy of work elements. At the root of the hierarchy there will be a definition of the whole project. Each layer below describes the constituent units. The items at the bottom-most level (leaves), when fully defined, describe the full project elements. Each element may be thought of as a 'module of work'. It will have a definition of its prerequisites, a description of the task, an estimate of the work product (dimensions: labour time) and an ideal resource level. It is intended that a critical path network or a Pert chart may be derived easily from it.

The source for the realisation of an object-oriented solution may be derived from the object dependency diagram (ODD). The ODD gives a hierarchical representation of all the objects that comprise an application. The ODD objects will map directly to a subset of the WBS. There will be additional project-based activities dealing with testing and integration and procedural activities that should be adhered to. The ODD also gives an indication of what objects can be delivered and when. This is for an application.

The object inheritance diagram (OID) can be used as a source for developing the enterprise object resources. Again, the objects at the supertype level are the units that are to be constructed and the subtypes (i.e. specialisations) are to be perceived as incremental developments upon the base unit (the supertype).

Estimation

The estimation of effort to build and deliver applications can fall into two regimes: those based upon some complexity coupled to an empirical production rate and those empirical measures based on lines of code and an empirical production rate. Estimation for project purposes in the software industry falls behind that of other industries, such as industrial and civil engineering, when considering accuracy and commensurate confidence. These industries typically deliver accuracies between 2 and 5 per cent whereas in software development we rarely own up to the degree of accuracy (or is it inaccuracy?); it is my suspicion that accuracies of 10 to 20 per cent are about the norm. In the software development industry it still appears a novelty to measure effort accurately and identify numerically empirically where effort and resources go in the development life-cycle.

A function-points-based method (Albrecht, 1979) offers a good basis for estimation of the complexity of a candidate system. The measure works by enumeration of the frequency of classified inputs, outputs, files, interfaces and inquiries against a grid with weighted cells. An extension of the frequency by the weights yields a function point score that is a measure of complexity. This complexity measure may be adjusted marginally by project-specific factors. However, for this estimation to work there must be a production rate of delivering a function point. This production rate is specific to the technology. So there will be a rate for source languages Fortran, Cobol, C or Smalltalk.

Function-point counting has been effective for structured systems complexity estimation. There is no reason why function points are not effective as the basis for estimation of complexity in an object-oriented scenario. The function-point grid still has relevance. Inputs have equivalence in the form of message and it is the number of arguments that determine complexity. Outputs remain as they are. Files in object terms are class objects; interfaces are the same. Inquiries and reports are again driven by means of messages and again it is the arguments that determine the complexity. At the time of writing this area is being investigated more deeply.

The other means of estimation is based on lines of code (e.g. the CoCoMo model of Boehm). Lines of code can be estimated from identified primitives or from some conversion measure from function points (for a specific language). This method works for structured developments but, in a more elegant environment, line estimates become difficult to enumerate when inheritance is used. Inheritance is something we should encourage. It is possible to derive an estimate of lines of code from a combination of the operation specifications used in the ODD and the OID. When an ODD uses objects that are specialisations of a more general class, the ODD will 'see' only the specialisation. The line-counting score is only incremented where the developers have to build any extra (or marginal) behaviour.

In no way has the estimating activity for development in software building stabilised.

Infrastructure

A development shop will have to be organised in a different style, with an emphasis on reuse of components across projects. This requires that the infrastructure in an organisation recognises that it must provide resources to accommodate modelling of all concepts that the organisation deals with and should have identified all the life-cycles of the components with appropriate custodial services (operations) all available as documentary objects. Additionally, there must be comprehensive class browsers with proper means to navigate around the browser for code units that will accomplish the desired behaviour.

This style of development requires a change in the 'mind-set' of developers. Project managers have in the past been encouraged to take a linear view of the project's development and not be concerned with their neighbour's development. With the advent of object-orientation the direction is still encouraged to be linear but with awareness as to what the infrastructure can provide. At one time it was a developer's 'pride and joy' to develop his/her own code; using prewritten code was 'somehow cheating'. The emphasis on team members should be to encourage reuse of class browser components.

Maintenance

Specifically maintenance takes the form of 'bug fixing', adaptation and enhancement. These are euphemisms for different scales of change to a system. Maintenance must be considered because of the life-span of systems (typically, information systems 5 years through to control systems 20 years). An object-oriented system should offer resilience through time. Object-oriented systems should degrade at a lesser rate than those developed as structured systems (Fig. 18.2).

First, this diagram is a sketch of the anticipated situation. Empirically, we know the relative shape of the two curves for structured and unstructured. Structured solutions degrade less rapidly than unstructured solutions because maintenance is applied, with a higher degree of likelihood, in the correct location. Unstructured solutions have the greater chance of maintenance being applied to the wrong location. A maintainer may not fully understand the workings of the unstructured solution and may reproduce, albeit unwittingly, whole pieces of behaviour because from his/her perception they need to provide a solution quickly. An object-oriented solution has the added advantage of units that already have a degree of self-contained behaviour. An object-oriented solution is at introduction less efficient than its structured counterpart, but because of its malleability it accommodates change more gracefully.

The first category of maintenance is bug-fixing, and this should be facilitated for an object-oriented solution because the search space should be much smaller than for a

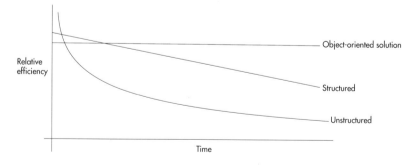

Figure 18.2   The relative efficiencies of unstructured, structured and object-oriented development.

solution based on function units. It should, of course, be easier to test in the first place. Additionally, the interface is much easier to work with by means of each object being sensitive to specific messages.

The second category adaptation refers to possible changes in technology being introduced. First, change should be isolated to a much smaller search space, which in effect isolates the change.

The third category, which I hope is encouraged, is an extension to a system. Advantage ought to be taken of the comprehensive class browsers to make use of what is possible as an extension to the systems. It ought be the ideal that systems will be extended. The cost for this extension is very small, in comparative terms, because one will be adding self-contained units, which may have the marginal behaviour added. This introduces the characteristic of malleability of objects.

It is also assumed that a developer/maintainer will have a comprehensive computer-aided software engineering (CASE) tool, which allows easy alteration of code, with appropriate safeguards, and alteration of the documentary objects.

Encouragement to use and supply class units

We can discuss the desired behaviour of the development of an object-oriented application by use of comprehensive class browsers but we must consider the 'what's in it for me?' aspect of human nature. Suppliers of class browsers could be given credit, possibly in the form of bonus remuneration. This would encourage people to supply viable class components. The activity of checking what was worthwhile may be handled by some administrative functionary who would check out its behaviour and document it fully and supply enough indexes to ensure that the class members were easily found.

Those who use units from these class browsers are saving themselves effort; however, they too should benefit, as users, by being able to assemble applications more speedily, with commensurate benefits. Further management encouragement can take the form of setting reuse targets over time. Say, for example, at the end of the first 6 months 50 per cent of all class units must be taken from the enterprise's own class browser. At the end of 18 months this target should be at least 75 per cent.

To apply successfully all of the above we are assuming an effective CASE environment from which a developer can usefully assemble his/her application.

The project phases

The phases suggested before of essential requirements followed by implementational considerations should still be the message. As mentioned earlier (Chapter 16), it is better to build some model of the concepts, for a wider scope than the application domain is useful to allow proper focusing of what is required. The implementational models follow as stated in Chapter 16. The models shown so far have always been based on the apparent net direction of logical to physical. The main concern is that there is some reference 'road map' of project stages.

A clear definition must be made concerning which particular kind of object-oriented is being used and what development style is to be adopted: synthesist or direct (mutually shaped). The former style requires the definition of what is to remain a structured activity, what is an object-oriented activity and where the objects are derived. With the direct (mutually shaped) style there will still be phases where the degree and scope of user participation must be defined.

A quick word on implementing object-oriented methods

It should also be recognised that on implementing an object-oriented development style (if one is a current structured methods developer) one can quite happily start with a synthesist approach and migrate to a direct approach. It is, of course, not useful to migrate in the other direction. If one does not currently use structured methods and wishes to proceed to object-oriented development style, one can proceed immediately to the direct (mutually shaped) style.

User roles

The degree of participation by end users in an object-oriented development scenario is up for debate. My opinion is that users should have an active and participatory role in the development of object-oriented solutions. It all depends on what degree of participation the user has been accustomed to so far. Structured methods work well in expressing requirements and in the main where users have been exposed to them in the role of reviewing and possibly developing them. They may not want to have additional notation to contend with. If you are adopting a synthesist posture you may well perceive that the object-oriented construction activity is something that developers do and the users do not do (Fig. 18.3). This 'chartoon' shows the various participant parties and what degree of visibility is presented. This style may be acceptable in the short term, but you will find that the users will want to know what 'objects' are.

The direct (mutually shaped) approach invites participation from users. The choice of symbols and diagrams was so that they were good graphical metaphors to be used effectively. The symbols were developed so that there would be the fewest possible concepts to juggle with (namely one symbol as opposed to the DFD, ERD and STD viewpoints). The first time the OIN was applied with users they had no problem understanding what was going on. It appeared as if it was a network of 'little object engines with plumbing-type connections'. In other words, users found that the symbols offered cognitive economy. The textual specification in the form of the object frame removes any of the mystery attached to 'those funny symbols'. The operation

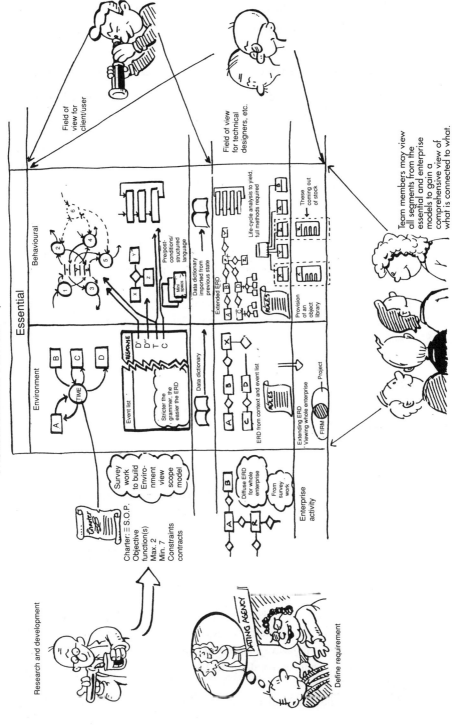

Figure 18.3 The analyst and user viewpoints of development (reproduced by kind permission of Yourdon Inc.).

specification expressed in pre- and post-condition form offers an effective way of expressing what a service (operation) should do 'before' and 'after'.

Procedures for participation (users and developers)

The end user should be involved as a stakeholder in evolving the fabric of applications. It is the view of this author that developers should not consider object-orientation development as part of their set of ritualistic 'black arts'. The object-orientation notation, as mentioned before, is user-friendly. As with other development styles there are formats to allow participation of users and developers, these are the JAD, blitzing and walk-through, plus prototyping.

JAD

JAD is an acronym for joint application development, which is a participation style that involves representative users in a session with recording devices like an electronic white board to allow the drawing/sketching out of visualised options. The session requires an animator knowledgeable in the object-oriented notation and users with specific subject area knowledge, the output from the sessions being diagrams outlining candidate objects and their projected interaction.

Blitzing

This is a similar format of session, with users and analyst developers, again with a rapid recording device.

Walk-throughs

These offer a format of participation that should encourage users to get involved in developments that affect their day-to-day work. This session is appropriate to a smaller number of people, is of shorter duration and relies upon an author of the projected product 'walking' it past a group of specialists for their comment.

Prototyping

As we saw in Chapter 14, prototyping relies on a user actually participating with an active model of his/her requirements. An object-oriented development, as stated before, makes rapid prototyping even easier and speedier. This accomplishes two things: it shows the user it is happening along the lines that he or she wants; and also the user can see the progress directly.

The bottom line of all this is a set of users who require a better quality of solution, which they will discuss more actively with developers. The developer is no longer in the role of a 'boffin who knows best'.

Conclusions

Most of this chapter recognises the aspects of project management such as the ideal sequence of activities to be undertaken. The spiral model has been introduced as another model for development, one that recognises risks and evolution to a solution set through prototyping. The work structure has been discussed, as have the appropriate sources, such as the ODD and OID. Additionally, the effects that object-orientation has on complexity and size have been discussed. The role of the developers and users is changing and will change more towards an active dialogue which is, in the long run, a good thing. Extension to systems ought not be seen as an admission of failure to anticipate change but as a recognition that your system is able to cater for change elegantly.

References and further reading

Albrecht, A.J. (1979) *Measuring Application Development Productivity*. In: IBM 'Share-Guide' Magazine, 1979, pp. 83–92. New York, NY: White Plains.

August, J. (1992) *Joint Application Design*. Englewood Cliffs, NJ: Yourdon Press/Prentice Hall.

Boehm, B. (1981) *Software Engineering Economics*. Englewood Cliffs, NJ: Prentice Hall.

Bouldin, B. (1989) *Agents of Change: Managing the Introduction of Automated Tools*. Englewood Cliffs, NJ: Yourdon Press/Prentice Hall.

Brooks, F.P. (1975) *The Mythical Man-Month*. Reading, MA: Addison-Wesley.

Coad, P. and Yourdon, E. (1991) *Object-Oriented Design*. Englewood Cliffs, NJ: Prentice Hall.

Cox, B. (1986) *Object-Oriented Programming*. Reading, MA: Addison-Wesley.

DeMarco, T. (1982) *Controlling Software Projects*. Englewood Cliffs, NJ: Yourdon Press/ Prentice Hall.

Gilb, T. (1991) *Principles of Software Engineering Management*. Wokingham, UK: Addison-Wesley.

Yourdon, E. (1977) *Structured Walkthroughs*. New York, NY: Yourdon Press.

CHAPTER 19

Conclusions

Great technological changes are always around the corner

(H.J. Hanham)

General issues have been raised, such as the various styles of development. Is OOA realistic? What object-oriented tools are helpful? What approaches are viable? What are the organisational changes required? What are the other object-oriented development methodologies doing? An outline is given of a few other object-oriented methods for development, such as Shlaer and Mellor (1992), Page-Jones, Constantine and Weiss (1990), HOOD and the Coad and Yourdon (1990) approach and various merits and defects of each are given.

General issues raised

Does object-orientation live up to its promises? Object-oriented system building as a style of development is evolving as a serious style. It has moved from appearing as a fad (fashion fads last two seasons at most) to a serious style of development. We are still at the early stages of development as we have no agreed 'royal road', as a definite proven way of proceeding. A prospective developer will still see a plethora of books about object-oriented programming languages (OOPLs) and some on OOD and a lesser number on OOA. There are still people who are not convinced of the contribution that OOA can make; there is also disagreement as to its scope. Is it for an application or is it for a whole enterprise? My own opinion is that it is for the enterprise as a whole, which can be more easily partitioned into individual parcels of development should you so wish.

What is the nature of the paradigm shift?

There is much debate still ensuing about how much the scale of difference is from structured development style and an object-oriented development style. Many consider that an object-oriented development is like a hyperversion of structured methods. I feel that this undervalues its contribution, although I can understand why people may perceive it that way.

The paradigm shift comes in terms of a similar perception that a hardware engineer may have when starting up some new enterprise. His/her thoughts are usually upon designing the right tools, which are the units he/she will anticipate using many times. This is in contradistinction to thinking of the specifics of the first engineering job to be undertaken. If he/she adopts the latter approach he/she is 'locked-into' what he/she constructed in that first instance.

Returning to software development, the situation is similar where we are suggesting that one thinks in terms of generalised units, that will be the basis for many subsequent specialisations. So the paradigm shift is reuse oriented. This is different from the structured methods where the units were the library functions that in hardware terms, are analogous to the nuts and bolts level of reuse. Another key characteristic is that application solutions will be customisations of these generalised units.

Is it easier than structured methods?

Structured methods did actually contribute much to making systems development a systematic activity. Object-orientation is in general a much more effective method. The structured methods also identified the function as the main unit of concern. Object-orientation has shown that the better unit to focus upon is the object. Effort to identify all the appropriate custodial and fundamental behaviour for that unit makes it a more self-contained and reusable unit.

The first time a developer applies an object-oriented approach he/she will inevitably consume more time and effort than for the structured equivalent. Object-orientation requires more effort in thinking of the object's use in many contexts.

Object-orientation as a development style is, in the long run, easier to use and more effective. It ensures we take an enterprise-wide view of our systems building activities.

The organisational changes required

To effectively use an object-oriented development style many infrastructural changes are required. In manufacturing industry there is an equivalent organisational unit that provides reuse across a company. This department is generally referred to as toolware. As mentioned elsewhere, application-only views are out. In manufacturing terms these are 'one-off' jobs, which do not usually reap great economic benefits for the company.

A company seriously constructing an appropriate infrastructure for development must think in terms of frameworks (Constantine, 1992). This requires that an appropriate set of CASE tools are in place to facilitate 'looking' across the individual applications domains (see Fig. 7.14).

Within each application development team there ought be a person from the framework to assist application developers in finding suitable reuse units. Again, there is a manufacturing equivalent in the form of a toolsmith, who will be aware of the variety of applications to which the tool will be subjected. Jacobsen (1987) suggests that we should see this style of development as similar to an object-factory with clients as individual application groups.

There are also procedures that should be put in place to encourage reuse. This takes the form of tools and possible financial inducements to encourage using class-held units and also to encourage the supply of units.

Other object-oriented approaches

There are many object-oriented development methods and styles and I believe it is appropriate to give a perception on a limited sample of some of the principal methods.

Grady Booch is a pioneer in the development of OOD. His methodology has developed significantly over the years. Booch has based much of his earlier work on Ada. More recently, he has developed the methodology to be availing itself on OOPLs like C++ and Smalltalk. Booch is of the revolutionary regime and takes an active part in the debate on the development of object-oriented method directions.

HOOD is an acronym for hierarchical object-oriented design, which is an oxymoron. The moment a hierarchy is imposed upon objects, we have imposed an unnecessary constraint on the associated objects at design time.

HOOD emanates from Estec (the European Space Technology Centre) at Noordwijk in The Netherlands. It is an object-based notation and uses a symbol for an object, which can be decomposed in to various object layers. The diagrams associated with HOOD closely approximate to object dependency diagrams (ODD). This method has a close following in the Benelux countries and the UK and France, particularly in the Astronautics communities.

Shlaer and Mellor are also pioneers, particularly in object-oriented analysis. Steve Mellor, along with Paul Ward, was the developer of the Yourdon Real-Time Structured Development methodology.

The Shlaer/Mellor approach relies on a data model being created at analysis time. The data model gives all attributes visibility. Each entity is subjected to a life-cycle analysis by means of a state diagram. This assists in collecting all the candidate methods for that entity when it is metamorphosed into an object. There are additional diagrams to depict aspects like activity flows by means of a type of data flow diagram (DFD).

More recently the method has been extended to depict classes and inheritances of object and decompositions of classes depicting all tokens used (a token being an attribute that participates in the coupling of one unit to another). This part of the notation is named OODLE (acronym for object-oriented development language).

The notation is highly granular. This whole approach is considered revolutionary and it offers much to a developer.

Page-Jones, Constantine and Weiss, from Wayland systems, offer another approach which is based upon a synthetic emphasis (i.e. derives objects from the products of structured methods). It uses the Yourdon structured notation as a basis. There is a notation for objects associated with this method called the uniform object method (UOM). This method is again very granular; every item in a message is modelled. This methodology has much to offer because it allows developers to migrate from structured methods to object-oriented approaches with minimum 'angst'.

Coad and Yourdon is an approach primarily developed by Coad at Object International. Coad is an 'enthusiastic' object aficionado who is a very active member of the revolutionaries. He was amongst the first of offer an object-oriented analysis method (OORA) 1989. This method has a notation that is a form of an object model, which displays class objects and their relationships to other objects. Each class object shows a list of its attributes and a list of its services. The connections between objects are depicted by message paths and relationship connectors. More recently this method has been extended into OOD areas. This method is a strong contender and is actively being developed.

Object behaviour analysis – Elizabeth Gibson

I am attracted towards this approach because the viewpoint taken is one of identifying candidate objects then subjecting them to a form of analysis to gather their behaviour in all identifiable contexts. Much emphasis is placed on textual analysis of interviews with subject area experts and the subsequent detailed analysis of phrases used to identify types of relationships between objects. This method has the charm of making systematic the early analysis stages of identifying candidate objects and relationships and behaviour.

What does the future hold?

So far the majority of object-oriented applications have been developed for small, stand-alone applications and control-type applications; business systems have largely been ignored. It will not be long before an object-oriented extension to Cobol is a reality which would certainly become a driving force for change. Object-oriented databases are also awaited. So far the only offerings have been extensions to OOPLs or test beds. When viable object-oriented databases and an object-oriented extension to Cobol are tangible and effective then we will have an avalanche of object-oriented development demand.

Approaches to object-oriented development will become easier. In my mind it is likely that a mutually shaped approach will evolve. The 'synthesist' route is at present a bridge between two styles of development (structured and object-oriented). The mutually shaped approach will become easier with use and experience.

Prototyping has been made easier and there is no excuse for not using object-oriented tools for use in this rapid prototyping activity.

The expert-system-type of application need no longer be considered as a separate flavour of system with its own cult. Many of the principles that were associated with expert systems, like the production rules and the objects they related to, can now be accommodated in the object relationship diagram (ORD) and the object frame.

Object-oriented development is a serious development direction and I do not believe we have seen anything that approaches the complete solution. The debate will continue as to how objects ought to be represented, what is important to model and how they are developed and maintained. It is a healthy state of affairs for the amount of discussion and debate that is being undertaken.

References and further reading

Coad, P. and Yourdon, E. (1990), *Object-Oriented Analysis*, Englewood Cliffs, NJ: Yourdon Press/Prentice Hall.

Constantine, L. (1992) *Objects on a Large Scale*. OOP '92, Munich, Germany.

Cook, S. (1992) *Introduction to Object Technology*. OOP '92, Munich, Germany.

Cox, B. (1992) *Information Age Consulting*. OOP '92, Munich, Germany.

Gibson, E. (1990) 'Objects – born and bred.' *Byte*, October.

HOOD, CISI Ingenerie, CRI A/S, Matra Espace (1988), *HOOD Manual Issue 2.2*, Noordwijk, Netherlands: European Space Agency.

Jacobsen, I. (1987) *Object-Oriented Development in an Industrial Environment*. OOPSLA '87.

Page-Jones, M., Constantine, L. and Weiss, S. (1990), 'Modelling object-oriented systems: the uniform object language', *Computer Language*, October, 69–87.

Shlaer, S. and Mellor, S. (1992) *Object Life Cycles: Modelling the World in States*. New York, NY: Yourdon Press.

Glossary of terms

Abstraction: The process of factoring out common behaviour and data to a superclass.

Actor: An object that is always a client and never a server.

ADT: An abstract data type. It is an abstraction that represents a set of attributes in terms of an encapsulated hidden structure and operations on that structure.

Aggregation: Identification of an object which is a composite of two or more objects.

AKO: An abbreviation for *a kind of*. It denotes a specialisation of a general class.

Anthropomorphism: A style of modelling that uses human-like behaviour for explanation.

Applicator: An operation (or method) that applies one of its arguments to other arguments.

Argument: A set of values, which is part of a message, which acts as operand data.

Attribute: A class. It is equivalent to a data item.

Backward chaining: A method of inference which works by taking the conclusions and working backward to the conditions. Associated with rule-based systems.

Base class: A supertype from which the behaviour of another class, the subtype, derives its data and behaviour.

Behaviour: The set of processing that an object exhibits, which originates from its object frame definition and operation specifications.

Binding: Commitment of a certain value or value set for execution. Late binding is considered desirable because it gives the latest possible commitment to certain values or value sets.

BNF: Backus Naur Form. In this tome, a relaxed form of BNF is used, which is derived from DeMarco (1978), is adopted which has the following operators:

'=' equivalence
[..|..] Selection of one option from a list
(..) Option
{..} Repetition
'+' along with

'@' Identifier.

As an example we may define a menu in a restaurant as follows.

Lunch = First_course + Second_course + Third_course
First_course = [soup | grapefruit]
Second_course = minute_steak + (french_fries)
Third_course = tart + {custard}

Browser: See class browser.

CASE: Abbreviation for computer-aided software environment.

Child: A child class is a specialisation of some general class.

Class-based: A source programming language in which the primary unit of implementation is the class, i.e. a collection of instances comprising a class.

Class browser: A facility to allow easy inspection of classes, their attributes and operations. Usually it will allow various styles access: serial, random and by class hierarchy.

Client: The party that is using an object (server) providing services. Synonyms: customer, user, caller.

CoCoMo: An abbreviation for Constructive Cost Model, devised by Boehm. Essentially a line-counting-based procedure for estimation of effort and duration and how the effort may be modified by cost drivers.

Cohesion: A measure of the strength of association of the constituents of a unit. It is in essence a structured methods term.

Collaborator: An association with another object to provide services.

Constructor: A method (or operation) which creates an initialisation of an object with the appropriate invariant. Constructor is an OOPL term.

Consumer: Synonym for a client.

Cost-driver: A factor which modifies the effort to build a solution. See CoCoMo model.

Coupling: A measure of interdependence of one unit upon another. It is in essence a structured methods term. In an object-oriented sense, coupling is catered for by the means messages.

Custodial: That behaviour associated with key life cycle actions.

Data abstraction: The process of factoring common data into a new supertype.

Data hiding: The activity of restricting visibility of data to the object's operations and attributes and those controlled to access it.

Demeter's Law: A law restricting the proliferation of varieties of object that any given object will call upon. It suggests that one should be minimalist in the number of objects a unit calls upon.

Destructor: A specialised function with an object to remove unrequired instances. This is important with respect to freeing storage. Destructor is a OOPL term and specific to C++.

DFD: Abbreviation for data flow diagram.

Dynamic binding: The situation where an operation's behaviour is determined at the latest possible time before execution (i.e. at run time). It is also the enabling mechanism for polymorphism.

Encapsulation: The conceptualisation of operations, data and state behaviour into one unit.

ERD: Abbreviation for entity relationship diagram.

eSTD: Abbreviation for entity state transition diagram.

Factorisation: The activity of decomposing a large unit into discernible and useful smaller units.

Forward chaining: A method of inference where the conditions are examined firstly and conclusions latterly. This is in contrast to backward chaining (c.f. above). This style of inference is used in some rule-based systems.

Frame: A conceptual device where a unit may be represented by means of a schema with slots for the individual textual items.

Friend: A concept from the OOPL C++ where an object may have direct access to another object's data without the host object providing services.

Function point: A dimensionless complexity measure devised by Alan Albrecht of IBM.

Fundamental: That behaviour associated with specific applications.

Genericity: The ability to define parametrised units.

Inheritance: The mechanism by which a specialised class of object automatically presents the more general class of behaviour in addition to its own behaviour.

Instance: An occurrence or a particular example of a class.

Interface: The means of communication between a client and supplier of object services. Each operation will have an interface such that it introduces the inbound messages to which it is sensitive and the responses that it will provide.

ISA: An abbreviation for is a. It introduces an instance of a class.

Layer: A level of detail in a diagram. Any object may be decomposed into an OIV to show another layer of detail. Any objects therein may in turn be decomposed into another layer.

Machine: A device capable of performing work. It will transform inputs to outputs, it will have state behaviour, it will use memory and its behaviour is governed by a set of rules.

Member function: A method or operation. It is a C++ specific term.

Message: A means of communication to an object. It is a package which ordinarily will include:

```
Class + (instance) + Service + {argument}
```

Message thread: A sequence of behaviour specific to an external event, which will list the objects and operations used to complete an external response, compare with Thread test.

Metaclass: A class whose instances are classes.

Metamodel: A diagram that expresses the interrelationship between components of a model type. Usually expressed as a data model (e.g. ERD).

Method: A synonym for an operation.

Normalisation: (i) Data normalisation. A procedure to place data more effectively (non-redundantly) into a structure. (ii) Behavioural normalisation. A procedure to place behaviour (processing operations) into its most effective position (non-redundantly).

Object: An encapsulation of data, operations and state behaviour as a single unit, with a distinct message protocol to facilitate usage of its operations. It is also an instance of a class. This book uses the Smalltalk ideas of everything being an object.

Object-based: A source programming language in which the primary implementation unit is the individual instance of the object. Ada and Oberon are object-based languages.

Object-oriented programming language: A desirable programming environment with the following characteristics: an encapsulation mechanism based on data; an inheritance mechanism; polymorphism and dynamic binding; an optional comprehensive class browser mechanism.

Object frame: The frame for definition of the object's name, description, attributes, its inheritance, the operations and the invariant.

OEV: Abbreviation for object external view. That is the external object symbol that will be visible in OID, OIN, ODD and ORD.

ODD: Abbreviation for object dependency diagram.

OID: Abbreviation for object inheritance diagram.

OIN: Abbreviation for object interconnection network.

OIV: Abbreviation for object-internal view.

OOPL: Abbreviation for object-oriented programming language.

ORD: Abbreviation for object relationship diagram.

Operation: A specific piece of processing that an object may provide. Objects provide operations which operate on the data encapsulated in the object. Synonyms: method, member function and service.

Operation frame: The documentation device for specification of the operation and its interface. Options for specification: pseudo-code, structured language or pre- and post-condition specification.

Overloading: The process of attaching more than one meaning to an operation name. It in turn will return behaviour specific to its object type. As an example, the use of the arithmetic operators '+' and '−' on numeric variables will yield appropriate arithmetic results. However, these two same operators may be used on strings for equivalent operations such as appending and removing strings.

Package: An Ada concept, which allows the combining of declarations and procedures to be bound as a single unit.

Parent: A supertype with respect to some reference class.

Polymorphism: The capability to send a common message to objects of different types. Each object will respond with its own particular behaviour.

Private: Those parts of an object other objects cannot 'see'.

Protocol: A set of rules, rigorously defined, for using a set of operations, encapsulated within an object.

Reference class: A base class upon which specialisation refers to.

Rule slot: A facility within the object frame to accept rule specification.

Server: An object that suffers operations upon itself and which may not call upon other other objects to supply additional services (i.e is not a client in its own right).

Service: Synonym for operation.

Sibling: A subtype that shares the same parent supertype.

Subtype: A specialisation of a general class.

Supertype: A generalisation of a set of subtypes.

Supplier: A party that supplies services and or data.

State: A specific situation of interest concerning the sensitivity of a unit such as a device, a system or subsystem or an entity. See STD.

STD: Abbreviation for state transition diagram. A diagramming method where one may model the sequence of entry and departure from states according to specified conditions and associated specified actions. There are two major styles of use: discrete control STDs and entity STDs.

Thread: A sequence of behaviour originating from an external event (through all the appropriate representational devices: such as OINs/ODDs) to alterations in memory through to the completion of its response.

Thread test: A sequence expressed in the form of a table which shows each external events progress through OINs/ODDs/ORDs and operation specifications to complete a response.

Transparency: The characteristic of being able to hide any complexity by showing any linkages through a complexity as if the complexity is not present.

Virtual function: A member function whose actions are deferred until execution time. A C++ source language specific term.

Virtual machine: This is the chracteristic of presenting to an observer a fictional processing unit which for all intents and purposes appears to behave to an external observer as if it is one working physical machine. It may in implementational terms actually be a collection of automated machines, not just one.

Visibility: The concept of showing only what is publicly available for clients to use.

WBS: An abbreviation for Work Breakdown Structure, which is a hierarchy of controllable work elements. Each work element will have a set of pre-requisites and post-requisites along with a description and an appropriate estimate of the work product's size.

Z: A formal language for expressing objects and object behaviour.

Case study: Continental Containers Inc.

Continental Containers Inc. is an international transport company which provides a containerised transport service for its clients. To bring Continental Containers Inc. (henceforth, CC Inc.) in touch with latest technology, we need to do some investigation to collect information to build an appropriate object-oriented analysis model. These investigations can be used as the basis for a prototype construction. The appropriate vehicle for this is a series of interviews:

1. The container business: Fred Holroyd, Container Inventory Manager.
2. Container tracking: Gladwys ForthWright, Container Tracking Specialist.
3. Outleasing: Neville Fairwether, Out Lease Manager.
4. CC Inc. field office: Mme Mazou, Area Administration Manager.
5. Container repairs and acquisitions. Maureen Delahaye, acquisitions, repairs and disposals; Harvey Wall, Chairman.
6. A prototyping session: Neville Fairwether, Fred Holroyd and Maureen Delahaye.

At the close of each interview the models may be elaborated to incorporate this new information.

Scene 1

The container business

Fred Holroyd, Container Inventory Manager. Scene: at Fred's office, which has a grand vista of the whole container terminal. One Tuesday mid-afternoon.

Fred H: Good afternoon, Cyril. I hope you didn't find it too much trouble to find my little eyrie?

Cyril Gainforth: (Continental Containers' Dynamic Systems Developer, an experienced analyst who has recently joined the company and therefore has a fresh view on systems) No, none at all sir.

Fred H: I believe you are here to find out about the container business?

Cyril G: Yes, that's right. I should be grateful if you would tell me all about the container business from your perspective. This is so that I can understand where the various systems fit in.

Fred H: Have you got one life to spare? Really, I think we ought start at the beginning and define our business. We are in transport, that is we offer a containerised transport service door to door from Western Europe to North America and vice versa. We have ships and inland transport to effect this service. Does that seem clear so far?

Cyril G: Yes, however I'd like a definition as to what your container is for the benefit of our readers.

Fred H: Fine! A container is a unit transport device; it is sized eight foot by eight-and-a-half foot by twenty foot long. Like this (pointing at a chart) (Fig. A2.1).

We also have ships that are specially configured to carry containers, called cellular vessels. These ships can carry anything up to 2000 TEUs (twenty-foot equivalent units). Look at this Hesperus class vessel (pointing at a picture of the vessel by Vernon Glabach, RA) (Fig. A2.2).

We also have an inland transport fleet (trucks and railway trains) that will handle these devices. The economy, from our point of view, comes from the manipulation of these containers between transport modes. To give you an idea, we can load the container vessel with 1600 container units in about twelve hours as opposed to an equivalent bulk cargo in about five days. Quite a difference, Eh?

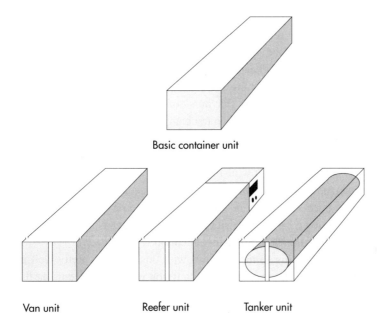

Basic container unit

Van unit   Reefer unit   Tanker unit

Figure A2.1   Container types.

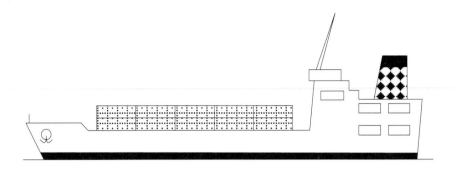

Figure A2.2   A container vessel.

Cyril G: That's interesting! Now, what pieces of information would you expect to need about all these areas of interest?

Fred H: Well, now you've got me thinking (he strokes his head and his beard, pensively). Well, there are containers of course and where they are, that and their location or even where they are travelling between. We also have to know what it is carrying and its bill of lading and often the trucker involved. Now, I need, also, to know the sailing schedule for the vessels, but for trucking the containers we use the 'spot market'.

Cyril G: What is the spot market?

Fred H: Well, it's not an acne prize! It's where a transport operator will anticipate what traffic is to be shipped and will offer transport at a given rate governed by the market ('spot market'). It is cheaper to have the transport organised this way. It means we do not have to run inland transport ourselves.

Additionally, we have various 'flavours' of container, such as vans, tankers and freezer units, to mention just a few. To track any of these container units I also need to know which transport operator has possession of the unit. We have a document called the EIR. It is an equipment interchange receipt, which is the document of exchange, and it enables us to track a unit whilst in the possession of a transport operator. (Phone rings and interrupts, Fred H answers using his executive-style cell phone whilst commencing to pace the office and carry on a phone conversation.)

Yes! I know, but we can't fix it with a spot weld, it needs size 34 grommets with a jubilee clip at least. (He then directs his attention to Cyril G.)

Listen Cyril, I am going to have to deal with this problem pretty well pronto, so I suggest that you call back at some later time if you want more details on the container business.

Cyril G: Thanks for your time. I'll contact you again. (Whereupon Cyril makes a gracious departure from Fred H's office, being careful not to injure the newly imported tropical plants.)

Commentary

The material given so far is useful for the construction of a data model which would introduce all the concepts and how they are interconnected.

Figures A2.3 and A2.4 show data models developed from the evidence so far.

Scene 2

Container tracking

Meeting at Gladwys ForthWright's office in Container Tracking. Mid-Wednesday morning just before 'elevenses' ritual.

Gladwys F: Would you like one, a delicious bun, I mean? (Gladwys offers a delightful confection with a full technicolourful topping.)

Cyril G: Thank you. You're most kind.

Gladwys F: Well, you've come to see me as well as learn about container tracking, right?

Cyril G: Yes. I would like to identify the container life-cycle from your perspective.

Gladwys F: Well, you're certainly in the right place. I'll start at the beginning. A container (or batch of them) is bought from a manufacturer and is painted to our logo scheme. The containers all have an identifier (unique number such as COCU100100). I create a magnetic chip for the tracking board at that instance and I write the identifier on the chip with a fibre marker. I also create a record of the container on my DBase3 file with regard to details such as data manufacturer and type. Oh, type, that reminds me, I create different coloured magnetic chips for each type of container: van, tanker, flat bed, reefer or whatever. The magnetic chips are put up on the magnetic board under the column of pool and status. Perhaps I should explain what a pool is.

Cyril G: Yes, please!

Gladwys F: Well, this board is very simple. It uses these magnetic chips to show where the containers are. Each region is divided off into pool regions. So, for example, Thwaite's Farm has, let me see, four vans, a tanker and a reefer. The coloured chips tells me exactly what types I've got and the quantity of chips gives an indication of how many units at a glance. I suggest we go over to the board and meet one of my 'toy boy croupiers'. (Cyril and Gladwys make their way through the maze to the magnetic board.)

Gladwys F: This is Gordon McCoy, one of my croupiers. Gordon meet Cyril, one of those boffins from HQ here to straighten us all out!

Gordon M: Nice to meet you!

Cyril G: Likewise.

Gladwys F: Gordon, tell Cyril how you use the board in your tracking activities.

Gordon M: Like Gladwys said, this board is our way of tracking containers by types and by individual units. I can tell at a glance how many units I've got. I can also

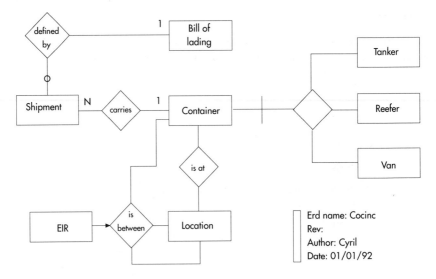

Figure A2.3   An ERD for containers.

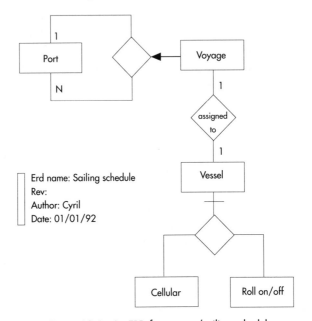

Figure A2.4   An ERD for voyage/sailing schedules.

anticipate when I've got unit shortages. If I need units, I need to know what type and if I can move containers in from another region.

If I need specialist units, I need to know if I can reuse another type. Also I can see where they are and I can manoeuvre them to where I want them in the least number of moves, a kind of large-scale game of checkers. We call this activity positioning.

It is ideal that we get the best utilisation out of these container units as possible.

Cyril G: Does offering more types of containers help?

Gordon M: Not really. The more specialised units you have the less utilisation you have. It is better to have a small core of flexible units, and the minimum you can get away with is a set of vans, tankers and refrigerated units (reefers). If you need specialist units you should ask yourself how often you really use them. The usual solution is to lease them just for the journey. (At this juncture Gordon is served his Captain Marvel mug freshly replenished with industrial-strength coffee.)

Cyril G: Thank you, Gordon, for your information. I'm sure that I will have to call back to see you with some additional questions if that is all right with you?

Gordon M: Yep! Fine. Be seeing you!

Commentary

This material is enough to enable construction of an outline of the life-cycle of a container unit, possibly described by an eSTD (Fig. A2.5). It also describes the actual tracking activity.

Scene 3

Outleasing

Neville Fairwether, Outlease Manager. Location: Neville's office, Thursday morning, 9:00.

Cyril G: Good morning! Thank you for granting me an interview.

Neville F: Top of the morning to you! You are here to find out about outleasing aren't you?

Cyril G: Yes, this is with a view to an organised information system that covers all aspects of the transport business.

Neville F: Well, that's a tall order! I've been man and boy and I don't know it all yet. Anyway, we'll start here.

We undertake outleasing because we can better utilise the containers and get revenue for it. Now, in the shipping business some continents have complementary business seasons. For instance, containers for use in shipping grain can only be used between March and October in the northern hemisphere and they can be used in the southern hemisphere over November to February.

Cyril G: How do you charge these folks?

Neville F: Well, first there is a set-up charge, which covers the start of a lease. Then there is a *per diem* charge for each container day that the leasee uses the unit. By the way, there is a minimum and a maximum duration. When a lease is up the leasee will

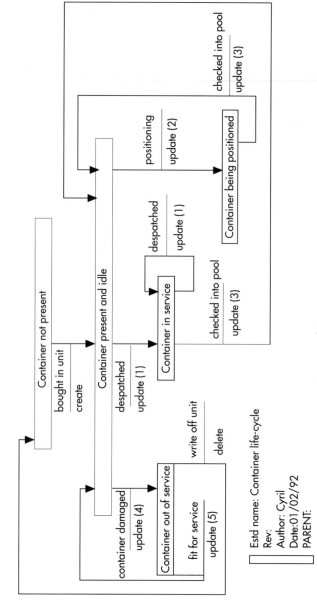

Figure A2.5   An eSTD for a container.

turn-in the box (container) at one of our pools. Associated with this there is a drop-off charge, which will vary from site to site. The idea behind this is to 'steer' the units to where we need them so that they become true Continental Containers Inc. revenue traffic.

Cyril G: So you use your leasees to position the containers for you?

Neville F: Right in one. Now, I need information concerning all my leasees and their specific leases. Also I want to maintain and keep track of the the drop charges. Additionally, I want to be able to bill my punters as quickly as possible.

Cyril G: This seems very specific?

Neville F: Yes, I think so, because I've been waiting for someone like you to come along. You're the answer to my prayers . . . . (Neville then continues to drone on . . . .)

Commentary

This is good description of the lease business. However, the data model from the earlier model should be extended to cater for this. Additionally, an ORD could be developed, and the earlier eSTD for the container life-cycle should be extended and the life-cycle behaviour of a lease may be described by means of an eSTD.

Figure A2.6 depicts the static aspect of the container business and Fig. A2.7, an ERD, depicts a preliminary model depicting the specifics of the rental sideline. A2.8 depicts an extension to the eSTD addressing outleasing.

Scene 4

CC Inc. field office

Mme Mazou, Area Administration Manager. Location: Mme Mazou's office in a small town in the hinterland. The office is located above a shopping precinct and it has a complement of two: the sales man and Mme Mazou, who handles everything in the office that is related with Continental Containers. The time is 11:00 on a Friday morning.

Mme Mazou: 'Ello 'ello! Are you looking for someone?

Cyril G: Yes! I was looking for Mme Mazou.

Mme Mazou: You have found herself. Zere is only one of myself (flicking the ash of a Disque Bleu in the pot of the house plant).

Cyril G: I've made an appointment with you to discuss automation.

Mme Mazou: So you did, I remember now.

Cyril G: So, would you like to describe to me all the activities you do in relation to container operations.

Mme Mazou: Certainement! Well, I shall start 'ere. I will take bookings from my customers. Zese bookings are essentially shippers who wish to send goods to a consignee, typically in another continent. I cut the way bill and I organise a trucker to

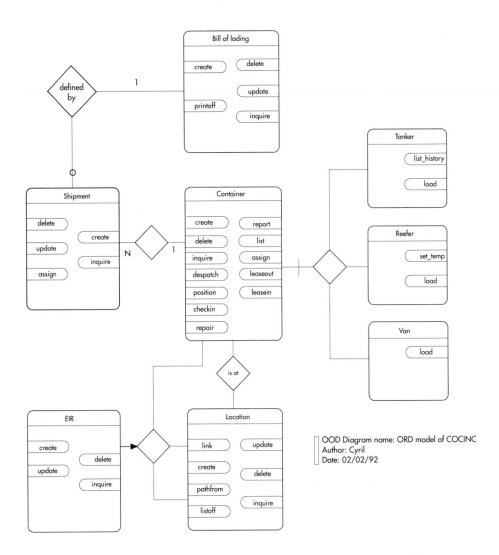

Figure A2.6   An ORD for the container tracking domain.

pick up an empty container and take it to zer shipper where it is loaded. Then zey are transported to a railhead and onwards to the boat. I will, of course, link the way bill to the container.

Cyril G: Hold on a moment. OK, that's the dispatching activity. What do you use to tell you who has what container and where they all are? Do you have a secret system to track the containers like at Thwaite's Farm?

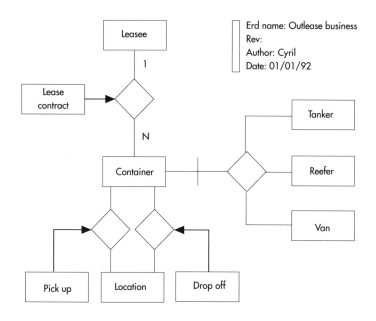

Figure A2.7 An ERD for container leasing.

Mme Mazou: What do zey 'ave at Thwaite's Farm that is so special?

Cyril G: They have a localised tracking system run on magnetic chips on a magnetic board.

Mme Mazou: Mon dieu! Why do I need such contrivances? When containers come and go from my region I remember them all. My secret system is my head! I should be in the Circus!

Cyril G: So you do all the dispatch documentation, the container control and what else?

Mme Mazou: I do the accounts, zen I produce the forecasts and I do ze . . . (then, at the end of the seemingly interminable list) . . . Well, I'm for lernching with perhaps a small aperitif. Will you join me?

Commentary

This is a good example of usage of the container system in the field. An OIN can be used to check out the network of messages and objects. Figure A2.9 indicates how objects shipment, container, location, EIR and trucker are involved.

Scene 5

A Group Meeting held to ascertain Cyril's progress and to identify anything that can

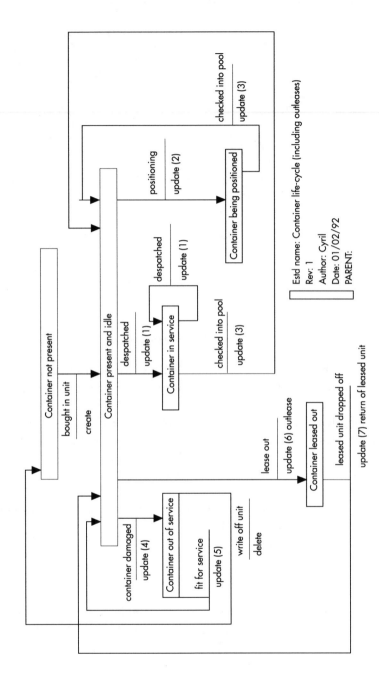

Figure A2.8 An eSTD for a container extended to accommodate leasing.

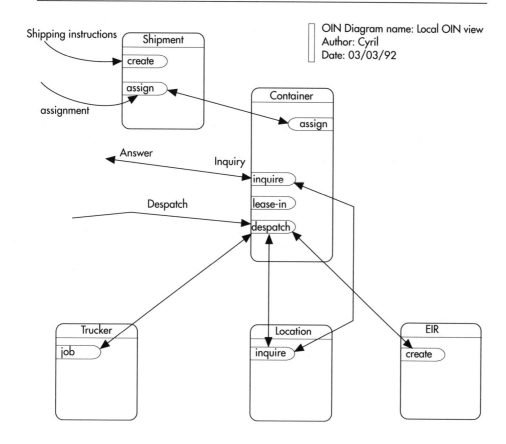

Figure A2.9 An OIN for container despatching activity.

assist in facilitating. The meeting includes Maureen Delahaye, Acquisitions, Repairs and Disposals and Vernon Goldglow, Market Planning Manager. Chairing the meeting is the 'El Supremo' of the container shipping business, Harvey Wall. The meeting is being held on a Tuesday afternoon at 15:00.

Harvey W: Good afternoon folks! You've all met Cyril, our systems analyst and automation specialist extraordinaire. Cyril, you've met everybody so no introductions are necessary. Mrs Patel will be our scribe. Now the agenda I wish to proceed with is where Maureen and Vernon will outline to you what they want. Then I want to know how you are going to link all these aims together. Maureen, ladies first. Off you go!

Maureen D: Thanks Harvey. I am interested in our system being able to accept new container units, and being able to tell their status and, furthermore, if they have been damaged, I wish to know what damage and how much it will cost to fix. If we lease out a unit I wish to know to whom and where it is going. I also want to know when and where a unit has been inspected. This I want on-line. I want to manage the fleet of units so that they give the most effective service. I wish to know which container manufactured units are best so that the best units are selected in future.

Harvey W: You got all that Mrs Patel?

Mrs Patel: Oh yes! Most definitely so.

Harvey W: Now you can go on, Vernon.

Vernon G: Thanks Harvey. Yes, my concerns are slightly different. I want to be able to steer the company into new markets where opportunities exist. To give you an example, in Latin America, I might wish to offer a containerised service to Argentina, Uruguay and Brazil. I need to have systems that I can erect in the field quickly and can 'bolt on' to the existing information systems we use here at HQ.

I might also wish to offer a system to control other folks' containers. You know, third party work. There's money to be made in that lark.

Harvey W: I think that's enough ideas for one day. We ought not overload Cyril's head with too much. We (with voice booming) can't let the grass grow under our feet. I didn't get where I am today by letting grass grow under my feet! Over to you, Cyril.

Cyril G: It is my intention that the system developed will be object-oriented. That means that the main conceptual units will be kept as if they are self-contained units of all the data and program units. This allows one to take the approach of being able to easily build systems. On my next visit I will show you a family of conceptual models, which should help verify my understanding of the system.

It is appropriate that a full set of the documentation so far be displayed for the esteemed gathering. This is where all the workings can be displayed, showing that there is more than one viewpoint of the container business.

Commentary

Note that there are many systems contexts at work here (Fig. A2.10 and A2.11). In Alexander's *Notes on the Synthesis of Form*, systems, as a rule, have multiple contexts.

In addition. this is a useful time to detail all the knowledge about all the objects (Figs A2.12–A2.15).

Scene 6

The prototyping session

This prototyping session involves Neville, Fred and Maureen and our ace prototyper Merv Morris. Merv has much experience with structured methods, object-oriented methods and prototyping, has taken the previous object models and has used them as source for a prototype built by means of Smalltalk. Smalltalk has a comprehensive library of features.

The dialogue opens with Neville.

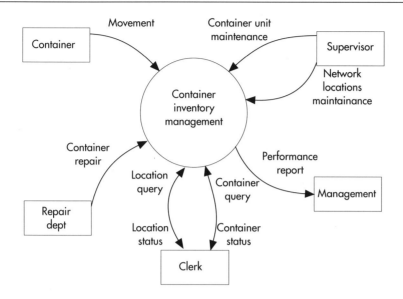

Figure A2.10 A context and event list for container inventory management.

Neville: Well, Merv, what contrivance are we to see today?

Merv: I had in mind to show you a style of interface which I think you may feel comfortable with. I've built three things for us to see: a window for interacting with the containers themselves; see if you feel that is OK for you? I've also got a window for container types (Fig. A2.17). Last, I have a sample of part of the system I used for that lot in Sales, and I've customised it a bit so we can use it to check out the window and screen design. I've allowed about an hour for this session. If that is OK? (Merv then proceeds to run the prototype and gather reactions from the gathered audience.)

Maureen: I like that style of window because it involves very little work to use. Any of my brain donors could use it! Ideally, I would like to see something I could use more in my day-to-day work. (Merv then proceeds to demonstrate the second prototype, showing the container types and details.)

Maureen: Hmmmm, yes, I think it is so easy to use. (Maureen then depresses the appropriate pull-down menu options and proceeds to enter details with facility.) Yes. OK, though it should format the details like this. (Maureen then proceeds to sketch out

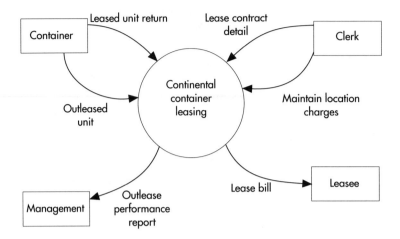

Associated external events:

Container unit is leased out
Container unit is returned
Time to generate outlease performance report
Time to generate leasee's lease bill
Clerk maintains location charges
Clerk adds a new lease contract

Figure A2.11   A context and event list for container leasing management.

some more elaborations of the window on an electronic whiteboard nearby. This is then discussed and transferred to paper automatically.)

Merv: This prototype (see Fig. A2.19) has been based on the sales tracking system and shows a scrolling list of containers, which may be selected by mouse positioning and a button depression. The selected container then has its details displayed on the right, and in the bottom left pane of the window we have a graphic that shows our distribution network as a graph and the position that the container is at is 'illuminated' by changing the background colour. How do you like that? (At this juncture, it is best to leave the session and discuss the construction steps that Merv underwent.)

Commentary

The diagrams shown so far have been developed on a case tool then using Smalltalk and have been developed from 'what is on the stocks' and what can be easily 'bent into shape' (or, in the correct parlance, objects should be malleable).

The style of development is straightforward. First, a style of window is developed. This window becomes a basic building block for subsequent steps. The window for individual containers and container types is, in essence, the same; the class behaviour

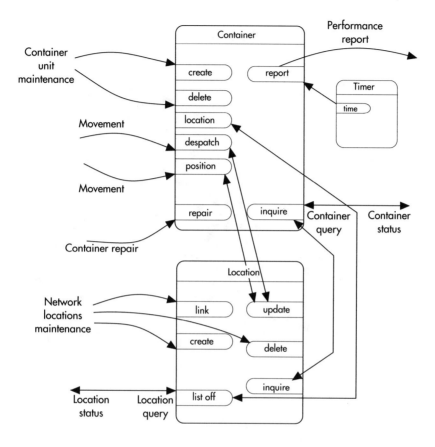

Figure A2.12   An OIN for container inventory activities.

was copied. Location requires some changes. First, it is a graphics pane and it will additionally use class resources such as Net, Network and NetworkNode. There are useful built-in methods to allow connections between nodes and to search for paths between nodes (locations). 'Dictionary', which is Smalltalk-*ese* for a file management system, allows use of a built-in filing system for prototyping purposes (Figs A2.16–A2.19).

Finally, the working transaction window has been based upon the development of easy-to-assemble components that have been proven and thence extended into a new context.

References and further reading

Alexander, C. (1964) *Notes on the Synthesis of Form*. Harvard paperback.

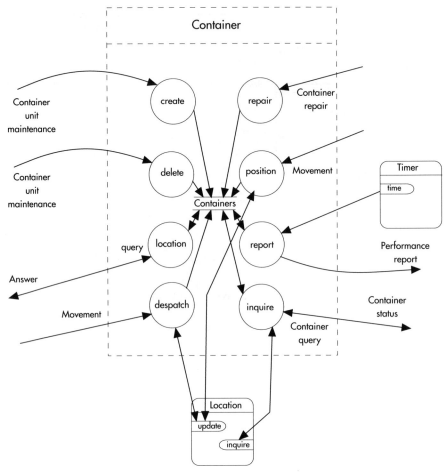

OIV Diagram name: Container internal view
Author: Cyril
Date: 01/01/92

Figure A2.13   An OIV for a container.

Smalltalk source code

```
ViewManager subclass: #ContainerType
 instanceVariableNames:
  'types selectedName '
 classVariableNames: ''
 poolDictionaries: ''
```

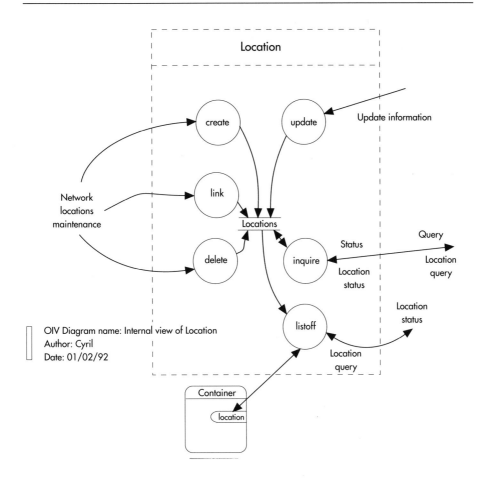

Figure A2.14 An OIV for location.

```
add
  " add a container type "
| key |
  self textModified ifTrue: [self].
  key := Prompter
   prompt: 'new name'
   default: String new.
 (key isNil or: [ types includesKey: key ] )
   ifTrue: [^self].
  selectedName := key.
  types at: key put: nil.
```

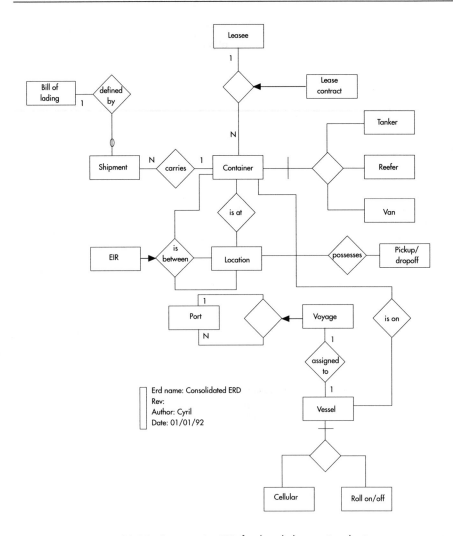

Figure A2.15   An extensive ERD for the whole container business.

```
self
 changed: #list:;
 changed: #list: with: #selection: with: key;
 changed: #text:
```

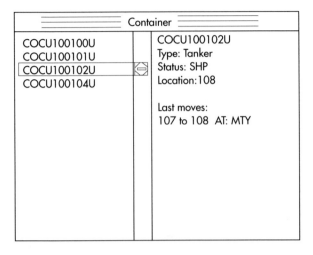

Figure A2.16 A container window.

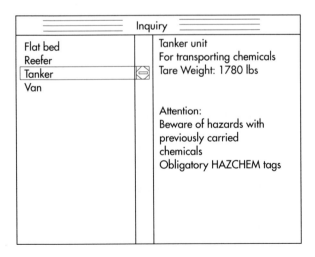

Figure A2.17 A container types window.

Plain locations described graphically as a network of nodes

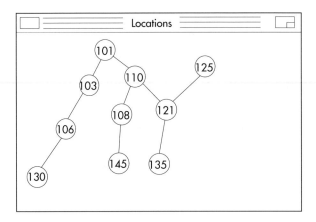

Locations plus a scrollable graphic pane

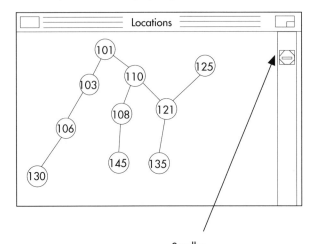

Scroller
Figure A2.18   A location window (graphics pane).

```
list: aListPane
   "Fill the list pane with the container types."

   aListPane contents: types keys asSortedCollection

listMenu: aListPane
   "Set the name list menu."
   aListPane setMenu: ( ( Menu
   labels: '~Add\~Remove' withCrs
   lines: Array new
```

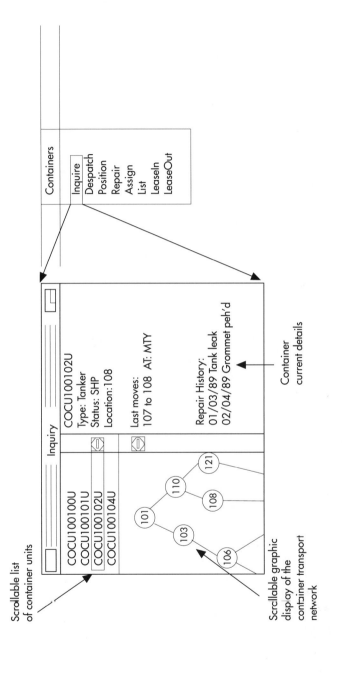

Scrollable list
of container units

Scrollable graphic
display of the
container transport
network

Container
current details

Figure A2.19   A consolidated transaction window.

```
    selectors: #( add remove ) )
     title: '~Types of container' )

 nameSelected: aListPane
   "Display the container typefor
   the selected name in aListPane."
   selectedName := aListPane selectedItem.
   self changed: #text:

openOn: aDictionary
    "Open a Container type window on aDictionary.
    Define the pane sizes and behavior, and
    open the window."
    types := aDictionary.
    self label: 'Container Types '.
    self addSubpane:
     (ListPane new
      when: #getMenu perform: #listMenu: ;
      owner: self;
      when: #getContents perform: #list: ;
      when: #select perform: #nameSelected: ;
      framingRatio: ( Rectangle leftTopUnit
       extentFromLeftTop: 1/3 @ 1 ) ).
    self addSubpane:
     (TextPane new
      owner: self;
      when: #getContents perform: #text: ;
      when: #save perform: #textFrom: ;
      framingRatio: ( (Rectangle leftTopUnit rightAndDown: 1/3
@ 0)
        extentFromLeftTop: 2/3 @ 1 ) ).
    self optext: aTextPane
     "Set the contents of the text pane
     with the container type string
     for the selected name."
    aTextPane contents: ( types at: selectedName
      ifAbsent: [''] )enWindow

   remove
    "Remove the selected name
    list entry."
    types removeKey: selectedName
     ifAbsent: [ ].
```

```
   selectedName := nil.
   self
    changed: #list:;
    changed: #text:

  textFrom: aTextPane
    "Get the contents of the text pane as the
    container type for the selected
    name and enter into dictionary."
   selectedName isNil
    ifTrue: [^true].
   types at: selectedName put: aTextPane contents.
    aTextPane modified: false

ViewManager subclass: #ContainerType
 instanceVariableNames:
  'types selectedName '
 classVariableNames: ''
 poolDictionaries: ''

add
   " add a container type "

 | key |
  self textModified ifTrue: [self].
  key := Prompter
   prompt: 'new name'
   default: String new.
  (key isNil or: [ types includesKey: key ] )
   ifTrue: [^self].
  selectedName := key.
  types at: key put: nil.
  self
   changed: #list:;
   changed: #list: with: #selection: with: key;
   changed: #text:

list: aListPane
   "Fill the list pane with the container types."

  aListPane contents: types keys asSortedCollection

 listMenu: aListPane
   "Set the name list menu."
```

```
    aListPane setMenu: ( ( Menu
      labels: '~Add\~Remove' withCrs

Object subclass: #Network
 instanceVariableNames:
  'connections '
 classVariableNames: ''
 poolDictionaries: ''

connect: nodeA to: nodeB
    "Add a connection from nodeA to nodeB."
  (connections
   at: nodeA
   ifAbsent: [connections at: nodeA put: Set new] )
    add: nodeB.
  (connections
   at: nodeB
   ifAbsent: [connections at: nodeB put: Set new] )
    add: nodeA

draw
    "Draw the network. For each node, it draws all the arcs and
    then the node. All the nodes visited are remembered to
    avoid double drawing."
  | visited pen |
  pen := (Window turtleWindow: 'Net') pen.
  pen erase.
  visited := Set new.
  pen drawRetainPicture: [
   connections keys do: [ :nodeA |
    visited add: nodeA.
    (connections at: nodeA) do: [ :nodeB |
     (visited includes: nodeB)
      ifFalse: [
      pen place: nodeA position;
       goto: nodeB position] ].
    nodeA drawWith: pen] ]

drawOn: aWindow      "** changed **"
    "Draw the network. For each node, it draws
    all the arcs and then the node. All the
    nodes visited are remembered to avoid double
    drawing."
```

```
| visited pen |
pen := aWindow pen.       "** changed **"
pen erase.
visited := Set new.
pen drawRetainPicture: [
 connections keys do: [ :nodeA |
  visited add: nodeA.
  (connections at: nodeA) do: [ :nodeB |
   (visited includes: nodeB)
    ifFalse: [
     pen place: nodeA position;
       goto: nodeB position] ].
  nodeA drawWith: pen] ]

initialize
   "Initialize the connections to be empty."
  connections := Dictionary new

pathFrom: nodeA to: nodeB avoiding: nodeSet
   "Answer a path of connections that connect nodeA
   to nodeB without going through the nodes in
   nodeSet. This result is returned as a new
   network. Answer nil if there is no path"
  | answer |
  nodeSet add: nodeA.
   (connections at: nodeA ifAbsent: [nil]) do:
  [ :node |
  node = nodeB
   ifTrue: [
    ^Network new initialize
      connect: nodeA to: node].
   (nodeSet includes: node)
    ifFalse: [
     answer := self
      pathFrom: node
      to: nodeB
      avoiding: nodeSet.
     answer isNil
      ifFalse: [
       ^answer connect: nodeA to: node]]].
  ^nil
```

```
printOn: aStream
    "Print a description of the receiver on aStream."
   connections keys asSortedCollection do: [ :node |
    node printOn: aStream.
    (connections at: node) asSortedCollection do:
     [ :neighbor |                              .
     aStream
      cr;
      nextPutAll: '>> '.
    aStream cr]

Object subclass: #NetworkNode
 instanceVariableNames:
  'name position '
 classVariableNames: ''
 poolDictionaries:
  'WinConstants '

<= aNode
    "Answer true if receiver name less or equal to
    aNode name."
   ^name <= aNode name

drawWith: aPen
    "Draw the receiver node with a
    circle around its name."
   | major minor |
   major := (SysFont stringWidth: name) + 16 // 2.
   minor := SysFont height + 16 // 2.
   aPen
    setTextAlign: TaTop;
    place: position;
    ellipseFilled: major minor: minor;
    centerText: name

hash
    "Answer receiver's hash."
   ^name hash

name
    "Answer receiver's name."
   ^name
    "Draw the receiver node with a
```

```
    circle around its name."
  active ifFalse: [^super drawWith: pen].
  pen
    foreColor: ClrRed;
    backColor: ClrLightgray.
  super drawWith: pen.
  pen
    foreColor: ClrNeutral;
    backColor: ClrBackground

info
  "Return the info instance variable for the receiver."
  ^info
```

Heuristics

Heuristics for object-oriented development

[0] An object class may be notated by a symbol representing an object engine, which is a hypothetical machine that displays (as buttons) available public services and hides its internal workings from a public user. It is communicated to by means of a message connected to the button (flow symbol). This is called an object external view (OEV) (Fig. A3.1).

Its facia may be removed to show a process symbol where every external service is offered and a store symbol to give the equivalent behaviour of memory. In the context of an object it is called an operation. Attached to the operation from the external world, may be inbound flows, which are equivalent to messages. It will access the object class's store (memory) in accordance with its preplanned response.

Any operation can call upon another object's services by means of a dialogue (flow) between them. This internal view of an object is called an OIV.

There are two styles of development synthesist and the direct approach. The next fifteen heuristics are associated with the synthesist approach.

[1] Data flow diagrams (DFDs), if decomposed to their most primitive form (one flow input one flow output and a store access), may correspond directly to a method for that store reincarnated as an object.

[2] DFDs are, as a rule, using more than one store. The process may become fragmented into n operations. Each operation will then be placed with the data. However, there are situations where a store is surrounded by processes each of which is solely servicing the store. This is a 'librarian'-type object. *Comment.* See Fig. 7.10 and note that the DFD configuration and the OIV are isomorphic.

[3] DFDs in a processor model, for an asymmetric distribution of the essential model to n processors ($n \geq 2$). To preserve the essence of the requirement the cut must be a minimum weight cut across essential flows (minimum weight = importance, volume, frequency). Cuts across a process tend to be equivalent to cuts across flow, between processes at a lower level. Very rarely is it a cut across a process *per se*.

[4] Processes in a serial relationship. A set of processes that are in a serial relationship

What is an object-oriented approach?

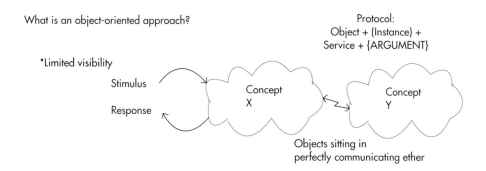

Objects sitting in
perfectly communicating ether

*More formally the notation is based on 'object engines'

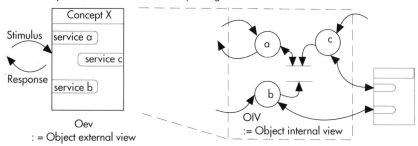

Figure A3.1   External object views.

(see Fig. 7.11) may be considered as a transducer. All the behaviour may be encapsulated as one transducer named after the subject that is being transformed.

[5] Control processes as controller objects. If a DFD uses a control process, this will be a candidate controller object. It will also gather the associated STD behaviour for that control process.

[6] Process specifications written in pre- and post-condition specification form tend to be more easily rearranged during the object construction activity. The fragmentation is by assertion group so it can easily be 'copied' and 'pasted'.

[7] ERDs. Each viable ERD entity is a candidate object. Supertype and subtype entities are candidate representations of inheritance. All the definition material for the entity is directly of use in the object definition.

[8] ERDs. Each relationship between entities will trace out a message connection between the corresponding objects.

[9] ERDs and processor models. As a provider of ERD services one will have to cut the ERD for each processor region. There will be a major portion of processing and a minor portion of processing:

1. Cuts are made across relationships.
2. Each cut will cause a 'ghost' entity to remain on the major portion ERD and a reduced entity on the minor portion ERD.
3. The service provider shall perceive a compressed entity that will migrate from the major processing portion to the minor portion periodically. This retains system integrity.

[10] The external event list is a source for candidate objects and operations. The event list is a list of external stimuli that the system must respond to. In object-oriented terms this is similar to the system being sensitive to certain messages originating from the environment. The event list takes the form of an external agent, being the source of an event which has a relationship to some specific subject area of the system. This style of structured development is derived from McMenamin and Palmer (1984).

This has the slot pattern of: Agent, action and subject area. This specific pattern maps directly to facilitating candidate objects and operations. Each event becomes a candidate to be decomposed into appropriate ERD fragments.

[11] The life-cycle for an entity is expressed by an eSTD. For a full life-cycle the actions associated with each transition condition become the operations for that entity. The source for the life-cycle is the external event list. The conditions correspond to external events and the actions are the minimal set of custodial operations.

[12] STDs. A state transition diagram is a representation of time and sequence (discrete control). For a translation of an essential STD to its corresponding object representation, states are preserved in a controlling object. Transitions remain as they were in the essential model. Conditions will be the same, actions, however, have different constituents (i.e invoking n objects instead of m processes) to accomplish the same time sequence behaviour.

[13] Processor model. In the case of asymmetric distributed processing (processor types $\geqslant 2$), one should think of a virtual observer who is familiar with the essential required behaviour and his/her view should remain the same. Therefore there will be a service object which will provide methods (services) which will preserve the virtual observer's viewpoint ('he/she should not see the join'). Note heuristic [3].

[14] Refinement. This in object-oriented terms may be a measure of the set of operation cohesion. In a DFD, for an application, there may a total of P_1 lines of process specification. This is an expression of the sum of all the transformations. This processing may be redistributed into objects operations. There is a degree of repeated behaviour in the processing when accessing stores as expressed by a DFD. The sum of the operation processing lines may be expressed by O_1. The ratio P_1/O_1 represents index of compression of the process specification into operation specification. This ratio can be further increased by use of object operations that may be drawn from a central library (say O_c). This may be expressed by $P_1/(O_1 - O_c)$, this increases the ratio

further. However, there is the added burden that each time an object operation is called it introduces an extra prescription line in the form of an object operation message O_m. The revised ratio takes the form of $P_1/(O_1 - O_c) + O_m$.

[15] Quality rules relating to traceability:

1. An object model shall perform the same end–end 'transaction' threading as with the original DFD. If positive it means there is equivalence, if negative it means there is incipient distortion.
2. Each essential process specification fragment shall be 'posted' to an operation specification. Unposted fragments from the essential model shall be considered an error. This is, in effect, a conservation of pre- and post-condition fragments.
3. Every ERD entity shall have as a minima a life-cycle, e.g. create, change, use and delete. The lack of any one of these operations should indicate possible omission of behaviour.

These next rules are related to the direct approach.

[16] The system context. The system context is an object that encapsulates all the behaviour (memory, states and processing).

[17] External events. External events to the system context, that are relevant, are raw messages where the system is viewed as an object. These messages will have the same structural pattern as in rule [10].

[18] Object behaviour. Object behaviour may be expressed by means of a network of objects interconnected by messages. The object-class-behaviour defined will be within the bounds of the system context. The messages from the environment are associated with events. All operations respond to the real world events by directly altering the object's disposition and/or communicating with other object services to complete the response. The object interconnection network (OIN) shows this configuration (Fig. A3.2).

Object static behaviour may also be expressed by means of objects with visible services interconnected by means of logical relationships. This diagram being called the object relationship diagram (ORD). This diagram has no limits as to its scope.

[19] When using ORDs and OINs, the relationships (ORD) between objects trace out message connections between object operations (as per OIN). These relationships are equivalent to the 'trunking' that connects objects and contains all the interobject messages.

[20] Objects may be textually defined by means of an object frame, which has the following minima of slots: description, inheritance, data items, operations available and an invariant for the object class.

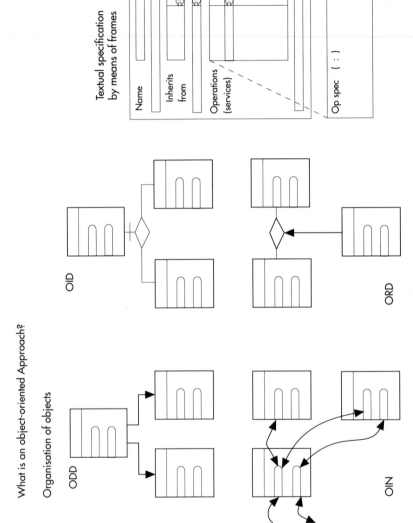

Figure A3.2 The family of object-oriented diagrams.

[21] Operations. Each operation's behaviour can be expressed in text (pseudo-code, pre- or post-condition specification). Its interface shall comprise a message and a response. The message and response shall have such visibility that they are able to be seen in an OIV and/or on an OIN.

References and further reading

McMenamin, S. and Palmer, J. (1984) *Essential Systems Analysis*. New York, NY: Yourdon Press.

Index

abstraction **8**
action 45, 46, 76, **79**, 82, 83,
ADA 53, 167, 203, 238
agent 79, 81, 82, 85, 214, 215
analyst 32,
argument 3, 19, 99, 100, 241

behavioural normalisation
  see normalisation
binding 160, 241
  late 160, 241
browser 37
button 18, 19, 25, 177, 189

C 36, 167, 170
C++ 36, 157, 167,170
CASE 15, 24, 41, 113, 181, 182, 188,
    191, 192, 211–17, 221–4, 231, 242
CASE Toolset 182
class browser 229, 231, 242
client-server 201, **207**
client/supplier 21, 205, 206
client/user 32–5,
code organisation
  model 197,198, 209
cognition 186, 187
cognitive aspects 187
cognitive economy 19, 188, 189
cohesion 186, 197, 242

collaboration 27
compatibility 9
compositor 193–4
concept linkages 103, 104
concreteness 38
concurrency 160
consistency 25, 54
cost 225, 228
cost driver 212, 225
coupling 155, 156
custodial 45, 46, 55, 57, 59, 60, 71, 72,
    75, 76, 95, 242

data dictionary 46, 122
  see project dictionary
definition
  of object 2, 10, 244
  of operation 85, 86, 244

Demeter's law 242
DDL 15, 125
DML 15, 125–7
DFD 1, 33, 41, 43–44, 51, 57, 58, 60–5,
    69, 71–4, 172, 178, 201–3, 213 242,
    274, 275, 276
dialogue 19
direct approach 77–80, 88, 92
Double-Helix 174, 175
dynamic binding 160, 243

efficiency 230, 231
effort 225, 228
encapsulation 3, 158, 243
ERD 1, 33, 41,42, 51–9, 71 –3, 81, 82, 84, 92, 101- 4, 109, **110**, 133, **135**, 137, **149**, 153, 175, 213, 250, 255, 264, 275, 276
eSTD 45, 46, 53, 57, 58, 71–3, **75**, 123, 137, 207, **214**, 252, 256, 276
estimation 225, 228
event 3, 74, 79–86, 94, 95,102, 123, 134
  thread 95, 123
extendibility 9
external
  view **18**, 54, 69, **106**, 274
  world 80

flex 147, 148, 179, 184
flow 18, 19, **78**, **79**
  as message 78, 79
  types of flow 78, 79
frame 115, 144, 147
function point 229, 243
fundamental 44, 57, 58, 243

genericity 159, 243
goal 37
granularity 11
  scale of 11, 12

HCI 185–7, 189, 190, 193
heuristic **50**, 67, 69–73
homunculi 2, 3, 4
human factors 189
Hypercard 177
Hypertalk 177

infrastructure 47, 229, 230
inheritance 4, 6, **22**, **29**, **111**, **112**, 145, **147**, 158, 243
instrument 79, 81

internal view **106**, 108, **140**, **141**, **146**
interrelationships 182
invariant 24, 116, 17, 130
isometric view 35

JAD 33, 35, 234

KBS 142, 144, 145
KDSI 144
knowledge based 148
knowledge based object 146
knowledge based systems 148, 152

layer 7
librarian 64, 69, 274
life cycle 14, 15
lump 156, 157

maintenance 10 , 230, 231
  mountain of 11, 13
mental model 186, 187
message 3, 4, 19, 25, 27, 78, 79, 86, 123, **161**, 243
message thread 123, 243
metaclass 244
metamodel 216–23
method 163- 5
model 40, 41, 47, 48
mutually shaped 54, 55
  see direct approach

normal form 126
normalisation 126, 244
  of behaviour 128
  of data 126
notation symbols 17–19, 20–5, 27–9, 278

Oberon 36
object 2–6, 10, 17–27, 30, 36–9, 46, 51, 56, 62, 63–5, 71, 73, 77, 87–9, 92, 98, 99, 113, 115, **116**, **129**, **133**,

138, 140, 158, 159, 161, 162, 190,
191, 192, 201–3, **223**, 244
communications with 19
definition of 2, 10, 244
derived object 55
frame 25, 115, **116**, **120**, 151
knowledge based 15, 146, 148
office 133
object databases 15, 207
object dependency diagram 21, 25, **29**,
61, **107**
see also ODD
object internal view 18, 20–2, 26, 69,
140
see also OIV
object inheritance diagram 20, 22, **29**,
59, 110, 164
see also OID
object interconnection net 23
see also OIN
object interconnection network 28, 30,
77, 97, **105**
see also OIN
objectness 10
object network diagram **28**, 30
see also OIN
object-oriented 2, 4, 5, 10, 15, 34, 35, 38,
49, 51, 53, 54, 65,179, 185, 189,
227, 236, 237
object-oriented languages 166–9
object relationship diagram 24, **28**, 29,
30, 77, 97, 139
see also ORD
object text frame 25
ODD 21, 22, 26, 29, 33, 61–3, 80, 89,
93, 97, 100,123, 151, 201, 202, **206,**
220, 228, 229, 235, 238, 245, 278
OEV 97, 99, 123, 203, **204**, 244, 278
OID 22, 27, 53, 92, 97, 100, 109, 110,
123, 151, 170, 202, 209, 211, 213,
220, 229, 235, 244, 278

OIN 22, 26–9, 77, 81–5, **88**, 89, 92, 93,
97, 100, 104, 105, 114, 151, 201,
203, 210, 211, 222, 232, 244, 257,
261, 277, 278
OIV 21, 53, 55, 84, **86**, 88, 97,100, 105,
116, 123, 146, 151, 203, 211, 244,
262, 263, 274, 278
OOA 236
OOD 236, 237
OODB 15,16, 80
OOKB 16, 146, 148
OOPL 35, 51, 55, 152, 154–69, 170,
179, 180, 209, 215, 239, 244
operation 3, 18, 20, 24, 25, 71, 72, 82–6,,
116–22, 191, 244
definition 82–85, 244
frame 25, 117–123, 244, 278
ORD 23, 26, 28, 29, 55, 77, 80, 81,
86–89, 92, 96, 97, 123, 127,
130–132, 136, 138, 140, 150, 153,
175, **176**, 202, 207, **208**, 210, 211,
213, 222, 245, 254, 277
organisation 21
orthogonal view **34**, 35
OSI layers 7
overload 160, 244

paradigm shift 35
physiological processes 2, 3
places 190, 191
polymorphism 159, 160, 245
postcondition 24, 117–21
redefinition of 121–2
precondition 24, 117–21
redefinition of 121–2
processor model 199–203
product culture 36
production rule 143
Prograph **180**
project culture 36
project dictionary 122

protocol 8, 99
prototype **173**
prototyping 171–84, 234

receiver 16
receptor 3
relational concepts 28–131
reproducibility 50
reuse 9, 11, 38
risk 227
road map 88, 90, 91, 227
robustness 9
rule based 179

service 3, 23–5, 99, 100, 245
  see also operation
Simula 5, 169
simulation 5, 9
Smalltalk 36, 161–6, 178, 179
software crisis 11
specialisation 7
  see also inheritance
STD 1, 33, 41, 45, 51, 66, 71, 177, 190,
    196, 204, 205, 207, 214, 275, 277,
    276

entity STD *see* eSTD
subject area 3, 71, 79, 81
symbols
  reference 278
Synthesist 52, 53, 56–8

task 203
text definition 23, 46
thread **114**, 123
thread test 245
three axes of emphasis 1, 174
transducer 65, 71, 203, 274, 275
transduction 64
typicality template 6, **7**

user 32
  user-role 232, 233

VDM 13
viewpoint 1, 33
visibility 4, 245

Walk throughs 35, 234
WBS 228

Z 13